Seventy-five Problems

With Central Baptist Theological Seminary's Book

The Bible Version Debate

Lloyd L. Streeter

First Baptist Church of LaSalle
P. O. Box 1043
LaSa

D1225595

The author does not endorse the various theological positions of all of the individuals who are cited or favorably quoted herein. Sometimes a disclaimer has been put into the text stating that a particular individual's position is rejected. Absence of such a disclaimer in the text does not constitute approval.

Library of Congress Control Number: 2001118989

Printed in the U.S.A.

To contact the Author

Mail:
P. O. Box 1043
LaSalle, IL 61301

E-mail:
fbc-lpcs@corecomm.net
street@theramp.net

To order additional copies of this book

1 copy	-	$14.00 + shipping
2-3 copies	-	$12.00 + shipping
4 or more copies	-	$11.00 + shipping

Send order to:
First Baptist Church
P. O. Box 1043
LaSalle, IL 61301

Or call :

(815) 224-3949

With Appreciation

I am indebted to Lisa Decker for typing the manuscript. She worked cheerfully as a good servant of the Lord. Thank you, Lisa.

I also thank those who proofread the book and made suggestions. They include Barb Foster, Barb Fulara, Brian Hamiel, Morgan Wilson, and Kevin Perryman.

I owe a great debt to my wife, Karen, for her suggestions. She helps me in all my work.

Thanks to all who pray for us.

For the people of First Baptist Church

FOREWORD

This book is more than a book review. It is a *handbook* for answering King James Bible critics. The seventy-five problems listed in the table, on pages 11-16, represent almost every objection or criticism that readers will ever hear regarding the KJV. Additionally, most of the weaknesses of the new versions are addressed. The material can be easily found by using the Table of Problems Analyzed, pages 11-16.

It is our prayer that the reader will be equipped to defend the King James Bible as the inspired, infallible, inerrant Word of God. "May we be challenged to love it, live it, understand it, and diligently study it as well as defend it!" (M. Simmons)

TABLE OF CONTENTS

TABLE OF PROBLEMS ANALYZED

<u>**PROBLEM**</u>   <u>**PAGE**</u>

PROBLEM   **PAGE**

PROBLEM   PAGE

PROBLEM   **PAGE**

PROBLEM   **PAGE**

PREFACE

I became a strong King James Bible believer in 1967.
It was a lonely position in those days with hardly any
preachers around who favored the Traditional Text over the
Critical Text. In those days none of us fundamentalist
preachers were taught the superiority of the Traditional Text
in our colleges or seminaries. We were not really taught
that there was any issue about the text. We were simply
taught that we have many newly found manuscripts now
that the King James translators did not have, and that these
newly found manuscripts "are older and better."

A preacher in California unintentionally turned me
on to a book which brought me to the truth. That book asked
an important question: *If God wrote only one Bible then
why is modern man moving away from the Bible which the
true people of God have always held, and why do the new
translations differ so profoundly from the time-honored
King James Bible?*

As I studied the Word of God on the subject of Bible
preservation, as I prayed, and as I read more books I had to
face some startling questions. If the Bible says that the

Word of God would be preserved (and I was convinced that the Bible says exactly that), then how could the true people of God go through eighteen centuries with an inferior, corrupted text? If the new versions represent a better more accurate text, then why would God not have made it available to the Church centuries and centuries ago? Is there a spiritual battle being fought over Bible preservation, and if so, then what has the Devil been doing to try to rob the Church of its Bible? Which Bible text and which versions are the strongest and truest on Bible doctrine and which texts and versions are the weakest? An honest examination of these questions resulted in my coming to the position that the texts underlying the King James Bible are the preserved Word of God and that the King James Bible, being accurately translated and being blessed of God, is the preserved Word of God in English.

In 1967 no one used the term "King James only." That term arose later as a term of derision. Some who, in the market place of new Bibles, resented those who insisted on staying with the Old Book sought for a term whereby they could ridicule KJV people. "King James only," we were called. Then we were told that "King James only" people are those who believe that the King James translators were inspired, those who are opposed to progress, and those who are ignorant rednecks.

I gladly accept the label "King James only" if that is what people feel that they must call me. However, I will not allow those who resent the King James Bible to say what I believe. I will say what I believe.

I am "King James only" because I preach only from the King James. I am "King James only" because I believe that the King James Bible has no errors of fact in it. I am

"King James only" because it is translated from texts which preserved all of the words of God. I am "King James only" because William Tyndale who translated the forerunner of the KJV was one of the most spiritual and scholarly men who ever lived. I am "King James only" because the translators of the KJV were the best, most qualified group of men who ever sat to translate the Word of God. I am "King James only" because I accept the KJV as my final authority in the English language.

The alternative to being "King James only" is to be "Critical Text only," which for all practical purposes is to be "Vatican Manuscript only." That position, to my mind, has insurmountable and indefensible problems. It is a position which had no Greek text of the New Testament until the last quarter of the 15th Century, a position which holds to the Roman Catholic text, a position which wants to overturn both the text of the Reformation and the text of the Philadelphian Age of revival and missions.

"Vatican Manuscript only" advocates always give lip service to the King James Bible. If they did not honor the KJV with their lips they would lose much of their audience. So they say, "I use the King James all the time;" "I love the King James;" "The King James is a dependable version;" and "I honor the King James, it has beautiful style." They say these things while continuing to criticize and correct the KJV, using as their standard the Vatican Manuscript.

I am "King James only" but I do not believe that the translators of the KJV were inspired. I do not believe in the **REINSPIRATION** of the Bible in A.D. 1611. The Bible was always inspired, ever since God gave it, and God **PRESERVED** His Word so that we still have the inspired inerrant Word of God today in the King James Bible. That is why the KJV has such life and power and authority. It is the inspired, inerrant Word of God.

By inerrant we mean that the KJV has no errors **OF FACT.** We do not say that there are no errors in printing, spelling, chapter and verse numbers, grammar, punctuation, or italicized words. However, it has no errors of fact, no discrepancies, no contradictions, and no mistakes. It has no errors about science, history, or any subject upon which it speaks.

Those who want to call the KJV the Word of God, but say that it is not inspired or inerrant have an obvious problem. **What kind of "Word of God" is it which is not inspired? What kind of "Word of God" is it that is not inerrant?** The truth is that if the King James Bible is the Word of God, as most "Vatican Manuscript only" people say, then it is also inspired and inerrant. Those who do not believe that it is inspired or inerrant should stop calling it the Word of God.

If the King James Bible is the Word of God, then the new versions are not the Word of God, at least not in the verses where they differ from the KJV. Two translations of the same verse saying two different things can not both be the Word of God.

I have never said that new versions are "no good." They are fine in those verses which agree with the KJV. In other words, the new versions **CONTAIN** the Word of God. However, those new versions have too many errors in them to be accurately called the Word of God. No one should say that the NIV **IS** the Word of God; it only **CONTAINS** the Word of God. But if it contains the Word of God it has some good **IN IT**, at least enough to make it dangerous. It also has enough of the Word of God **IN IT** that some people get saved reading it. But it does not have the power or the authority inherent in the real Word of God, the KJV.

Some of my KJV-only brethren will probably find fault with me, but I must say this: If a person has only the NIV or the NASB and they are reading it, I am glad that they are reading it, rather than reading no Bible at all. I would much rather that they were reading the KJV, of course. However, it is better to be reading a book which **CONTAINS** some of God's Word than to be reading nothing at all.

I do not call new versions "trash," "garbage," or "toilet paper" as some have done. I think that kind of language is intemperate and does not help anyone.

One of the most tragic consequences of the crass commercial promotion of the new translations is the denigration of the King James Bible. In advertisement after advertisement we are told that the King James Bible is out-of-date, inaccurate, difficult to read, archaic, and based on poor manuscripts. The new translations can not be sold unless the faith of people in their Old Bible is destroyed. Perhaps this is why God made His true people (rather than publishing houses!) the keepers of the Word of God. "The love of money is the root of all evil" (I Timothy 6:10) and the ungodly will do **ANYTHING** for filthy lucre. The main reason that new Bibles are published is so somebody can make money. If the main concern was evangelism or the promulgation of the Word of God, the publishers would be publishing Bibles in Chinese dialects which have no Bible, or in another language, not in English. But, alas, people in Third World countries do not have much money to

21

buy Bibles. About three thousand languages and dialects have no Scripture at all, but since it would not be profitable to publish Bibles in those languages the publishers of the modern English versions are not going to do it.

Advocates of the Critical Text and of the new translations are almost always intellectually dishonest. When they want to prove the need for new versions they **MAXIMIZE** the differences between the Traditional Text and the Critical Text and between the King James Bible and the new translations. However, when they want to justify the additions, deletions, and changes they **MINIMIZE** the differences. They can not have it both ways!

When trying to prove that new translations are **NEEDED**, the Critical Text advocates say that there are tremendous differences in texts and Bibles. "We've got to have a more accurate Bible," they say. "There are huge differences in the manuscripts," we are told.

However, while trying to calm the fears and suspicions of King James Bible believers those same Critical Text advocates say, "The changes are very minor;" "Not a single doctrine is impacted;" "The differences in the Greek texts would fill only a half a page in your Bible."

If Critical Text advocates had said, "Yes, some words and verses have been eliminated, but we can still find some Scripture to prove all of the doctrines," at least that would be more truthful. However, when they say, "Not a single doctrine is affected or impacted," that is double-dealing duplicity. That kind of duplicity is the height of dishonesty.

When the words of Scripture are changed, doctrine is **WEAKENED**. And **MORE** than doctrine is affected.

Comfort, faith, assurance, evangelism, and Christian growth are all weakened.

What are the facts? The facts are that the differences between the Traditional Text and the Critical Text **ARE HUGE**. It is utterly false that "not one doctrine is affected." It is not true that "the differences do not affect any doctrine in any way."

I do not make the issue of the text a test of fellowship. I would not separate from those who prefer the new translations unless their preference is causing a problem. I must break fellowship with rabid anti-King James only people. I can not fellowship with those who insist on using a new version in their preaching and teaching. However, as long as a fundamentalist preacher preaches from the King James Bible and does not correct it nor denigrate it, I will fellowship with him, even if he prefers the Critical Text and even if he disagrees with me about the KJV being the best and most accurate translation. I remember that I was a Christian for a long time and made only the KJV my Bible before I came to the convictions which I now hold regarding the text. So, I believe in giving others time to think, study, and investigate. I have seen literally hundreds of people embrace the Traditional Text and the King James Bible. The KJV-only group is getting larger all the time. I have seen churches and colleges and mission agencies come over to the King James only position. So there is no reason to break fellowship with Critical Text believers **ON A WHOLESALE BASIS**. We need to keep talking to each other. Thousands more are going to yet embrace the Traditional Text and the King James Bible.

I am no longer lonely holding the King James position. Since 1967, thousands of fundamentalists have turned away from the Westcott and Hort position and away from the Critical Text. Multitudes are coming over to the King James position.

Fundamentalist colleges and seminaries are becoming more King James friendly and Traditional Text friendly.

Finally, I am not a scholar. I am just a country preacher. This work was begun to provide information for my own people. I tried to avoid being too technical. Rather than using endnotes or footnotes, the decision was made to put some citations into the text itself.

It is my hope that this little volume will serve as a handbook in dealing with criticisms against the King James Bible. The same criticisms are met over and over again. We hear nothing new. D. A. Carson, Kubo and Specht, James White, J.B. Williams, and all the rest level the same criticisms. The only differences with McLachlan, Pettegrew, Beacham, and Glenny is that they have gone further than the others. I hope this little book will help some King James Bible defenders to answer its critics.

Lloyd L. Streeter
First Baptist Church
LaSalle, IL 61301
March 14, 2000

INTRODUCTORY REMARKS

Central Baptist Theological Seminary of Minneapolis has put out a book which is critical of "King James only" people, and critical of the King James Bible itself. The book, _**The Bible Version Debate**_, has an introduction by Central's president, Douglas R. McLachlan, and six additional chapters written by three of Central's professors; four chapters by W. Edward Glenny, and one chapter each by Larry Pettegrew and Roy Beacham.

I have found the book to be somewhat unfair in its judgments, too general in its characterizations, and unnecessarily harsh in its tone as well as deficient in its doctrine.

In discussing this book, I do not have any ax to grind. I do not have ill will against Central or any of its personnel. In fact, in the past I have recommended the Seminary and have had considerable confidence in its people. I think some of the professors are militant separatists. Some of them have written helpful articles on many subjects. The Seminary has contributed significantly to the fundamentalist cause. I have admired the founder of the school and some who have led the school in the past. I do not intend, in any of my remarks here, to be personally unkind. I will not call anyone names. I will not say that any of the authors of Central's book are "less of a fundamentalist" than myself. [*The Bible Version Debate*, p. 13] I will not call my opponents Nazis or compare them to Hitler's supporters. [*Ibid*, pp. 79-80]

However, there are problems with the book which must be faced honestly. Some of the statements by Central's professors must be challenged. It is my hope that those who read my words will have a greater confidence in their Bible, and that they will know that nothing is better than the King James Bible for clarity and accuracy. The KJV is the best we have and the best we will ever have, so it is time to stop finding fault with it and to begin to more earnestly believe it and obey it.

In discussing *The Bible Version Debate*, I will enumerate **SOME** of the problems I see in the book stating the problem first and then giving an analysis of the problem.

CHAPTER ONE

1. In his introduction, Doug McLachlan speaks of the inspiration of the Bible saying, "The end result was a book which manifests the imprint of both God and man and which was both inerrant and infallible **in the autographs**" (emphasis McLachlan's). [p. 2]

Analysis: The autographs were never "a book." McLachlan is talking in circles to try to make us think that he believes in **A BOOK** that is in some way inerrant and infallible. He does not. He does not believe that there is an inerrant and infallible book anywhere on the face of the earth. He does not believe that there ever was such a book. He believes only that the autographs were inerrant and infallible. The autographs were never in any book. The **BIBLE** is a book. That is what the word **BIBLE** means. The Bible is not the autographs. When McLachlan, and many others, say they believe in the "inspiration and infallibility of the Bible," they are only misleading people about what they really believe. They do not want to **PLAINLY** say that

27

what they really believe is that the only place the perfect Word of God ever existed was in some verbally inspired original manuscripts, the ones actually penned by the human authors. Since none of those manuscripts exist today, and since God did not **PERFECTLY** preserve His Word anywhere on earth, not in any or all of the copies, versions, translations, quotations, or books which do exist, **THERE IS NO INSPIRED AND INFALLIBLE BOOK OR BIBLE.** That is Central's position. McLachlan believes the Bible has the "imprint" of God upon it, but he does not believe it is inerrant or infallible.

2. McLachlan writes that the "overwhelming majority of these variants are of minor importance. Significant variants number about 2000." [p. 3]

Analysis: McLachlan (and others who hold to the Critical Text) has no final authority **EXCEPT HIS OWN MIND.** He is going to decide which variants are significant, which of the variants are correct, and which variants are important. He does not have **A BOOK** which is the final authority. He may **SAY** that the Bible is his final authority, but he does not **BELIEVE** it. He does not **BEHAVE** toward the Bible as if it is his final authority. His final appeal is to the human mind. He approvingly quotes Black saying, "The expositor will inevitably be called upon to **MAKE AN INFORMED JUDGMENT**" [emphasis mine]. So, *HE* is going to decide what is and what is not the Word of God instead of subjecting himself to the Book.

3. The president of Central goes on to say, "None of [the variants] impacts the overall theology of Bible-believing Christians. Textual variants do no harm to one's overall theology because no element of theology is constructed on only one text of Scripture." [p. 3]

Analysis: The above is used as an excuse for the differences in the English versions and for the changes, additions, and subtractions to the Word of God. This is a very strange view of the Bible. Apparently, Central (and others) do not believe we should be concerned at all about any of the changes, additions, or subtractions of words, verses, and passages of God's Word because we can still find all the doctrines in the Bible **SOMEWHERE.** McLachlan's conclusion is that doctrine and theology is not "impacted." This is shallow and foolish thinking which does not portray the high view of Scripture which we presume McLachlan holds.

Every word of God is all important (Matt. 4:4). The devil attacks the words of God, attempting to delete them, add to them, change them, and question them (Gen. 3:1). Servants of the Lord are charged to be on guard to defend the integrity of the words of God (Deut. 4:2; 12:32; Prov. 30:5-6; Rev. 22:18-19).

Every time a doctrinal word is added, subtracted, or changed it impacts doctrine in a destructive and harmful way. Doctrine is weakened. The support for doctrine is undermined. Those who really believe that the Bible is the Word of God **SHOULD NOT BE WILLING TO HAVE ONE SYLLABLE OF IT CHANGED,** even if all of the doctrines can still be supported in other Scriptures.

However, it is simply not true that doctrine is not impacted by new version omissions and changes. For example, take the doctrine of the Ascension of Jesus Christ. There are several oblique and obscure passages that *relate* to (but do not directly *state*) the Ascension, such as, John 1:18 ("which is in the bosom of the Father"), John 3:13 ("The Son of man which is in heaven"), John 20:17 ("I ascend unto my Father, and your Father"), John 17:13 ("I come to thee"), and Hebrews 9:24 ("Christ is not entered into the holy places made with hands, which are the figures of the true; but into heaven itself"). But beyond these indirect and oblique references there are only three *accounts* of the Ascension of Jesus Christ into Heaven. They are Mark 16:19, Luke 24:51, and Acts 1. Of these three, the NASV wants to omit Mark 16:19 and Luke 24:51. This would leave only one account of the Ascension! How can it be said that two of the three accounts of the Ascension may be omitted without impacting the doctrine? Who is kidding whom? Especially are the above considerations important if we accept the position of some that a major doctrine should not stand on a single verse!

Add to the above the fact that many of the changes in the new versions strengthen the position of the anti-supernaturalists, Romanists, humanists, and liberals. It is simply not true that none of the variants impact theology or doctrine.

4. McLachlan laments that there are advocates of the KJV-only position, and says, "There is no evidence that previous generations of fundamentalists have used the translation issue as a hallmark of an authentic kind of fundamentalism." [p. 4]

Analysis: The statement is unfair, misleading, and a generalization. There is no evidence that whole previous generations of Bible-believing Christians agree **WITH MCLACHLAN** on this issue. He wants his readers to think that all real Christians in all previous generations agree with him. That, of course, is untrue. There has been a debate about versions since the days of Westcott and Hort and the first efforts to revise the Bible. Most people rejected the revisions and stayed with the KJV. Furthermore, the true Bible-believing churches through the ages from A.D. 300 until the 20th Century accepted the Traditional Text of Scripture. When the liberal RSV came out, fundamentalists rejected it and stayed with the KJV. That RSV is much closer to the NASV and NIV than it is to the KJV. The RSV is based on the same text as the NIV and NASV and to quote an American politician, "There is not a dimes worth of difference between them."

Contrary to what the president of Central thinks, almost all fundamentalists have been KJV-only people. Almost all common, ordinary, Bible-believing fundamentalists have accepted the KJV as their final authority. We speak not of professors or scholars but of the vast majority of fundamentalist Christians. Their final authority was never the autographs, nor Nestle's Greek, nor any other Greek text, nor any scholar. The final authority for Bible-believing fundamentalists has been the King James Bible.

It is not true, as brother McLachlan would have us believe, that all advocates of the King James only position

31

use the issue as "a hallmark of an authentic kind of fundamentalism." Most KJV-only people do not do this. With most of us it is not a test of fellowship. Most of us do not want a guest preacher to preach from a new version in our pulpits. This is understandable and should be acceptable to everyone. Most of us want our missionaries to use the KJV for their preaching in English-speaking countries. What is wrong with that? Some KJV-only people prefer to promote colleges that hold to the superiority of the KJV and its text. Is this unreasonable? However, the vast majority of KJV-only people believe it is possible to be a fundamentalist and still hold to the Critical Text. Most KJV-only people still fellowship with Critical Text people on many levels. I personally, do not demand that all of our guest preachers agree with me about the KJV, but I do demand that they preach from the KJV **FROM MY PULPIT**. Is there something wrong with this? I know, love, and respect many preachers who disagree with me on this issue and so do almost all of the KJV-only people I know. McLachlan's statement is unfair because he is trying to dishonestly characterize the beliefs of all previous generations and the position of all KJV-only people today.

While I think it is reasonable for a pastor to prefer to support only colleges and seminaries which take a KJV-only position, I do not personally do this. For more than thirty years I have accepted the KJV as my final authority, but I have continued to support both KJV-only and Critical Text colleges. It takes a long time for some men and schools to come over to the KJV position. I believe we must work with one another, keep talking to one another, and keep praying for one another. I have lived to see many men and schools come over to the KJV position. I have lived to see other schools become more accepting, flexible, and understanding of the KJV position. Some "Critical Text" schools, for example, now have more than one position represented on their Bible faculty. Many new colleges have begun which hold the KJV-only position and these schools are growing and prospering.

I take the same position on fellowships of churches, camps, mission agencies, evangelists, and other ministries. I have not rejected Critical Text people as "less than fundamentalists." I have not refused to fellowship with them. Of course, there are some rabid anti-King James only people with whom I do not care to fellowship. They are the exception, rather than the rule. So, I have not made the KJV-only position a "hallmark." Most of the KJV-only people I know have not done so.

5. McLachlan accuses KJV-only advocates of "absolutizing only one English translation or one narrow family of Greek manuscripts while ignoring all the rest of the textual evidence." [p. 4]

Analysis: McLachlan and the Critical Text advocates are guilty of the very thing of which he here incorrectly accuses his KJV-only brethren. It is the practice of the new version translators and advocates to ignore the vast majority of the evidence in favor of **THREE** newly found manuscripts. The new versions have "absolutized" Siniaticus, Alexandrinus, and especially Vaticanus while largely ignoring 5,000 Greek manuscripts and 15,000 other ancient witnesses where they differ. New version advocates systematically accept the Vatican manuscript reading over the Traditional Text in almost every case where they differ.

While I plead guilty of "absolutizing" the King James Bible, I do not believe it can be said that advocates of the Traditional Text have *ignored* the Alexandrian readings. It would be more accurate to say that Traditional Text advocates *considered* the Alexandrian readings **AND REJECTED THEM**. That was certainly the case with Erasmus, Beza, Burgon, Scrivener, Miller, and Hills.

6. Finally, McLachlan makes the very prejudicial, egotistical statement that those who agree with him about the text and about versions can "then preach and teach with the authority of a true biblicist, speaking God's absolute truth accurately, passionately, and relevantly into the hearts and minds of our post modern world." [p. 4]

Analysis: The implication is that KJV-only preachers can not teach and preach with the authority of a true biblicist, and cannot speak God's absolute truth accurately, passionately, and relevantly. McLachlan's unkindness in this remark is superseded only by his pride.

The fact is that preachers throughout the past 380 years who have preached only the King James Bible (have accepted the KJV as their final authority, and have not corrected the KJV) have preached with **MORE AUTHORITY** than new version advocates. The vast majority of King James Bible preachers during the past four centuries have not said "a better translation would be...," "this is an unfortunate translation," or "according to the original Greek this should say..." They just preached the King James Bible because they believed it, trusted it, and loved it. They preached it across Wales, England, Scotland, and Ireland. They preached it in the hills of Appalachia, in the Ozarks, and on the frontiers from Kentucky to California. They preached it in the slave churches on plantations. They preached it in brush arbors from South Carolina to Texas, and from Michigan to Key West. They preached it across India, the Caribbean, and Liberia. Most of those preachers were trained in their own local church by a godly pastor with a King James Bible in his hand. At least 99% of those preachers could not recognize even one letter of the Greek alphabet, much less even think of making the non-existent autographs their final authority! Yes, and for the most part those preachers **DID** preach the Word of God "accurately, passionately, and relevantly." The King James Bible was being preached by those "unlearned and ignorant" preachers when the vast majority of souls were saved in the English-speaking world. It was the King James Bible which was being preached when almost all true gospel preachers were called to preach in the English-speaking world. The preaching of the King James Bible produced all of the revivals in the English-speaking world. All of the great hymns in the English language were written by King James Bible readers. And almost all soul-winning and Christian growth which has ever occurred among English-speaking people has resulted from the preaching and teaching of the King James Bible **BY PEOPLE WHO ACCEPTED IT AS THEIR FINAL AUTHORITY.**

If anyone doubts that those who preach only the King James Bible are able to preach the Word of God "with authority," "accurately, passionately, and relevantly," all he has to do is compare the results of the preaching of the King James Bible to the results of the preaching of the NIV, Living Bible, NASV, and Phillips. What a sorry confused mess is this charismatic, ecumenical, Promise Keepers, CCM, compromising, church marketing culture which passes for Christianity! The new versions have helped produce this mess.

I would not want to say that brother McLachlan is not "a true biblicist," however, I must admit that it is difficult for me to understand how anyone can "preach and teach with authority" when he does not **HAVE** a final authority. How can he preach the "thus saith the Lord" accurately, passionately, and relevantly when his final authority is to "make an informed judgment" about what the Word of God is? McLachlan cannot claim the autographs as his final authority because he does not have them. He has never seen them and does not know exactly what they say. McLachlan cannot claim a reconstructed, restored Greek text as his final authority because he does not believe the work of restoration is completed or ever will be completed. As a matter of fact, as time goes on, there is **MORE AND MORE DISAGREEMENT ABOUT WHAT A RE-STORED TEXT SHOULD SAY**, and many students of the issue believe the textual critics are moving farther and farther away from what a restored text should say.

The closest that Central and other Critical Text advocates can come to having a final authority is to trust in the human brain. They must **DETERMINE** in their **OWN MIND** what the Word of God is and where it is.

The Bible says that "in the last days perilous times shall come...evil men and seducers shall wax worse and worse, deceiving and being deceived" (II Timothy 3:1 and 13). And yet we have fundamentalists who believe that in the last days there will be better and better Bible versions! I do not think so.

This is the age of apostasy, the age which Jesus described saying, "when the Son of man cometh, shall he find faith on the earth?" (Luke 18:8). Jesus meant that the faith of even some saved people will be shaken, but He also meant that the last days would be times of spiritual declension and unproductivity. Nothing better is going to develop during this age of apostasy—not better evangelism, scholarship, or organizations; not better churches, culture, or standards; **and certainly not better Bible versions**.

CHAPTER TWO

Larry Pettegrew wrote the second chapter of Central Seminary's *The Bible Version Debate*. He claims to give an historical overview of the King James only position. Unfortunately, his article makes too much use of generalization and propaganda techniques to be considered an honest piece of work.

7. He mentions as a part of the King James only position that, "Even non-English Bibles must be translated out of the King James Version, rather than Greek and Hebrew." [p. 5]

Analysis: This is a generalization. It is not true of most KJV-only people. I am King James only in my position, but I do not believe that non-English Bibles **MUST** be translated out of the King James Version, rather than Greek and Hebrew. In fact, I do not know **ANY** KJV advocate who believes what Pettegrew carelessly attributes to all KJV-only people. In all of the multitudinous books and articles which I have read which promote the KJV position I have never found a single writer who says what Pettegrew attributes to the KJV-only view. There may be one, or a few, somewhere who believe as Pettegrew says but he certainly does not make an accurate characterization. I think I read somewhere that on a certain mission field, perhaps in the Ukraine, that there were some people who thought their Bible had to be translated out of the KJV in order to be the Word of God. However, that is very unusual, not at all typical of KJV-only people. So why would Pettegrew make this very unfair and inaccurate blanket generalization of KJV-only advocates?

Did Pettegrew check with the Bible faculty at the KJV-only schools to see if any of them teach what he says they believe? Did he check with Massillon Baptist College, Crown College, Pensacola Christian College, West Coast Baptist College, Heritage Baptist University, Trinity Baptist College, Providence Baptist College, Landmark Baptist College, Hyles-Anderson College, Texas Baptist College, Tabernacle Baptist College, or Ambassador Baptist College? I doubt that he tried to find out the truth. Did he care if he characterized his KJV brethren accurately?

The truth is that hardly any King James only men believe that all non-English Bibles **MUST** be translated out of the King James Version. Without a doubt, a good translation **COULD** be made that way if competent people were doing it, (after all it has already been done approximately 700 times!), but that is not the only way; and we do not believe that it **MUST** be done that way.

It should concern us that there are foreign language versions being translated out of the NIV, Good News for Modern Man, The Living Bible, and other new versions. If a foreign language version had to be translated out of an

English version I would much rather have it translated from the KJV than from any of the others. The new versions are notoriously inaccurate and clumsy **IN ENGLISH**, and it is extremely doubtful that they would be better after being translated into another language.

However, almost all KJV-only men believe the King James is far superior to the new versions, among other reasons, because the Traditional Text underlying the King James is far superior to the Critical Text. Therefore, if the Traditional Texts are used to make foreign language translations, and if the work is done accurately, it would result in an inspired Bible in the receptor language.

Pettegrew, it would seem, has tried to make all KJV-only people to appear extreme and unreasonable through his use of inaccurate generalizations.

8. Pettegrew's entire article is shot through with the above kind of generalization and dishonest characterization. He says, "Some of those who are arguing for a certain Greek text apparently are only using the argument concerning the Greek text as a sophisticated cover for their real concern. The real issue for them is that only the King James Version is God-breathed." [p. 6]

Analysis: This is judging motives and intentions, which Pettegrew is not competent to do. It certainly is not generally true that KJV-only advocates do not care about the Greek text. It is not true, as Pettegrew charges, that KJV-only people are insincere in their advocacy of the Traditional Text.

KJV-only people could make the same type of charge against new version advocates, **AND WITH MUCH**

MORE JUSTIFICATION. Though many of the new versions laud the newly-found manuscripts as their reason for making a new version, they depart from their own Greek text over and over again, do not translate it accurately, and use a dynamic equivalency which results in little more than a paraphrase. So, we could more honestly question whether their proclaimed allegiance to a Greek text is just a ruse, and whether they could not have done just as good a job if they had not had a Greek text at all! But, that's another subject.

Does Pettegrew know of a single KJV-only preacher or teacher who does not believe sincerely that the Greek text underlying the KJV is superior to the Critical Text? He does not name one. Why would he question their sincerity? Why suggest that KJV people do not think that the underlying Greek text is important? His only "proof" of his assertion is that KJV-only people, "reject the New King James Bible, even though it is translated from the Greek manuscripts to which they are committed." But, most KJV-only people know that the NKJV is not translated strictly from the Traditional Text. The newly-found Vatican manuscript influenced this translation in many places. The notes are unfaithful to the Traditional Text. It is highly deceptive in many ways. Besides the issue of the underlying Greek text, the NKJV is a poor translation because it makes many of the same mistakes as the NIV, NASB, RSV, NEB, and New World Version. It weakens the deity of Christ, for example, in Acts 3:13, 26; Acts 4:27, 30 **WHERE THE GREEK TEXT IS NOT AN ISSUE.**

9. Pettegrew again generalizes and misrepresents KJV-only people when he says, "The King James only position teaches that the King James Version alone is the inspired Word of God in the English language." [p. 7]

Analysis: The preceding statement is wrong for the following reasons: (1) Most KJV advocates believe that there were English Bibles before 1611 which were the Word of God. (2) Most KJV-only people believe the Traditional Text of the Word of God when translated into English results in an inspired English Bible **WHEN IT IS TRANSLATED ACCURATELY.** This is true no matter where the English words are printed or written, no matter who prints them or writes them, no matter on what the words are printed or written. If the English words mean exactly the same as the Greek and Hebrew words then that English translation would be the inspired Word of God. **BUT, OF COURSE, THAT WOULD MEAN THAT THE WORDS OF THE NEW ENGLISH TRANSLATION WOULD MEAN EXACTLY THE SAME AS THE WORDS OF THE KJV.** So, Pettegrew is making a generalization, an accusation, about KJV-only people which is not true for the great majority of them.

It would be more accurate to say that the KJV-only advocate is one who accepts the KJV as his final authority in English. He is satisfied that it pleases the Lord for the KJV to be believed and practiced, and not corrected or undermined. So, wherever any new version of the Bible changes, adds to, or subtracts from the words of God, a KJV-only preacher will accept the KJV reading as the Word of God and will reject all other English readings. What Pettegrew says is an over-statement and a generalization.

We believe that English versions other than the KJV **CONTAIN SOME** of the Word of God and that it is

POSSIBLE that another accurate translation **COULD** be made.   However, we are not in favor of anyone trying to make any new English version, and we do not believe any could be **BETTER** than the KJV.

10. Pettegrew says, "Because the Scriptures were God-breathed in their original form, they *are* without error or inerrant." [p. 8]

Analysis: The originals do not exist, therefore Pettegrew should have said, "They *were* without error."   Apparently the professor wants people to think that he **HAS** something which is inerrant, hence the use of the present tense. However, he believes nothing of the kind. Since the originals do not exist, and since copies and translations are not inspired, there *is* no inerrant, perfect Word of God anywhere on Earth.   That is what Central believes.

11. "Translated documents," writes Pettegrew, "cannot be God-breathed in the same sense as the original documents.   God has not chosen to extend the miracle of inspiration beyond the work of prophets and apostles to include translations." [p. 9]

Analysis: Pettegrew, et.al., does not believe **ANY** copy, or **ANY** translation, or **ANY** group of copies or translations are the inspired, inerrant, perfect Word of God.   He seems grudgingly to say that "translations do partake of derivative inspiration."   In an end note, he finally admits that "a copy or translation is the Word of God to the degree that it reflects and reproduces the original text."

By "original text" in the above statement we assume Pettegrew means the autographs, and if that is the case, then he will never know to what **"DEGREE"** any copy or translation is the Word of God, because he will never know to what **"DEGREE"** it agrees with the original text.

The term "derived inspiration" is a good and useful term if it is used correctly and in a way which is consistent with plenary inspiration (meaning all Scripture is equally inspired) and verbal inspiration (meaning that every word of Scripture is inspired). Many King James Bible defenders correctly use the term to indicate that the King James Bible is inspired because it is translated from words which were breathed out by God. However, King James Bible critics, including Central Seminary, use the term, "derived inspiration," in an unscriptural and incorrect way. To Central, the term "derived inspiration" means that the KJV has a lesser inspiration or a lower degree of inspiration ("not in the same sense as the originals"; "not in the absolute sense," etc.).

There is no lesser inspiration or lower degree of inspiration. Inspiration is inspiration. Either the King James Bible has the quality of God-breathedness, or it does not. Either it is inspired the way Scripture claims that the Bible is inspired or else it is not inspired at all. The idea of a lesser inspiration, lower inspiration, or lower degree of inspiration is not consistent with the plenary and verbal inspiration of II Timothy three, verse sixteen.

The King James Bible does have a derived inspiration. However, that does not refer to the **EXTENT** that it is inspired, but to the **REASON** that it is inspired. The term, "derived inspiration" can not refer to the **QUANTITY** of inspiration, but to the **QUALITY** of God-breathedness which it possesses.

The King James Bible is the plenarily and verbally inspired Word of God **BECAUSE** it was translated from words which were breathed out by God, and because those words **DID NOT LOOSE THEIR INSPIRATION WHEN THEY WERE TRANSLATED.** The quality of God-breathedness did not leak out or evaporate from the words which were accurately translated. So, "derived inspiration" can not refer to **HOW MUCH** the KJV is inspired, but only to the **PROCESS BY WHICH IT RETAINED THE INSPIRATION** of the words God breathed out.

All of this business about the KJV being the Word of God only to a **"DEGREE"** and saying that it is not inspired **"IN THE SAME SENSE"** as the original text is to downplay the inspiration of the Bible, the only Bible most people have. This seems unwise. Unwise and without scriptural authorization. Where is the chapter and verse for **DEGREES** of inspiration, one degree for the original and a lower degree for copies or for the KJV?

When Paul wrote to Timothy and said, "All scripture is given by inspiration of God" (II Tim. 3:16), the Holy Spirit was not referring to the original autographs but to a Greek translation **WHICH TIMOTHY HAD.** It was a Greek translation of the Old Testament which was profitable to Timothy for doctrine, reproof, correction, and instruction. This was the same Scripture which Timothy had known since he was a child (v. 15), the same Scripture which had made him wise unto salvation (v. 15). This was the same Scripture which had been taught to him by his grandmother, Lois, and his mother, Eunice (II Tim. 1:5). It was not the original autographs, for they had been long before lost or worn out. The Scriptures which Timothy **HAD** and **USED** for doctrine, reproof, correction, and instruction, and which God the Holy Spirit said were "given by inspiration" was a translation. And Paul did not downplay it. He did not say, "Well, there are degrees of inspiration, Timothy, and **YOUR** Scriptures are not inspired to the same degree as the originals." Paul did not use the kind of language used in *The Bible Version Debate*, i.e., "Your translation is not inspired in the same degree as ..." (p. 129) or "Your translation is not inspired in the absolute sense" (p. 130). It is inspired only in "a practical, virtual sense but not in a technical sense" (p. 120).

Inspiration is not in degrees, nor is it a higher o r a lower level. Either the Bible we have is inspired, breathed out by God, or it is not.

We are not arguing here for, so called, "double inspiration" i.e., that the translators of the KJV were used by God to "reinspire" the Word of God. The fact is that the words of God were **ALREADY INSPIRED** before the KJV translators ever handled them or read them. Those words did not have to be "reinspired" in order for us to have an inspired Bible in the KJV.

As Dr. Ian Paisley, the Free Presbyterian fundamentalist from Ulster, has said "The inspiration of the Bible **DID NOT EVAPORATE**" just because it was translated.

More than twenty-five years ago, before there was much awareness in fundamentalism of the dangers of downplaying the accuracy of the KJV, H. O. Van Gilder wrote about the importance of believing in the inspiration of the King James Bible. Writing in the February, 1972 issue of the *Baptist Bulletin*, Van Gilder wrote that it was disturbing to him to discover "a widespread malaise within our own ranks, a weakness and debility arising from a strange view which leaves the preacher holding a weapon which he believes **WAS** the Sword of the Spirit, deriving his texts from a source book from which he believes the divine element evaporated centuries ago!"

"This ailment comes from a defective view of inspiration," wrote the former National Representative of the GARBC (1944-1948), "a faulty and inadequate definition."

After explaining that inspiration does not refer to **WRITERS** but to the Scriptures themselves, Van Gilder says of II Timothy 3:16 that, "the assertion concerning the Scriptures was made in such a way as to indicate that the quality of 'God-breathedness' is not limited to the original autographs. Paul was speaking of the Scriptures which Timothy had known from his youth...."

Van Gilder goes on to argue that what Timothy read, the "Scripture" to which Paul referred, was not the autographs nor even a copy. It was a Greek translation of the Old Testament.

Van Gilder was not a King James only man and there is much he said with which this writer disagrees. Some of those he quotes favorably held very different views from ours. But, he was right to say that the Bible we use is the inspired Word of God. And he was right to find it disturbing that many people seem to think that inspiration evaporated from the Bible when it was copied or translated. He was wise to attempt to build, rather than to destroy, confidence in the King James Bible as the inspired Word of God.

Van Gilder wrote, "the Holy Spirit who gave the Word is affirming through Paul that the **TRANSLATION**

48

Timothy used, whether the Septuagint or some other, had that divine attribute of God-breathedness which made it profitable...It is a strange phenomenon of our day that men who believe in verbal inspiration of the original autographs lost sight of the real nature of inspiration as 'a quality which Scripture possesses' [Warfield and Basil] and so **HAVE NO INSPIRED SCRIPTURE** [emphasis mine]. The person who rejects the doctrine of verbal inspiration but who does believe in the inspiration of concepts, propositions, truth [in a translation] actually holds a **HIGHER VIEW OF INSPIRATION** than the person who contends for inspiration of the words [of the autographs] but believes the element of God-breathedness evaporated when the last autographs disappeared."

Those who believe the text underlying the KJV is a corrupted inferior text, and think that the KJV is an "unfortunate," "poor," "inaccurate" version cannot imagine how the Book could be called "inspired" in any **UNQUALIFIED** sense. They think it must be qualified with "not in the same sense," "not in an absolute sense," "only in a secondary sense," "only in a derived sense," and "not in a technical sense." These critics of the KJV and of its underlying texts cannot imagine how anyone could believe in its inspiration unless they believe the translators were inspired to "reinspire" it.

As a matter of fact, neither the KJV translators **NOR THE ORIGINAL PENMEN OF THE BIBLE** were inspired. It is the **WORDS** of Scripture which are inspired, not the writers or translators. The words were breathed out by God, and therefore are inspired. Those words are the inspired words of God wherever they are found, no matter who writes them, no matter in which language they are translated. So, when Pettegrew says in bold headlines, **"The King James not 'Breathed-out' by God"** (p. 7), he is simply wrong.

Contrary to the way KJV-only preachers are misrepresented, hardly any of them believe that the KJV translators were inspired. This writer cannot name even one. As often as this issue is raised by KJV opponents we might think that it is a big problem and that many KJV-only preachers hold to that position. Not so! Most KJV advocates would say that the translators were well prepared for their work, that they were helped by God in their work, that they were the best educated in languages and the most reverent of the Scriptures of any group of translators who ever sat to do that work, and that the result of their work is that we have the inspired Word of God in English. But, that is the process of **PRESERVATION** and not of "reinspiration."

12. Professor Pettegrew says, "God has not chosen to extend the **MIRACLE** of inspiration beyond the work of prophets and apostles to include translations." [p. 9]

Analysis: This dogmatic denial of the possibility of any miracle in the process of the preservation of God's Word is a theme which is repeated throughout the book. W. Edward Glenny says, for example, "We do not believe that God has perfectly, preserved His Word by **MIRACULOUS, SUPERNATURAL** means..." (p. 71). "The Scriptures do not teach that God will **MIRACULOUSLY** PRESERVE His Word..." (p. 92). "...God has not **MIRACULOUSLY** and perfectly preserved His Word in any one manuscript or group of manuscripts or in all the manuscripts" (p. 99). "We do not believe that God has preserved His Word perfectly and **MIRACULOUSLY** in any one manuscript or group of manuscripts, or in all the manuscripts" (p. 131).

We are dealing at this time only with the assertion that there are no miracles (or anything supernatural) involved in the preservation of the Bible, we will deal later with the issue of whether God preserved His Word **PERFECTLY** or **IMPERFECTLY**.

Neither Pettegrew nor Glenny can prove that God did not perform any miracles in the providential preservation of the Bible. Yet, the possibility of miracles is dogmatically excluded. In his end notes, Pettegrew says, "The preservation of Scripture has been normally accomplished through providence rather than through miracle" and, "Historically, God providentially, rather than miraculously, preserved the text of the Old Testament" (p. 14). Pettegrew cannot prove this, and no proof is offered except that he mentions that the Books of the Law at one time were lost for almost fifty years. But, that incident does not prove Pettegrew's point. If anything, the fact that the Law was lost (or hidden by God!) for fifty years, and then found at the right time may admit of miracles in preservation rather than divine inattention and non-involvement. It was not a mutual coincidence that the Word of God was rediscovered by the high priest at the right time for King Josiah to lead his people to repentance and revival (II Kings 22:8-13). It was not an accident that a copy of the Law was hidden and kept safe in a time when evil men were destroying all the copies they could find. Whether or not there were miracles involved in this concealing and the resurrecting of the precious Word of God is not a matter we should be dogmatic about. However, it is certain that the Book was not hidden from God! And it is certain that the entire incident resulted in the Word of God being **PRESERVED** and not destroyed, corrupted, or changed. We fail to see how the incident is any proof that miracles do not happen in the preservation of God's Word.

In discussing the passage in II Kings, Matthew Henry takes a more reverent and realistic view of Bible preservation than does Professor Pettegrew. He says,

> Whoever were the instruments of its preservation, we ought to acknowledge the hand of God in it...I am sure we now have reason to thank God, upon our knees, for that happy providence by which Hilkiah found this book at this time, found it when he sought it not...If the Holy Scriptures had not been of God, they would not have been in being at this day; God's care of the Bible is a plain indication of his interest in it.

A miracle is an event obvious to the senses, produced for a holy purpose by the immediate agency of God; an event, therefore, which (though not necessarily conflicting with any law of nature), the laws of nature, if fully known, would not, without this immediate agency of God, be competent to explain [Bancroft].

A miracle is a result which comes about from the direct volition and intervention of God. The result is not necessarily contrary to nature, or **UNNATURAL**.

Someone said, "The daily miracles of God have grown cheap by repetition." God has intervened so often in the preservation of His Word through the hearts and minds of His true people and through the teaching, convicting ministry of the Holy Spirit that God's people have failed to take notice of it. However, we can be sure that God has not withdrawn from something so important as the keeping of His Holy Words. He has not left this work to the sole government of creatures.

The very fact that Satan hates the Bible and wants to destroy it leads us to believe that it is not at all unreasonable that God miraculously preserves His Word. Satan brings all of his supernatural power against the Word of God in the translating of it, in the keeping of it, and in the teaching of it, but God protects His Word. Why would He not do supernatural, miraculous things in this spiritual battle? It is difficult for us to see how God could keep His promises to preserve His Word without doing some miracles all along the way. Jesus said, "My words shall not pass away" (Matt. 24:35); "Till heaven and earth pass, one jot or one tittle shall in no wise pass from the law, till all be fulfilled" (Matt. 5:18). How could this be done without God's miraculous involvement?

The very antiquity of the Bible tells us that God has miraculously preserved His Word. How many books do we have which were written nineteen hundred years ago or three thousand five hundred years ago? Yet, we have a multitude of copies of the ancient texts of the Bible. **How can this be explained apart from the miraculous intervention of God?**

This writer does not claim to know if God performed any **SPECIAL** miracles (what some theologians call "absolute miracles") in, or among, the KJV translators, but we do not believe Pettegrew knows either. He should not elevate his opinion in the matter to the level of Bible doctrine.

Central makes a mistake when the professors contrast "miraculous" with "natural" and "miraculous" with "providential" (p. 14) as if these terms are mutually exclusive. It is entirely possible that God used some miracles in the providential preservation of Scripture. It is also true that some of those miracles may have used natural means since miracles are above nature but not necessarily contrary to nature, or unnatural. Indeed, God sometimes uses nature to bring about His miraculous works.

13. Professor Pettegrew charges, "since the King James Version was first produced, it has undergone five revisions." [p. 9]

Analysis: The King James Bible has never been revised. There have been many new editions which corrected printing and spelling errors. And with each of the earlier new editions, new spelling and printing errors were introduced. But, the King James Bible has never been revised. It is a ruse to say it has been revised.

The spelling and printing errors of the 1611 edition are talked up by KJV critics to try to show that the "first KJV" was far from perfect, and to show that it is okay to make new revisions of the Bible. But it is a hoax to say that the KJV has been revised.

In new editions of any book the printing errors and spelling errors are corrected. Printing and spelling errors always occur when new books are published. In Central's book, _**The Bible Version Debate**_, for example, there is a sentence fragment on page VI. This will probably be corrected in any future editions of the book, but no one is going to find fault with Central's scholarship or doctrine because of this printing error. And no one will say the book has been **REVISED** if only errors of this sort are corrected. A new edition is not necessarily a revision. The language was changing very rapidly in A.D. 1600. In fact, modern English was only recently created. There was still no "correct" way to spell many English words. Almost all of the spelling and printing errors were corrected in the KJV in 1629 when the second edition came out. It was not a revision. Many more of the spelling and printing errors were corrected by 1769. We refer to "spelling errors" by today's standards.

Almost all of the changes made in the KJV were spelling and printing errors. There were only 421 phonetic changes (changes in any sound of any word), according to Waite. That is 421 words out of 791,328. Of those 421 words, 283 of them were changes in the form of a word. The remaining 136 changes were such things as an extra "of" or "and," "towards" instead of "toward," "burnt" instead of "burned," "lift up" instead of "lifted up," "among" instead of "amongst," and "you" instead of "ye" [*Defending the King James Bible*, p. 4].

As Dr. Kirk D. DiVietro has very aptly pointed out, "The text of the King James Bible is the intended text of the translators, not the physical text of a printing machine" [*Disproving the Myths*, p. 77].

The KJV has remained exactly the same for nearly 250 years, and **VIRTUALLY** the same for 350 years! It has never been revised! A "revision," as the word applies to the Bible versions, is a much more wholesale change. "Revision" does not refer, and has never referred anywhere in the history of publishing, to changes in spelling, punctuation, printing errors, and forms of words. All of the changes to the KJV came very early in its history, most of them made by some of the original translators. And having been providentially guided by God, the Book, as we now have it, is the one we defend as the inspired Word of God, all of those minor changes having been worked out long ago.

The only two possible reasons that I can think of for anyone to talk about the KJV having been "revised" because "thousands of changes have been made since 1611" are (1) They are trying to justify making revisions of the Bible, and (2) They are trying to destroy the confidence of people in the Bible which they have and hold. These two reasons always go together because the only way the publishers and merchandisers of new versions can sell them is by destroying the confidence that people have in the KJV.

14. When Brother Pettegrew gets around to giving examples of "some poor translations in the King James Version" (p. 10), he begins by appealing to our desire to be good baptists. He says, "When the Anglicans needed to translate the Greek word, *baptizo*, for example, they were unable to translate it as immerse because of their personal doctrine...most Bible-believing baptists would consider that a mistake." [p. 10]

Analysis: Pettegrew is simply wrong about the word *baptism*. The word was an English word in 1611. It was not a Greek word. **It had been an English word for hundreds of years before the King James translators were born.** The word was in common English usage. The fact that the word had a Greek origin does not make it a Greek word.

Baptisid and *baptym* were found in Wycliffe's Bible in A.D. 1380. This was 220 years before the King James translators used the word.

Tyndale's Bible in 1534, said *baptysed* and *baptim.*

Coverdale's Bible said, *baptysed* and *baptyme*, in 1535.

The Great Bible said, *baptysed* and *baptyme* in 1539.

The Geneva Bible of 1559 said, *baptized* and *baptisme.*

Even the Rheims Bible said *baptized* and *baptisme,* in 1582.

For Pettegrew to say that the King James translators made a mistake because, as he implies, they put a Greek word into an English Bible without translating it is like saying that we should not use the word **MILLENNIUM**, and that we should say **THOUSAND YEARS** instead, because millennium is a Latin word. The fact is that millennium is an English word which has a Latin origin.

Furthermore, baptize means immerse and immerse means baptize and both of them mean "to dip." So what could be wrong with the word?

The word *baptizo* does indeed mean to immerse, or to dip. That is the very literal meaning of the word. However, in using the word *baptizo* **FOR THE ORDINANCE OF WATER BAPTISM**, the Holy Spirit obviously meant more than that. The ordinance of baptism is more than a burial. It is also a resurrection (Romans 6:4). Burial is only half of baptism. The ordinance takes its name from only one part of the activity involved. We should keep in mind that baptism pictures not only that Christ was buried but that He also came out of the grave. And we must remember that the believer is not just dead to self, but also spiritually raised to walk in newness of life. All of this is pictured in baptism. Therefore, we must conclude that the Holy Spirit helped the

KJV translators to wisely use the word baptize rather than immerse.

There is nothing wrong with occasionally transliterating a word. When this writer was in college, he took an English course called Origin of English Words. We found that most English words came from other languages, usually by transliteration, which is to say that a Greek word (for example) was changed phonetically to make its pronunciation easier and it was brought right over into English usage. There is nothing wrong with that. It happens often, especially when a single word equivalency cannot be found in the receptor language which conveys all of the meaning of the original word. There is nothing dishonest or prejudicial about that process. However, the KJV translators did not do that with the word *baptize*. They did not have to. The word *baptize* was already a common English word with which all English speaking people were familiar.

Of course, with the professor saying that "baptize" is a poor translation in the King James, we can expect the "new," "better," and "clearer" versions to translate it "immerse," right? Now that Brother Pettegrew has found fault with only the King James, and with no others, we can be sure that the NIV, NASB, RSV, NEB, Phillips, LB, and all the rest, have gotten BEYOND this "poor translating." We can expect these new, improved, up-to-date versions to be more baptistic, right? They say "immerse," right? But wait! When we turn to these new versions we see that they have been translated by a bunch of Anglicans, just like those who translated the KJV! Every new version we checked says "baptize." Not a single one of them says "immerse." Why do you suppose that the professor did not criticize the new versions on this point? We find it rather disingenuous and unfair to criticize the KJV for "poor translations" while finding no fault with the new versions which have identical renderings.

15. Pettegrew offers as a second "mistake" in the King James Bible that "The King James translators also often translated the Greek word for demons as 'devils'...The Bible teaches that there is only one devil, but many demons; therefore, this is an instance of poor translation." [p. 10]

**Analysis:** The professor is simply wrong. It would be correct to say that the Bible teaches that there is only one Satan. It is not correct to say that the Bible teaches that there is only one devil. The word devil (in both 1611 and today) in the English language has always referred to both demons and Satan.

We turn to _**Webster's Encyclopedic Dictionary of the English Language**_. The first definition for devil is "an evil spirit, a demon."

**Webster's New Universal Unabridged Dictionary** divides the first definition into two parts, "(a) The Chief Evil Spirit... (b) any of such subordinate beings who reside in hell; a demon."

**The World Book Dictionary** says, "any evil spirit, fiend, or demon."

Noah Webster's first edition, 1828, says, "In Christian theology, an evil spirit or being; a fallen angel, expelled from heaven for rebellion against God."

The _**American Heritage Dictionary**_ divides it's first definition into two parts, saying, "(a) the major spirit of evil, especially in Christian theology, (b) a demon or similar evil spirit."

It appears that in the English language both Satan and demons are called devils. If Central had to find fault on this issue, it is the receptor language which should have been blamed, not the KJV.

The Greek words *Daimonian* and *Daimon* are found about seventy-five times in the New Testament. These words refer to demons, or devils.

The Greek word *diabolos* is found about thirty-one times in the New Testament. In most cases it refers to Satan, but not in every case. It refers to Judas Iscariot (John 6:70); to seducing spirits (I Tim. 4:1); and to false accusers (II Tim. 3:2; and Titus 2:3).

All of the above words are translated "devil," or "devils," but the King James Bible always makes the distinction between Satan and demons when the word *devil* is used. It is in the plural fifty-one of the 106 times the word "devils" appears. When it is plural it cannot refer to Satan. In the cases where the word is singular (devil) the definite article is used in every place where it refers to Satan (the devil).

An indefinite article is used in almost every instance where the word refers to demons (a devil). In the few places where "the devil" refers to a demon it is referring to a **SPECIFIC** demon, and the context makes it clear that Satan is not being referenced.

So, what is the problem? The words are all properly translated in the KJV because English usage clearly allows *diabolos* to be translated for either the devil (Satan) or for devils (evil spirits); and still, the KJV makes it clear whether it is Satan or demons which are under discussion.

When Professor Pettegrew decided to show us "some poor translations" and "mistakes" in the King James Bible he came up with two well-worn mantras. He came up with two "truisms" which are not true, two "facts" which are not factual, two complaints which have been heard so often that those who repeat them have begun to believe them. Upon closer examination these examples are found to be false accusations against the King James Bible. If these two examples are what Pettegrew sees as "mistakes," then there is nothing wrong with the KJV.

16. The professor continues by saying that "fundamentalists are not necessarily King James only." [p. 10]

**Analysis:** Of course, fundamentalists are not necessarily King James only. No one, to our knowledge, ever said they were. But, **FUNDAMENTALISTS ARE NOT NECESSARILY _NOT_ KING JAMES ONLY, EITHER.** This is a fact that Central seems to be having a difficult time accepting. The King James only person is "less of a fundamentalist" (p. 13), according to Pettegrew.

The issue of the text was never a huge issue in fundamentalism until about thirty years ago. Fundamentalists just trusted what they were taught by conservative scholars, who, in turn, had been misled by liberal scholars. In the past thirty years, as the subject of the text and translations has been studied more, thousands of fundamentalists have come to the position that God has preserved His Word perfectly in the Traditional Texts of Scripture and in the KJV. Indeed, when presented with the evidence, many ordinary preachers and Christians find the evidence underpinning the KJV to be irresistible, which is to say that to believe in the superiority of the Traditional Texts and the KJV is often the most reasonable and the most logical.

On the other hand, many of us do not find the Critical Text position or Eclectic Text position, such as is held by Central, to be convincing. We do not believe God preserved His Word **IMPERFECTLY**. We do not believe that God would fail to protect the **WORDS** of the writings of the canon of Scripture after He had given them to man under a process of plenary verbal inspiration. We do not find it credible that the words of God were best preserved in the Roman Catholic Church, rather than among God's true people. We do not think that two or three newly found manuscripts outweigh the evidence of the other 5,000 manuscripts. We do not believe that the translators of the NIV, the NASV, and the RSV were better scholars or more qualified than the translators of the KJV.

No, "fundamentalists are not necessarily King James only." However, the KJV-only position is a growing movement among fundamentalists. The momentum is in the direction of the KJV position. More and more preachers, Bible colleges, and seminaries are coming to the position that the King James Bible must be our final authority in the English language.

We do not believe that Critical Text people cannot be fundamentalists. Most of us once held the Critical Text position, and it took quite a long time and much study for us to come to the KJV-only view. Most of us KJV-only people love and respect many who differ with us on this issue. We have not made the text a test of fellowship. We do not believe it is helpful for people on either side to call names, cast aspersions on others, or treat one another with contempt.

It is fine to try to convince one another of sincerely held positions. Let us talk, debate, discuss, and write to each other. But, let not either side pretend that truth will die when they do, nor pretend that only they have ownership of the name "fundamentalist."

CHAPTER THREE

Professor Roy E. Beacham wrote the third chapter of Central Seminary's book **_The Bible Version Debate_**. He continues to develop the presupposition that there are mistakes in the Bible (in all of its copies, translations, and versions) because God has not perfectly preserved His Word. He finds many faults with the Old Testament Masoretic Text which he believes made it impossible for the King James translators to give us a perfect Bible in English. Indeed, it seems strange and incongruous to see a fundamentalist critically attacking the text of the Bible instead of trying to build the confidence of God's people in their Bible. Instead of detailing the many, many positive factors about the copying of the Old Testament text, reasons for believing that our Bible can be trusted, Beacham chooses to develop all of the destructive negatives.

17. The professor begins by listing "arguments against perfect preservation in the Masoretic Text." Stating that the Masoretic Text needs "critical analysis" and that it is a "simplistic answer" to say that the Masoretic Text best represents or perfectly preserves the Old Testament text. [p. 18]

Analysis: Naturally, we wonder which text Beacham would prefer. If he does not believe that the Masoretic Text is the best nor the perfectly preserved text then which one **DOES** he think is best? Or does he, as we suspect, just want a more **COMPLEX ANSWER**?

If Beacham gets his way and believers are forced to accept only complex answers, then the vast majority of ordinary Christians will never know what the Bible says! At least 99.99% of all Christians who have ever lived have not understood anything about the methods of Masoretic scribes, recensions, textual families, linguistic develop-ments, the history of orthography, or grammatical constructions and pronunciations in the Hebrew language. These are the things Beacham thinks we must understand in order to critically analyze the text. However, if believers have to go to Beacham, and scholars like him, in order to know what the Bible says, then those scholars will be the final authority in all matters of faith and practice, **NOT THE BIBLE**.

We have to ask ourselves, did God really intend for it to be that **COMPLEX**? Did God really intend that here in the last days of the Church Age we should not be able to be sure of what the Bible is or what it says?

18. According to Professor Beacham, "numerous significant factors were at work in the development of the text of the Old Testament Scriptures" which make it impossible to have a perfect Bible today. He mentions linguistic developments with their spelling, grammar, and

pronunciation changes. These, he says, "affected the text."
[p. 19]

Analysis: Without a doubt there were changes in spelling,
grammar, and pronunciation in the medieval Hebrew
language. This is true of every language. There are changes
over time, and there are even greatly differing dialects
within the same language and in the same generation. Some
of these differences are indeed profound enough to make
what could almost be considered to be foreign languages.
**BUT HOW DOES THIS PREVENT US FROM
HAVING A PERFECT BIBLE?** Changes in spelling do
not prevent the Bible from being accurately translated. The
Bible can be accurately translated no matter how the words
were pronounced in Hebrew. Changes in accepted Hebrew
grammar could not possibly preclude an accurate translation
into English. Changing of consonants and adding vowel
points does not make it impossible to translate the Old
Testament into English. Not only was God able to give us a
perfect Bible, **IT WAS HIS STATED INTENTION TO
DO SO.**

19. Beacham downplays the influence of God in the
preservation of the Old Testament text while magnifying the
destructive influences. He says the Masorite's copies were
copied "apart from the direct supervision of the Holy Spirit
(for the Bible never speaks of Spirit supervision apart from
the original authors and autographs)." [p. 19]

Analysis: God promised to preserve His Word. Of course,
Central Seminary "explains away" all of those promises (pp.
86-93). God's role in the preservation of Scripture is thus

greatly limited. Central dismisses the scriptural statements on preservation as follows: "not speaking of the exact words" (p. 87); do not "guarantee that every word…will be preserved" (p. 88); do not mean that the text of God's Word will remain intact centuries after the [Psalmist] dies" (p. 89); have "nothing to do with the words of Scripture being preserved perfectly" (p. 89); and "does not refer to the words" but to the "poor and the needy" (p. 91). After dismissing all of the pertinent scriptures as irrelevant, it is easy for Central to defend her position; but, at what cost?

We take God's promises to preserve His Word for the plain statements which they are. We believe that those plain words mean what they say and say what they mean. It is not a matter of interpretation, nor is it a matter of what the Bible "teaches." It is simply a matter of believing what the Bible plainly **SAYS**. The historic position of God's people throughout church history has been that these promises do indeed refer to God perfectly preserving the words of Holy Scripture.

In a later chapter we will deal more completely with the promises of God to preserve His words, and with Central's comments on those promises. For now let us simply read one of God's promises.

Matthew 24:35

"Heaven and earth shall pass away,
but my words shall not pass away."

If that is not a clear promise of the Lord Jesus Christ to preserve His words then language does not mean anything, there is no meaning to anything that God said, and we might as well forget about taking any words anywhere at face value. All of the Bible's words are the words of the Lord Jesus Christ, and He said His words would not pass away (disappear, be destroyed, or be lost). It is a clear promise that the world would always have the words of God.

According to the words of our Lord in John chapter fourteen, the Holy Spirit is (contrary to Beacham's statement) directly involved in the supervision of the preservation of the truth of God. The Holy Spirit is called "The Spirit of truth" (John 14:17; 15:26; 16:13). The Bible is the truth (John 17:17). The Holy Spirit (who gave the words of truth) living in believers will teach them to know the truth, and keep the truth. The truth is equal to "the words" that Jesus gave us (John 14:10). If a man loves the Lord he will know how to keep God's words and will be motivated to do so (John 14:23). The Holy Spirit has taught true believers (collectively) "all things" about the words of God, not just some things about some of His words (John 14:26).

In John, chapter sixteen, Jesus speaks again about how the Spirit of God would work in believers to help them to know and keep the words which He gave us. Jesus said that the Holy Spirit would guide us into all truth (John 16:13). Surely no one would want to **EXCLUDE THE WORDS OF SCRIPTURE** from the Holy Spirit guidance which Jesus promised! Jesus was referring to all truth, even the words of truth about the things of God as found in the Bible. Jesus said, "All things that the Father hath are mine: therefore said I, that he shall take of mine, and **SHALL SHOW IT UNTO YOU**" (John 16:15).

To summarize what the Lord Jesus said about Holy Spirit supervision in preserving the words of Scripture we note the following:

1. All of the Bible is included in "the truth" (John 16:15).
2. The Word of God is the truth (John 17:17).
3. Jesus promised that the Holy Spirit (the Spirit of truth) would be especially concerned with helping believers to **REMEMBER, KNOW,** and **KEEP** His words (John 14:10, 21, 23, 24, 26; 16:4).
4. The Holy Spirit has been active throughout the Church Age **TEACHING** all things to believers about what the Bible is and which words are the true words of God (John 14:10, 23, 26).
5. Jesus promised that the Holy Spirit would **GUIDE** us into **ALL** truth (John 16:13).
6. Jesus promised that the Holy Spirit would **SHOW** us all things which belong to God and Christ (John 16:14-15).

Beacham has several charts (pp. 21-29) which purport to show how imperfect copies were copied over and over, making more and more copies with errors perpetuated ad infinitum. What is wrong with this picture? In his charts errors are never corrected, corruptions are never destroyed, and poor readings are never eliminated. In Beacham's charts the only things which are **PRESERVED** and perpetual are the errors!

Charts help to make things **SEEM** scientific and accurate. People look at charts and think sometimes that all of the factors are represented in the chart. None of this is true about Beacham's charts.

His charts are theologically and historically incorrect for two reasons. First, the influence of God is left out of the charts. God was there all down through the centuries influencing the correcting of the errors which crept into the manuscripts.

Secondly, the charts do not even reflect the fact that careful scribes were searching out any errors before manuscripts could be copied.

The fact is that the errors which were copied were very few.

20. Beacham mentions all of the problems, all of the negative factors that he thinks makes it impossible for us to have a perfect Word of God today in English. There were differences in the Hebrew copies of the First Century, he points out. The Masorete scribes made changes during the Dark Ages, he says. The Masoretic Text is a late recension, he claims. [pp. 18-21]

Analysis: Yes, there were problems and challenges for God's people to overcome all through history in preserving the Old and New Testament Scriptures. Yes, some (relatively few) who copied the text made errors. Some of the errors were intentional while some were accidents. Yes, there were, and are, variants in the manuscripts. But, always the true words of God were there in the manuscripts and other biblical materials. In almost every case, the correct word was there in overwhelming numbers. Usually, where an error crept in it was corrected in scores of other manuscripts, and in some cases it was corrected in hundreds of other witnesses. And always, the Holy Spirit was "with" believers (in the Old Testament dispensations) or "in" believers in the Church Age. Yes, the Spirit of God was there to teach and guide the true people of God about the words of God, so that none of the words were lost, so that additions to the Word were rejected, and alterations were found out.

Why not focus on all the positive reasons why it is likely that we have the Word of God perfectly preserved? Why raise all of the destructive critical factors which tend to destroy the faith of ordinary Christians in their Bible? And why would anyone raise all of those destructive factors without even mentioning some of the wonderful confidence enhancing facts about how God worked in His people to preserve His Word?

We should focus on how God instilled in the Jews a holy reverence for His Word. The Jews were uniquely prepared by God to love His Word and to be zealous of it. To the Jews was given the responsibility of keeping the Word of God pure. "Unto them were committed the oracles of God" (Romans 3:2). And those Jews identified the Word of God with the very name and person of God and were determined to preserve it accurately, keeping out all additions and deletions. Those Jews considered it more important than life itself to prevent changes and corruptions from coming into the texts.

We should focus on the almost absolutely never failing methods the Jews used in copying the Word of God in order to prevent errors. The materials (animal skins, ink, and pens) had to all be properly prepared by holy hands.

The words and letters on each line had to be read and read again, pronounced aloud again and again before the scribe could go on to the next line. The letters had to be **COUNTED** on each line and on each page. A mistake, once found, meant the entire page or manuscript must be destroyed so that the mistake would not be perpetuated. Only professional, trained scribes could copy the Word of God, and the strictest possible rules had to be followed. When manuscripts became worn from reading and copying, they were destroyed so that they would not become illegible and allow mistakes to be made.

We should focus on the fact that Jesus authenticated the Old Testament text. Time and time again, Jesus endorsed the Old Testament **JUST AS IT WAS** in His day. He did not correct it. If there had been something wrong with the text, He would have straightened it out. He found not a word of fault with it. Jesus encouraged people to search the Scriptures and did not discourage faith in any part of the Old Testament (John 5:39). Jesus quoted the Old Testament all the time and never questioned a word of it. He said of the Old Testament which existed in His day, "These are the words which I spake unto you, while I was yet with you, that all things must be fulfilled, which were written in the law of Moses, and in the prophets, and in the psalms, concerning me" (Luke 24:44). Yes, Jesus put His holy, omniscient character behind His words as given in the Old Testament and did not say that anything should be changed about them.

We should focus on God and not upon man when we discuss Bible preservation. The Bible is God's Word, and He is zealous of His Word, holding it as dear to Him as His own Holy name! He gave us a verbally inspired, inerrant

Bible. Why would He not preserve it as an inspired, inerrant Bible? Especially since He promised to do so! God has the power to preserve His Word, even while He allows men to copy it and translate it. God has the volition and the desire to preserve His Word. So why would anyone downplay His influence in this process?

The text of the Masorete scribes (A.D. 500 – 1000) was the same Hebrew Old Testament text that Jesus read and approved. We know that this is true because of the wonderful things we have just mentioned about how the Old Testament was preserved. No copies of the Hebrew Old Testament exist which were copied between the time of our Lord and the time when the Masorete school began at Tiberius in A.D. 500. No doubt, all of the copies the Masoretes had when they began to copy the Word of God were destroyed. The copies would have been destroyed as they began to become illegible from use. But the Masoretes, continuing in the old Jewish tradition, were used of God to preserve His Word (changes in consonants, vowel points, and pronunciations not withstanding!).

Now why would the Central Seminary professors say negative things about the Masoretic Text? Could it be that they are simply trying to promote the NIV and the NASV? The NIV and the NASV do not strictly follow the Masoretic Text, choosing instead to follow some Greek translations of the Old Testament, the Samaritan Pentateuch, the Dead Sea Scrolls (copied by a cult), quotations of various men, and even their own guesses.

21. The final problem in Beacham's chapter which we will address is his teaching on the subject of faith. He rightly points out that true biblical faith must be faith in what God has said; however, he then advances to the erroneous conclusion that "the Bible does not teach, much less imply, that God providentially or supernaturally preserved his Word perfectly in the supposed standardized text of A.D. 100, the Second Rabbinic Bible of Jacob ben Chayyim, or any particular English translation, be it the King James version or some other translation." [p. 33]

**Analysis:** First, those who believe that we have a perfectly preserved Bible today base their faith on the promises of God. Of course, Central explains these verses away. We have cited the verses which tell us that God would show His people, guide His people into all truth, teach His people all things about the truth, and help God's people to keep the words of God and the things which belong to God.

Since the Masoretic Text is the only Hebrew text there is for the entire Old Testament, we know that that is the very place where God preserved His Word.

How does Beacham know that the canon of Scripture which all of us accept is correct? How does he know that the sixty-six books of the Bible are all of the books God intended for us to accept? How does he know that some of the books were not left out? How does he know God intended for them to be canonical? After all, God did not give us a list of canonical books. So, what is Beacham's faith based on?

The answer to the above questions should be that the canon of Scriptures is based on the same verses which I cite for promises of Bible preservation. If God could lead and guide His people to accept the right Books for the canon could He not also guide His people to accept the right words?

A considerable amount of faith is required if we are going to believe at all that we have God's Word, even in "a practical virtual sense." When we consider some of the facts in the history of the Old Testament text, we must conclude that God was overseeing and caring for the words of Scripture just as He had indicated in Matthew 5:18; 24:35; Psalm 119:152; Psalm 119:160; Isaiah 40:8; I Peter 1:23-25; Psalm 12:5-8; and John 14 and 16.

Yes, it requires faith to believe that we have God's Word when we consider the fact that some books of the Bible were written at least fifteen hundred years before Christ's first advent and that until the Dead Sea Scrolls were discovered there were no copies of any Old Testament book copied before A.D. 900.

The Codex Cairenis, copied in A.D. 900 by the Masoretes, contains the books of Joshua, Judges, Samuel, Kings, Isaiah, Jeremiah, Ezekiel, and the twelve minor prophets. That was the oldest copy of any part of the Old Testament that anyone had until 1947.

The Biblia Hebraica Stuttgartensia was copied from the Codex Leningradensis which is dated A.D. 1008.

Of course, since there are no copies of the Old Testament between 1500 B.C. and A.D. 900 we must have faith in God that He preserved His Word through those 2,400 years. We know that the Masoretes of Tiberius had copies in A.D. 500 which have long ago disappeared. The same is true of every generation of godly Jews who copied God's Word back through all of those centuries; they copied from copies which then ceased to exist.

Those 2,400 years constitute a huge gap of time. In whom will you have faith for the preservation of Scripture during that gap? You can either have faith in God or you can have faith in man. Those are the only two possibilities. The Dead Sea Scrolls are not much help, except in the case of the book of Isaiah. There is a complete copy of the book of Isaiah which dates back to about the time of Christ. Almost all of the biblical literature in the Dead Sea Scrolls consists of small fragments of animal skins and paper. The manuscripts had for the most part fallen apart, and the 60,000 fragments can not even be handled to this day lest they disintegrate. Some have been photo-copied, but they have not been studied much.

There is a scroll containing the minor prophets in Greek which dates to A.D. 130, found in a cave. There is a copy of the Ten Commandments (Nash Papyrus), dated A.D. 150. There are 200,000 fragments found in Saint Michael's Church in Cairo, dated A.D. 880. And, there is a Samaritan Pentateuch which dates back to 100 B.C., but it was copied by a group which rejected all of the Old Testament as Scripture with the exception of the books of Moses; and the work has great flaws, with 6,000 changes from the Jewish text in the five books of Moses. This is the sum total of the Hebrew manuscript evidence for the text of the Old Testament. **IS THERE A NEED FOR FAITH IN GOD THAT HE HAS PRESERVED THE OLD TESTAMENT TEXT?** Yes! And there is no room for faith **IN MAN** for the preservation of the text if you expect to have an Old Testament with even "derived inspiration."

Aside from the Hebrew manuscripts, we have some Greek translations of the Old Testament (although the stories about the seventy or seventy-two scribes copying the

Old Testament in seventy days and all of the seventy or seventy-two agreeing exactly with each other is probably an apocryphal story). There are some Latin, Syriac, Aramaic, and Armenian versions of the Old Testament (all late). However, **THERE ARE NO EARLY ORIGINAL LANGUAGE MANUSCRIPTS OF THE OLD TESTAMENT.** The Old Testament text is never going to be settled on that basis.

I have complete faith in the Old Testament as we have it in the King James Bible and in the process by which it came down from the Masoretic Text in Hebrew. This faith is not based on man's scholarship or intelligence. **I AM NOT A HUMANIST!** God prepared men and used men to help preserve the perfect Word of God, but I do not have faith in the men themselves. My faith is in God and His promises. I do not have faith in any men **TODAY** to make improvements in the text of the Old Testament as we have it in the KJV. The Lord God promised to preserve His Word, and I believe He has done it.

Our point is that if God preserved His Word (which He most assuredly did), He did it through the Masoretic Hebrew Text since that is the only one we have; and we fail to see any wisdom (or even any purpose) for anyone to question if it "best represents" the autographs. Furthermore, our point is that the Old Testament text **COULD NOT HAVE BEEN PRESERVED AT ALL** except for the intervention and oversight of God. The remaining question is, "How good of a job did God do caring for His Word?" Did He preserve it perfectly, as we believe; or did He allow errors which could not be found and corrected? If God allowed undetectable and uncorrectable errors, then how much error was God willing to keep in His Word?

CHAPTER FOUR

The fourth chapter of Central Seminary's book, _**The Bible Version Debate**_, was written by W. Edward Glenny. His purpose seems to be to defend modern textual criticism, show that the Greek text underlying the King James Bible is inferior, attack Erasmus and his work, and show that there are differences in the various editions of the King James Bible since A.D. 1611.

22. Professor Glenny defends modern textual criticism as a practice that "need not" be destructive. [p. 41]

**Analysis:** While it is true that textual criticism has not **ALL** been destructive, much of it has been **VERY** destructive, especially in the past 150 years.

Any textual criticism which has as its purpose to overthrow the Greek text underlying the King James Bible is **EXCEEDINGLY** destructive indeed. To overthrow the text of the King James Bible is to overthrow the text of most of the Bible-believing churches of the second and third centuries. To overthrow the Greek text underlying the KJV would be to overthrow most of the ancient Syriac and Italic versions of the Second Century. It would be to overthrow the text of most of the Anabaptist churches, Waldensian churches, and Albigensian churches. It would be to overthrow the text of the Protestant Reformation, the text of Tyndale, Luther, and Calvin. And to overthrow the text underlying the KJV would be to overthrow the text of the great Philadelphian Church Age of revival and missions. All of the above named people of God knew about the Origen-Eusebian-Constantine-Jerome-Jesuit Critical Text, **AND REJECTED IT**. For the modern day evangelical church to now allow the Traditional Text to be supplanted by the Critical Text is to be disloyal to (and to reject God's guidance of) the most faithful people of God in every generation of church history. That would be **VERY DESTRUCTIVE!**

Not **ALL** textual criticism has been destructive because there is a spiritual, biblical method of textual criticism. There have always been **TWO METHODS** of textual criticism. The method which has given us the King James Bible is a biblical and spiritual method; whereas, the method which brought to the world the new versions is a naturalistic and humanistic method.

After the King James Bible was delivered to the English world, in A.D. 1611, there was not much need for any further textual criticism (at least, not for the purpose of producing more English Bibles). It is only the unbelief of the critical method, a position that says we do not yet have the true Bible text and must still search for it which feels compelled to revise, and revise, and revise again.

The King James Bible was brought into existence through a biblical process. The texts and ancient versions which comprise the family which are behind the KJV were used by the true Bible believers, not by the Romanists. These Bible believers, considered enemies by Rome, were indwelt by the Holy Spirit and were led by the Holy Spirit to keep the Word of God pure. This was accomplished through the reality of the priesthood of the believer and through the guidance of God. The Traditional Text of Scripture was kept, copied, translated, and preserved by Bible-believing Christians and Bible-believing churches.

The only alternative to the above is a sort of humanist, neutralist, almost deist view of preservation. It is a view that suggests that God practices a laissez-faire attitude toward His Word; that God takes a "hands off" position and says, "Let people do what they choose about My Word."

The textual criticism which supports the Critical Text says that **MAN** preserved the Scriptures, and **MAN'S** own wisdom and scientific procedure will determine what the Bible is. On the other hand, the textual criticism which gave us the King James Bible says that **GOD** preserved His Word and the **HOLY SPIRIT** made the determination about what the Bible is. In other words, the Critical Text position is consistent with **HUMANIST** principles (this is very destructive!); whereas, the Traditional Text position is **THEISTIC** in its assumptions.

The textual criticism which supports the Critical Text believes in treating textual documents in a neutral way. Adherents to this position believe in treating the biblical textual documents in exactly the same way as texts of other ancient works. The holy words of God, it is said, should be treated just like we treat the extant manuscripts of Cicero,

Sophocles, Virgil, Thucydides, or Euripicles in determining the true text of these works. Why? Because it should be assumed that God was not involved in leading His people to know and keep His words. It should be assumed that the Holy Spirit did not teach God's people "all things," nor did He help God's people to keep the things which belong to Him. Therefore, it is believed, it is a good idea to accept shorter readings over longer ones, to accept "older" readings over those copied later, and to accept more difficult readings over more understandable ones. This is called "a science" by modern textual critics.

What are the facts? (A) God has been successfully involved in the preservation of His Word; (B) the Devil has attacked the Word of God in every way possible, especially in the copying and translating of it; (C) God's true people have been led by the Holy Spirit of God to know what the truth is and to hold fast to it; (D) the enemies of God, (i.e., the Devil and his false church) have tried, with some success to corrupt the Word of God; (E) God has never been neutral about His Word; (F) the Devil has never been neutral about God's Word; (G) the true people of God have never been neutral about God's Word; and, (H) there is nothing scientific about modern textual criticism.

Dr. Edward F. Hills wrote of the differences between the two approaches to textual criticism, the approach which produced the critical text and its new versions, on the one hand, and the approach which delivered to us the Traditional Text and its King James Version on the other. In his book, *The King James Version Defended* (pp. 111-112), Hills wrote:

Bentley, Zahn, Warfield, and countless others have tried to devise a theory of the special providential preservation of the Scriptures which leaves room for naturalistic New Testament textual criticism. But this is impossible, for the two concepts are mutually exclusive. Naturalistic New Testament textual criticism requires us to treat the text of the New Testament like the text of any other ancient book, in other words, to ignore or deny the special providential preservation of the Scriptures. Hence if we really believe in the special providential preservation of the Scriptures, then we cannot follow the naturalistic method of New Testament textual criticism.

For a believer, then, the only alternative is to follow a consistently Christian method of New Testament textual criticism in which all the principles are derived from the Bible itself and none is borrowed from the textual criticism of other ancient books....we...summarize [these Bible] principles briefly.

Principle One: The Old Testament text was preserved by the Old Testament priesthood and the scribes and scholars that grouped themselves around that priesthood.

Principle Two: When Christ died upon the cross, the Old Testament priesthood was abolished. In the New Testament dispensation every believer is a priest under Christ the great High Priest. Hence the New Testament text has been preserved by the universal priesthood of believers, by faithful Christians in every walk of life.

Principle Three: The Traditional Text, found in the vast majority of the Greek New Testament manuscripts, is the True Text because it represents the God-guided usage of this universal priesthood of believers.

Principle Four: The first printed text of the Greek New Testament represents a forward step in the providential preservation of the New Testament. In it the few errors of any consequence occurring in the Traditional Greek Text were corrected by the providence of God operating through the usage of the Latin-speaking Church of Western Europe. In other words, the editors and printers who produced this first printed Greek New Testament text were providentially guided by the usage of the Latin-speaking Church to follow the Latin Vulgate in those few places in which the Latin Church usage rather than the Greek Church usage had preserved the genuine reading.

Principle Five: Through the usage of Bible-believing Protestants God placed the stamp of His approval on this first printed text, and it became the Textus Receptus (Received Text). It is the printed form of the Traditional Text found in the vast majority of the Greek New Testament manuscripts.

Principle Six: The King James (Authorized) Version is an accurate translation of the Textus Receptus. On it God has placed the stamp of His approval through the long continued usage of English-speaking believers. Hence it should be used and defended today by Bible-believing Christians.

The view of textual criticism expressed by Professor Glenny is a "Johnny-Come-Lately" view among Protestants (and Baptists!). Not until the last half of the Nineteenth Century were Protestants convinced that the Alexandrian Text was superior. Of course, the Roman Catholic Church always believed what Central now teaches. The official text of Rome has been the Vulgate since A.D. 380, and the Vulgate agrees with the Critical Text. For Protestants, the change in belief started in England with some high church (Catholic-Lite) Anglicans by the names of Foss Brooke Westcott and Fenton John Anthony Hort.

Westcott and Hort were textual critics with strong Catholic leanings. Their Mariolatry, their sacradotalism, their baptismal regeneration view, their devotion to the pope, and their doctrine of purgatory have been widely reported. Their rationalism is so well established that it is simply a fraud to refer to them as conservatives. They were deeply influenced by liberals Tischendorf, Griesbach, and Lachmann. They seem to have been also influenced by Kreble (who said that England leaving Rome was "national apostasy"), Newman, and Pusey, all part of the Oxford movement.

Kreble was the originator of the Oxford movement (also called Puseyism or the Tractarian Society). The purpose of the movement was to take the Church of England back to Rome. John Henry Newman did leave the Church of England to join the Roman Catholic Church and was made a cardinal many years later.

Westcott and Hort's Greek Text was produced in the 1870's and was translated into the English Revised Version in A.D. 1881. Their text was produced from the Bible of the medieval Roman Catholic Church and followed some recently found Roman Catholic manuscripts of suspicious origin. The Vatican manuscript which was found in the Vatican Library, c.1480, the Sinai manuscript which was found by Tischendorf in 1859 in a Greek Orthodox monastery at the foot of Mt. Sinai (St. Catherines), and the Alexandrian manuscript which surfaced as a gift to the King of England from Cyril Lucar (patriarch of Constantinople) in 1627 became the basis of Westcott and Hort's efforts to dethrone the Traditional Text of the New Testament.

Unfortunately, the scholarship of Westcott and Hort was followed, with few questions, by liberals (such as Ellicott and Schaff) and conservatives (such as Warfield and the

Princeton scholars) alike. The reason for the unquestioned acceptance of Westcott and Hort's radical views by most liberals and conservatives seems to have been an inordinate respect for scholarship. Dr. Edward F. Hills writes of Benjamin Warfield's influence and his philosophical and theological dichotomy in his book, ***The King James Version Defended***, p. 110. (After finding fault with J. H. Skiton for saying, "Textual Criticism, in God's providence, is the means provided for ascertaining the text of the Bible.")

> And half a century earlier Dr. B. B. Warfield (1893) expressed himself in a very similar manner. "In the sense of the Westminster Confession, therefore, the multiplication of copies of the Scriptures, the several early efforts towards the revision of the text, the raising up of scholars in our own day to collect and collate manuscripts, and to reform them on scientific principles – of our Tischendorfs and Tregelleses, and Westcotts and Horts – are all parts of God's singular care and providence in preserving His inspired Word pure."
>
> Dr. B. B. Warfield was an outstanding defender of the orthodox Christian faith, so much so that one hesitates to criticize him in any way. Certainly no Bible-believing Christian would wish to say anything disrespectful concerning so venerable a Christian scholar. But nevertheless it is a fact that Dr. Warfield's thinking was not entirely unified. Through his mind ran two separate trains of thought which not even he could join together. The one train of thought was dogmatic, going back to the Protestant Reformation. When following this train of thought Dr. Warfield regarded Christianity as true. The other train of thought was apologetic, going back to the rationalistic viewpoint of the 18th century. When following this train of thought Dr. Warfield regarded Christianity as merely probable. And this same divided outlook was shared by Dr.

Warfield's colleagues at Princeton Seminary and by conservative theologians and scholars generally throughout the 19th and early 20th century. Even today this split-level thinking is still a factor to be reckoned with in conservative circles, although in far too many instances it has passed over into modernism.

Dr. Warfield's treatment of the New Testament text illustrates this cleavage in his thinking. In the realm of dogmatics he agreed with the Westminster Confession that the New Testament text had been "kept pure in all ages" by God's "singular care and providence," but in the realm of New Testament textual criticism he agreed with Westcott and Hort in ignoring God's providence and even went so far as to assert that the same methods were to be applied to the text of the New Testament that would be applied to the text of a morning newspaper. It was to bridge the gap between his dogmatics and his New Testament textual criticism that he suggested that God had worked providentially through Tischendorf, Tregelles, and Westcott and Hort to preserve the New Testament text.   But this suggestion leads to conclusions which are extremely bizarre and inconsistent. It would have us believe that during the   manuscript period   orthodox Christians   corrupted the New Testament text, that the text used by the Protestant Reformers was the worst of all, and that the True Text was not restored until the 19th century, when Tregelles brought it forth out of the Pope's library, when Tischendorf rescued it from a waste basket on Mt. Sinai, and when Westcott and Hort were providentially guided to construct a theory of it which ignores God's special providence and treats the text of the New Testament like the text of any other ancient book. But if the True New Testament Text was lost for 1500 years, how can we be sure that it has ever been found again?

Modern textual criticism (A.D. 1850-2000) has been highly destructive as it has attempted to overthrow the text of the Bible used by Bible-believing Christians for the past seventeen centuries. It has used naturalistic methods to attack the Bible text of the Reformation, the Bible of Luther, Calvin, Beza, Zwingly, Tyndale, and Knox. **THE CATHOLIC COUNTER-REFORMATION NEVER HAD A BETTER FRIEND THAN MODERN, NATURALISTIC, HUMANISTIC TEXTUAL CRITICISM**, because it has been partially successful in foisting upon unsuspecting Protestant and Baptist Christians the Bible of the medieval Roman Catholic Church (in the NIV and the NASV). This modern form of textual criticism has caused millions of Christians to question their Bible and lose faith in the inerrancy of Scripture because it has taught them that the Bible they hold in their hands is "a poor unfortunate translation" of a text which God has not perfectly preserved anywhere on earth.

This new form of textual criticism, which has given us all these new versions, has caused division and confusion in the church. Many churches have been split. Schools and fellowships have been torn asunder because it is insisted that new versions (with their huge differences in text) must be considered as superior to the Bible which God's people have used all along (for the past 400 years!). Contrary to what some have said in this regard, **IT IS THOSE WHO BRING IN THE NEW TEACHING TO A GROUP WHO CAUSE THE DIVISION,** not those who walk in the old paths.

So, when brother Glenny says that modern textual criticism "need not" be destructive, he is not being realistic. Modern textual criticism has already been extremely destructive.

23. Professor Glenny writes a full page of negative criticism of the Majority Text. He says it is "generally judged inferior"; it has conflations; it has "harmonization," which means to Glenny that the text has been tinkered with; it has "liturgically-motivated readings"; it is "scarce in the early manuscripts"; and it has "inferior style and content." And after all of this tirade against the text underlying the KJV, the professor mentions the Western text-type and the Alexandrian text-type, but **DOES NOT MENTION EVEN ONE PROBLEM WITH EITHER ONE!**

<u>*Analysis:*</u> There is plenty wrong with the Alexandrian Text (The Alexandrian and the Western are almost exactly the same thing with one of them being derived from the other.) (A) The newly found manuscripts (late 15th through 19th centuries) were discovered in places which should be considered suspicious to Bible believers. Egypt is a type of the world and Rome is Babylon in the Bible. More importantly, it is obvious that the manuscripts were not copied by Bible-believing Jews. The Jews were God's choice as the preservers of the ancient text (Rom. 3:2). The Traditional Text, on the other hand, is the Antiochian Text, the Syrian Text, the Palestinian Text which was copied and preserved by God's people in the earliest centuries of the church. The Traditional Text comes from the place where believers were first called Christians, where missionary work began, and where many of the autographs were written.

(B) Since Vaticanus and Siniaticus were both discovered late (A.D. 1480 and A.D. 1859) and their defenders admit that these two manuscripts are the very heart and core of the Critical Text, should we not ask ourselves why God allowed them to be lost for 950-1200 years? If they were the best manuscripts why would God not have them out there for His people to read?

(C) Vaticanus contains the Apocrypha as Scripture, and Sinaiticus contains the "Shepherd of Hermas," the "Epistle of Barnabus," and other pseudepigrapha.

(D) The best of the very earliest manuscripts were worn out from continuous use and were destroyed; but Vaticanus, Sinaiticus, and Alexandrinus survived because they were inferior (corruptions) and, therefore, not used.

(E) The readings of the Alexandrian Text (Critical Text) **ARE NOT AS OLD** as the readings of the Traditional Text. We know this because the ancient versions, the Syriac, the Italic, and especially the Peshitto (which may have been used by the Apostle John) most resemble the Traditional Text. These ancient versions which date from the Second Century are at least 150 years older than Vaticanus or Sinaiticus. The quotations of the Second and Third Century Palestinian and Syrian church fathers also favor the Traditional Text over the Alexandrian Text. So, it is simply not true that the Critical Text readings are the oldest.

(F) In addition to all of the above is the very strong probability that the Alexandrian Text is a corruption by Origen, copied under Eusebius' direction after having been ordered by Constantine for the newly formed Roman Catholic Church. Edward Miller, in his book, _**A Guide to the Textual Criticism of the New Testament**_ (1886), explains what almost certainly happened. [pp. 81-83]

...whilst Constantine was in the midst of his Semiarian stage, he gave the celebrated order to Eusebius, probably between A.D. 330 and 340, to send him fifty magnificent copies of the Holy Scriptures. They were to be written on the best vellum by skillful and accomplished penmen, and in a form well fitted for use. Orders were at the same time issued to the Governor of the province to supply the materials for the work, which was to be accomplished with all possible speed. Two carriages were placed at the disposal of Eusebius for conveying the copies to Constantinople, and he sent them off soon under the charge of a deacon.

Now there are various reasons for supposing that B and Sinaitius were amongst these fifty manuscripts. They are referred by the best judges to about the period of Constantine's letter, to speak generally. In Tischendorf's opinion, which is confirmed by Dr. Scrivener, the scribe of B wrote six "conjugate leaves" of Sinaiticus. These manuscripts are unrivaled for the beauty of their vellum and for their other grandeur, and are just what we should expect to find amongst such as would be supplied in obedience to an imperial command, and executed with the aid of imperial resources. They are also, as has been already stated, sister manuscripts, as may be inferred from their general resemblance in readings. They abound in omissions, and show marks of such carelessness as would attend an order carried out with more than ordinary expedition. And even the corrector, who always followed the copyist, did his work with similar carelessness to the scribe whom he was following. Besides which, it is expressly stated in Sinaiticus that it was collated with a very old manuscript corrected by Pamphilus after the Hexapla of Origen. And Caesarea was the place where manuscripts of Pamphilus and Origen would be found.

There is therefore very considerable foundation for the opinion entertained by many that these two celebrated manuscripts owe their execution to the order of Constantine, and show throughout the effects of the care of Eusebius, and the influence of Origen, whose works formed the staple of the Library of Pamphilus, in the city where they were most likely written.

Such was probably the parentage, and such the production of these two celebrated manuscripts, which are the main exponents of a form of Text differing from that which has come down to us from the Era of Chrysostom, and has since that time till very recent years been recognized as mainly supreme in the Church. And the question arises, which of the two was the generally accredited Text in the period which has just passed under review.

It is both strange and unreasonable for a seminary professor to find no problems with the Alexandrian Text, given the foregoing facts, and yet find a whole page of negative criticisms about the Greek text underlying the KJV. An honest and unbiased Eclectic Text man would reject Vaticanus and Siniaticus readings where they differ from the majority reading.

Glenny imagines that there are conflations in the Traditional Text, but the proof is simply not there that there are any conflations. Westcott and Hort thought they had found eight places where conflations exist in the KJV and its underlying text. That is eight places where two short readings are combined to form a longer reading (supposedly done by copyists to harmonize differences). There is at least as much proof that **ALEXANDRIAN COPYISTS SHORTENED THE ORIGINAL READINGS.**

I personally believe it is past time for the advocates of the Critical Text to stop the talk about "conflations," "harmonizations," "liturgically motivated readings," and "inferior style and content." All such talk is foolish. I say this in kindness and with due respect. There is not even any solid **EVIDENCE** for such subjective opinions, much less any **PROOF** that these charges are true. It appears that these same old canards are repeated—one professor copying another—without any original thinking. These unsubstantiated charges started with liberal critics of the Bible; and many conservatives, beginning with Warfield, have followed on like the proverbial sheep jumping off a cliff.

Professor Glenny charges that there is a "scarcity" of the Majority Text in early manuscripts. But, the fact is that there is a scarcity in both text-types, in both the Alexandrian family and the Majority family. There are no complete Greek manuscripts of the New Testament which were copied before the last half of the Fourth Century.

The Chester Beatty Papyri includes P^{45} which consists of most of the Gospels and Acts; P^{46} which has some of the Pauline Epistles; and P^{47} which is a copy of the Revelation. In addition to these we have the Bodmer Papyri which includes P^{66} consisting of a copy of John's Gospel; and P^{75} which is a copy of the Gospel of Luke and one verse of the Gospel of John. The Chester Beatty Papyri and the Bodmer Papyri are usually dated from A. D. 225 – 275. Beyond these, we have only some fragments dating before the last half of the Fourth Century. Some of the fragments contain part of a verse or part of a chapter.

Vaticanus and Sinaiticus are dated to the last half of the Fourth Century. They are nearly complete, but not quite. They have great problems. Vaticanus omits most of the book of Genesis, some of the Psalms, the Pastoral Epistles, about one-third of Hebrews, and the Revelation. In addition to containing various forms of Pseudepigrapha and Apocrypha, they present the problems of who wrote those manuscripts and where were they written. Tischendorf said that both Vaticanus and Sinaiticus were written by the same man. He was probably right about this. There is little doubt that these two manuscripts are two of the fifty Constantine-Eusebius productions—that is, **they are as Roman Catholic as the church which they helped to create.** Both seem to have been hurriedly and carelessly copied, and yet they are made of material that only a king could afford.

It is worth noting that Bible believing Christians have not been allowed to handle the Vatican manuscript. For the most part, Protestants have simply taken the Vatican's word for the date and composition of the document since it is kept under lock and key in the Vatican.

The Alexandrinus manuscript was copied in the Fifth Century. It can hardly be called complete since it is missing parts of Genesis, some of I Kings, some of the Gospel of Matthew, part of the Gospel of John, and most of II Corinthians. It contains some Pseudepigrapha.

There are only about four or five other manuscripts containing portions of the New Testament copied prior to the Sixth Century. There are also some fragments containing parts of verses or parts of chapters. There is the Ephraemi "C" manuscript, which no one believes is a good or trustworthy copy. "W" has only the Gospels. "O" has the book of Acts and the Gospels. "Q" has 235 verses from Luke and John.

That is about all there is for "the early manuscripts." There is an extreme "scarcity" of pre-Sixth Century Greek manuscript evidence for either the Critical Text or the

Traditional Text. There are three copies which are fairly complete (but not quite), about eight other manuscripts which contain a book (or books) of the New Testament, and some fragments. And the three more-or-less complete copies are not very good ones, but are corruptions with theological and philosophical bias. This is scarce evidence, indeed!

The truth is that most of the extant Greek manuscripts were copied in the Sixth through the Twelfth Centuries. This includes almost all of the important witnesses to the New Testament (between five and six thousand manuscripts). And the truth is that the vast majority of these manuscripts (between eighty-five and ninety-five percent), whether uncial or cursive, whether vellum or paper, are of the Traditional Text and agree with the King James Bible.

Vaticanus, Sinaiticus, and Alexandrinus are not enough to overturn all of the other evidence for the King James Bible. They are not enough to overturn the majority of the ancient versions (especially Syriac and Italic) which hold the Traditional Text. Nor are they enough to overturn the quotations of the church fathers.

The New Testament could be almost completely reconstructed from the quotations of the early church fathers' sermons and writings. Many parts of the New Testament could be reconstructed several times using this source. Those quotations favor the Traditional Text.

Edward Miller, in his book, **_A Guide to the Textual Criticism of the New Testament_**, writes of the evidence found in the early fathers and in the ancient versions (pp. 84-85).

...there is remaining even now to us sufficient demonstration of the existence and use of the Traditional Text in the first ages. The witness borne by the early Fathers to controverted readings proves that they used Manuscripts belonging to the Traditional Class which were much older than any now in existence. Take, for example, fifteen passages which are at the present time under discussion, and the following Fathers are found to testify upon them to the Traditional readings: --Ignatius (I), Papias (I), Justin Martyr (5), Irenaeus (6), Tertullian (7), Theophilus of Antioch (I), Hegesippus (I), Athenagoras (I), Vincentius (I), Marcion (I), Clement of Alexandria (3), Hippolytus (6), Acta Pilati (2), Origen (II), Dionysius of Alexandria (3), Apostolical Constitutions (6), Ps. Taian (2), Cyprian (Ii), Macarius Magnes (2), Julius Africanus (I), Titus of Bostra (2), Archelaus with Manes (I), Ps. Justin (I), Clementine Homilies (I), Arius (I), Eusebius (9), Athanasius (8), Aphraates the Persioan (4), Didymus (10), Epiphanius (11), Ephraem Syrus (6), Ps. Ephraem (1), Gregory Nazianzen (9), Gregory of Nyssa (26), Basil (8), Cyril of Jerusalem (2), Lucifer (2), and Leontius (1). That is to say, in 165 places as relating to only 15 chance passages in Holy Scripture Ecclesiastical Writers living before the Era of St. Chrysostom are proved to have followed Manuscripts thus witnessing to the Traditional Text. It should be borne in mind that it was only at the close of this period that Vaticanus and Sinaiticus, the two oldest manuscripts now existing, were produced.

In a similar manner, the Peshito and Italic Versions— including under the latter class the best of the Old Latin Versions -- were made two hundred years before those two Manuscripts, and – especially of the former — support the Traditional Text. Nor is occasional evidence subsequently wanting in the Egyptian Versions which, as has been seen, came out later in the same period.

There is therefore, as these specimens show, no warrant for asserting that the Traditional Text is not traceable back as far as the earliest age of the Church.

The fifteen passages Miller refers to are some over which we are still battling today, namely Matthew 1:18; Matthew 17:21; Mark 6:20; Mark 16:9-20; Luke 2:14; Luke 22:43-44; Luke 23:34; Luke 23:45; Luke 24:40; John 3:13; John 5:3-4; Acts 20:28; and I Timothy 3:16. It is good to know that these readings existed in the Second Century, proving that they are genuine and authentic in the Traditional Text and in the KJV. The fact that these obviously genuine readings are not in Vaticanus and Sinaiticus is evidence of the poor quality of those two manuscripts.

Should it trouble us that there is a "scarcity" of Greek manuscript evidence (especially of **TRUSTWORTHY** Greek manuscript evidence) in the earliest centuries of church history? **ABSOLUTELY NOT!** The text survived on through the Sixth through the Fourteenth Centuries, and beyond. God promised to preserve His Word and He did so. The witnesses other than Greek manuscripts (ancient versions and quotations of the fathers) corroborate the testimony of the Traditional Text.

FURTHERMORE, IF WE CAN TRUST GOD FOR THE AUTHENTICITY OF THE TEXT OF THE OLD TESTAMENT, WITH NO HEBREW MANUSCRIPT EVIDENCE BETWEEN 1500 B.C. AND A.D. 900, WE SHOULD BE ABLE TO TRUST GOD FOR A FEW HUNDRED YEARS ON THE NEW TESTAMENT TEXT.

We have no original language manuscripts for the book of Job except those copied in A.D. 900 by Massorite scribes. That is a gap of approximately 3000 years. Actually, we do not even know the language in which Job was originally written. Think of it, dear reader— **3000 YEARS WITH NO MANUSCRIPTS?** How would you know that Job is God's Word if you had to depend on "early manuscripts"? There is **ONE** way to know and that is by faith. God said He would preserve His Word and He kept His promise.

We have no Hebrew manuscripts for the Pentetuch until A.D. 900. Assuming that those five books were written in approximately 1500 B.C., that is a 2,400 year gap! With a gap of 2,400 years with no Hebrew manuscripts how do you know that the books of Moses are the Word of God, that they were properly copied? **YOU WILL NOT BE ABLE TO SETTLE IT ON THE BASIS OF EARLY MANUSCRIPTS!**

There is very little in the Old Testament (except for Isaiah) for which we have any Hebrew manuscripts copied before A.D. 900. We have two copies of Isaiah found in the Dead Sea Scrolls dated to about the time of Christ. With the exception of Isaiah, there is at least a 1300 year gap with no Hebrew manuscripts to support the text of most Old Testament books. The gap with Isaiah is only 800 years!

We have Greek and other versions of the Old Testament which are very old (and other evidence), but if we had to depend on early copies of Hebrew manuscripts to know what the text said we would have to throw out two thirds of our Bible (the entire Old Testament) as untrustworthy.

So it means absolutely nothing that there is a "scarcity" of Greek manuscript evidence in the first several centuries of church history. Our confidence is in the God of the Bible Who said that He would not allow His words to fall by the wayside never to be known to man again. Early copies were worn out and destroyed (especially the best ones!) but the Word of God is indestructible and unalterable. God always saw to it that the best copies were copied. The Holy Spirit taught God's people to know and keep the words of God.

24. Glenny finds fault with Erasmus, saying that he was a Catholic humanist (p. 48). The Central professor indicates that Erasmus made great errors because he had few manuscripts and translated occasionally from the Latin Vulgate. [pp. 49-51]

Analysis: First, it is not really necessary for us to defend Erasmus because the King James Version of the Bible is not based on the work of Erasmus alone. The Textus Receptus of Erasmus went through many improvements A.D. 1516 through A.D. 1611. Theodore Beza, John Calvin's scholarly and able associate, brought forth ten editions of the Receptus. Beza, who also served on the translation committee of the Geneva Bible (1560), worked tirelessly to make refinements in Erasmus' work. So what the King James translators had was not simply Erasmus' Greek text, but also Beza's text, Robert Stephanus' four editions of the Receptus, and other manuscript material.

If the King James translators kept a verse which Erasmus had put in (even though Central Seminary does not think the verse should be there), or if they kept a passage which Erasmus had translated from the Latin Vulgate (even though Central Seminary abhors this), we should assume that the King James translators looked at all the evidence (not just Erasmus' text) and decided the verse or the passage belonged there.

Even though it is not essential that we defend Erasmus, in the interest of truth and fairness we will point out that Erasmus was never a humanist in the modern sense of the word; and he was never a good Catholic (at least he was not a better Catholic than Luther).

Desiderius Erasmus was born in Rotterdam in about 1466. His parents both died when he was a young lad, leaving him in the care of guardians who misused and consumed his father's estate and placed him in a Catholic monastic school against his will (he wanted to attend a university). He was addicted to learning and to books from the very beginning and is widely believed to be not only the greatest scholar of his day but also one of the greatest scholars of all time. He is known to have done more to bring about the Reformation than any man except Luther.

Erasmus was not a humanist in the modern sense of the word, at least not in the sense in which fundamentalists use the word. Today's fundamentalists would say that humanism is the false belief that man is basically good and in complete control of his own destiny and does not have to resort to a belief in the supernatural. Erasmus did not believe in this kind of humanism.

Erasmus was a humanist only in the sense that he was a renaissance man who believed in new learning—new learning because he disliked the Roman Catholic scholastic theology of his day which did nothing to meet the needs of man for whom Erasmus mourned. According to **_Britannica_**, he attacked the established form of scholasticism and tried to learn from antiquity, and in the tradition of the Northern humanists (as opposed to the Southern or Italian humanists who were essentially secularists) his purpose was to serve religion. He had a conception of the Christian life grounded in the rhetorical, historical, and ethical standards of the Word of God and wanted to restore the Gospel to the center of Christian piety where it would serve the needs of ordinary people. Erasmus, therefore, opposed the arid intellectualization of faith and deplored ritual religion as practiced vicariously through a priest. According to Erasmus, peace and simplicity should be the aim of the good Christian, and the life of Christ should be his perfect model.

Erasmus did not believe man should be deified, nor did he believe that God was irrelevant in the world. So the only sense in which he was a humanist was in a sort of classical way in which he believed in "new learning" [Henry Cowan; **_Landmarks of Church History_**].

Erasmus was never a good Catholic. He was trained in Catholic schools but never felt comfortable with the teachings nor the practice of his church. According to Will Durant [**_The Story of Civilization: Part VI The Reformation_**], he opposed such Catholic institutions as indulgences, fasting, pilgrimages, auricular confessions, monasticism, clerical celibacy, relic worship, and prayers to the saints. He vociferously criticized the church, the popes, and the cardinals.

According to Jesse Hurlbut [*The Story of the Christian Church*], Erasmus accepted ordination to the priesthood but left the active priesthood in 1492 and was a relentless critic of the Roman Catholic Church.

According to B. K. Kuiper [*The Church in History*], Erasmus became attached to the Brethren of the Common Life, a movement which attacked indulgences, rejected transubstantiation, believed in justification by faith alone, and believed in salvation by grace alone.

Erasmus was attacked by Roman Catholic theologians as a "fomenter of the revolt" (reformation). The Council of Trent branded him an heretic and his works were forbidden to Catholic readers [Durant]. He was kicked off the faculty at Louvain.

Erasmus also did such un-Catholic things as defending Luther to Fredrick of Saxony, introduced Luther's ninety-five theses into England by sending them to John Colet and Thomas More, and when he knew he was dying he did not ask for a priest or confessor.

It would be difficult to distinguish between the core beliefs of Luther and Erasmus. They both contended for the same doctrines of the faith, and they both opposed the same evil practices of the Roman Catholic Church. For several years Luther collaborated with Erasmus and thanked God for him. It was only when Erasmus thought that Luther was going too far, too quickly, that division came. Neither Luther nor Erasmus left the Roman Catholic Church **VOLUNTARILY**. Luther was ex-communicated and Erasmus was not, but this had more to do with personality than with core beliefs. Latourette says in his book, *A History of Christianity*, Vol. II, chapter 32, that Luther and

Erasmus "were so much alike that there were those who attributed some of Luther's works to Erasmus."

Erasmus was more of a pacifist than was Luther (Luther had not a pacifist bone in his body!) and urged caution on the part of the Lutherans. Much like today's new evangelicals, Erasmus was a compromiser. He had other faults as well. But to call him "a Catholic humanist" and just let that accusation lie there with no qualification or explanation is not fair to this man who did some great works for God.

According to Kuiper, Erasmus' Greek Text was translated into German (by Luther), into French (by Calvin), into Dutch, and into English (by Tyndale). So the man did a good work for the Christian world for which we are indebted.

No doubt, Glenny hopes to prejudice his readers against the Receptus and against the KJV by attacking Erasmus in this way. However, Erasmus' faults are somewhat exaggerated, and even if Erasmus had been a Catholic humanist, it would not necessarily mean that his work was worthless, dishonest, or untrustworthy.

Glenny is critical of the Receptus because Erasmus had only seven manuscripts, none containing the whole New Testament. He says, "One was complete except for Revelation, and all the rest had various parts of the NT (1 had only Revelation, except for the last 6 verses; 2 had only the Gospels; 2 had only Acts and the Epistles; 1 had only the Pauline Epistles). All are from the 11th to 15th centuries" (p. 49).

What shall we say of this criticism by Professor Glenny? It should be mentioned first that Erasmus had read and studied hundreds of manuscripts of the New Testament. Searching out and studying those ancient manuscripts (both Greek copies and ancient versions) was Erasmus' forte. He was an expert textual critic (not of the neutralist-naturalistic type, but of the biblical-spiritual type). He went all over Europe searching for those manuscripts. He made notes on the variants in hundreds of manuscripts. He combed the great libraries at Paris, Rome, Oxford, Cambridge, Freibuch, Basel, and elsewhere. Erasmus read almost everything and remembered everything he read. So, the fact that he had only a few manuscripts available **at the time of his construction of the Textus Receptus** was not as great an impediment in arriving at the true text as Glenny would have us think.

Furthermore, the perfection and trustworthiness of the King James Bible should be looked upon as a winnowing or refining process extending from Tyndale through 1769. God used such men as Erasmus, Beza, Stephanus, Tyndale, the translators of the English versions which preceded the KJV, the translators of the KJV itself, and those who corrected printing and spelling errors between 1611 and 1769.

In response to Glenny, we must also point out that Beza, who refined Erasmus' text, **HAD MORE THAN SEVEN COPIES** of the New Testament with which he was familiar and which he studied.

The translators of the Great Bible, the Coverdale Bible, the Geneva Bible, and the other predecessors of the KJV **HAD STUDIED MORE THAN ERASMUS' SEVEN MANUSCRIPTS.**

Add to the above the fact that the King James translators themselves **HAD MORE THAN SEVEN MANU-SCRIPTS** and published texts with which to work, and Glenny's criticism of Erasmus' text, as it relates to the KJV, does not seem very important.

Glenny continues his criticism of Erasmus, "Because Erasmus had no Greek manuscript(s) containing the last six verses of Revelation, he translated these verses from the Latin Vulgate into Greek" (p. 49). This, according to Glenny, resulted in at least twenty errors which have no support whatever in any Greek manuscript and yet are found in the Textus Receptus today. Glenny does not specifically mention what these "errors" are, so we can not respond to them. Does he mean theological errors? Spelling errors? And more importantly, does Glenny believe these "errors" were followed by the KJV translators?

Not knowing exactly what Glenny means by "errors," we can only answer in a general way by saying that we do not believe it was wrong for Erasmus to use the Vulgate in order to construct those six verses. The Vulgate was not wrong about **EVERYTHING**. Erasmus was very critical of the Vulgate because of its pro-Catholic readings and because it was a translation from corrupted manuscripts in the genre of Vaticanus. However, Erasmus understood (what all of us should realize) that there were places where the Vulgate preserved the correct reading even when the Greek church did not.

Glenny then finds fault with Erasmus, saying, "In Acts 9:6 Erasmus added to his Greek text the words '**AND HE TREMBLING AND ASTONISHED SAID, LORD, WHAT WILT THOU HAVE ME TO DO? AND THE**

LORD SAID UNTO HIM..."' (p. 50). Again these are words which Erasmus found in the Vulgate. But, the reading is also found in the old Latin versions, the ancient Syrian versions, including the Peshitto. So, the reading is at least 200 years older than Vaticanus. The reading is also found in some Greek manuscripts, including "E". Erasmus, it seems was on solid textual ground when he left these words in the text.

Brother Glenny then says that it was a mistake for Erasmus to include I John 5:7-8 (The Johannine Comma) in his Greek text. The professor repeats all of the usual information: that Erasmus found it in only one Greek manuscript; it has been found in only four Greek manuscripts to date; and Erasmus did not include the verses in his first two editions.

The verses are the strongest testimony to the Trinity to be found in the Word of God. **"FOR THERE ARE THREE THAT BEAR RECORD IN HEAVEN, THE FATHER, THE WORD, AND THE HOLY GHOST: AND THESE THREE ARE ONE. AND THERE ARE THREE THAT BEAR WITNESS IN EARTH,** *the spirit, and the water, and the blood, and these three agree in one"* (I John 5:7-8). No doubt some copyists had a prejudice against the doctrine of the Trinity and so left out those words.

Glenny seems to be somewhat behind in the information about the number of Greek manuscripts which contain the disputed words. Several sources list the supporting manuscripts as G, Ravianus, Dubliniensis, 61, 88 mg, 429 mg, 918, 636 mg, 629, 634 mg, Omega 110, 60, 173, 221, and 2318.

In addition to the Greek manuscripts, the disputed words are found in the Vulgate and in many other Latin manuscripts dating back to the 4th Century. They are also found in some old Latin versions. They were quoted in Africa in the 5th Century by several writers. And the words are quoted by such fathers as Cyprian, Tertullian, and Athanasius.

Defending the authenticity of I John 5:7 are such commentators as Bengel, Knittel, R. L. Dabney, Ezra Abbot, Fredrick Nolan, and John Gill (who said that Stephanus found the Comma in nine manuscripts and that there was never any controversy about its authenticity until Erasmus left it out of his first edition).

Edward Hills argues that the passage would be incomplete without the Comma, and that the verses could not be grammatically correct in Greek without it (the gender of the nouns do not match).

Neither Glenny nor anyone else has yet proved that Erasmus or the KJV translators made a mistake by including I John 5:7 in the text.

Glenny completes the chapter by discussing "changes" in the "many hundreds of editions and revisions of the King James Version" (p. 57). But, the list of supposed changes he presents (p. 59) are spelling and printing errors. We have already dealt with this matter. We repeat here that the text of the King James Bible is the intended text of the translators and not the text of a printing press. No theological error is in view when "Thou art Christ" is changed to "Thou art the Christ" (Matt. 16:16). It is an error when Ps. 69:32 was printed as "seek good" instead of "seek God," but it was **NOT A THEOLOGICAL**

ERROR. It was a printing error.

None of the problems presented by the professor from Central prove that we do not have the inspired, inerrant Word of God in the KJV. The methods of modern textual criticism are obviously inferior to the methods and practices of the King James translators. Ad hominem attacks upon Erasmus, Beza, and the KJV translators only serve to point up the weaknesses of the critical (eclectic) text position.

CHAPTER FIVE

Chapter five of Central Baptist Theological Seminary's book, *__The__ __Bible__ __Version__ __Debate__*, was written by W. Edward Glenny. It is the most dangerous chapter in a very dangerous book. This chapter has more problems and errors than any of the other chapters, almost as many as all of the other chapters combined. These problems and errors consist of everything from an outright denial of the Bible's doctrine of the preservation of Scripture to an obvious misinterpretation and misuse of history.

I do not know Edward Glenny. As far as I can recall, I have never met him. I have read a few short articles which he has written through the years. Some of them were helpful articles on timely subjects. I am sure that he is faithful to the Bible in most of his teaching, helpful to his students, and devoted to his Lord. I want to believe that he is subservient to Christ in his scholarship, desiring to be thoroughly biblical in his approach, careful in his research, and honest in his conclusions. I do not intend this article as an attack on the professor.

Having said all of that, I must now remind my readers that scholarship has not only its own limitations but also its own set of temptations, prejudices, and blind spots. Those of us who have studied the Bible and taught it for more than forty years, and have spent many hours in college and seminary classrooms, and have read most of the major theological, devotional, biographical, and sermonic writings have learned that modern scholars **OFTEN** are as wrong as they are sincere. Now and then, an otherwise good man writes a very bad book. In this case, what is very likely an otherwise good seminary faculty has written a very bad book. There is probably some good scholarship at Central, but it is not in evidence in ***The Bible Version Debate***.

The problems in chapter five are so numerous that we will have to be rather sketchy in our analysis; otherwise, our review of this chapter would be much longer than Central's book.

25. Glenny begins chapter five by saying that the Bible has been preserved "by natural processes." [p. 71]

Analysis: Glenny seems to believe that God was involved in some minimal, incidental way in the preservation of the Bible, but only in the sense that God is sovereign in the events of history, not in the sense that God took any special care of His Word. This view is not at all consistent with what God said He would do. God gave promise concerning His Word that He would preserve it perfectly. He said, "The Word of God" is that "which liveth and abideth forever" (I Peter 1:23). Jesus said, "Heaven and earth shall pass away, but my words shall not pass away" (Matthew 24:35). It is written concerning the words of

God that "Thou hast founded them forever" (Psalms 119:152).

If God had left His Word to "natural processes," if He had let nature take its course, and if He had let the Devil have his way, the Bible would have been destroyed. It would not have survived. Glenny does not want us to believe that the Word of God has been preserved perfectly. If God has perfectly preserved His Word, then God's people had the perfect Word of God in every age. The Church had the perfect Word of God long before the Vatican manuscript was discovered in the pope's library in the later part of the Fifteenth Century.

If God perfectly preserved His Word, then the church already had it before the Sinai manuscript was discovered, and Glenny does not want us to believe that!

If God perfectly preserved His Word during the first eighteen centuries of church history, then we already have the Word of God in the King James Bible; and we do not need modern, destructive textual criticism. Glenny does not want us to believe that!

If God perfectly preserved His Word, then all the modern scholars who believe the critical/eclectic text theory are wrong; they misled several generations of theological students, and they have endorsed a lot of Bible versions which are highly inaccurate. Glenny would not want us to believe that!

So now Central Seminary has come with this new, novel doctrine that God has preserved His Word (sort of!) through "natural processes," a kind of *laissez-faire* preservation wherein God did not do much and did not get much involved in protecting His Word. There was no direct intervention by God, Central thinks, in the keeping of the Word of God, and certainly **NOTHING MIRA-CULOUS** occurred.

The result of Central's kind of preservation is an imperfect Bible. The unavoidable conclusion is that God preserved His Word, but He did not do a very good job of it! God did it **IMPERFECTLY**. The obvious implication of Central's theory is that through inattention, lack of power, or lack of desire **GOD FAILED** to preserve His Word perfectly. This is a blasphemous thought!

This new doctrine of preservation should be rejected by Christians everywhere. Both Traditional Text advocates **AND CRITICAL TEXT ADVOCATES** should turn their backs on the doctrine that God preserved His Word through "natural processes" and that the Bible was not preserved perfectly.

The standard Bible-believing position on preservation has always been that God personally and carefully superintended the transmission of the text and that God intervened in the affairs of men to keep His Word pure. **EVEN THOSE WHO HOLD TO THE CRITICAL TEXT HAVE CREDITED DIVINE ACTION AND NOT "NATURAL PROCESSES" FOR THE PRESERVATION OF GOD'S WORD.**

Both Traditional Text advocates **AND CRITICAL TEXT ADVOCATES** should turn their backs on Central's position that there is no doctrine of preservation of the words of the text anywhere in the Bible. We call on **ALL** Bible believers to reject the view that there were no miracles involved in the preservation of the Bible. **ALL** should resent the view that God was not much involved in Bible preservation and consequently we do not now know how the Hebrew text should read. **ALL** should reject the idea that there have been no miracles in the preservation of the words of God. Central's position is not the historic position of either Received Text advocates or Critical Text advocates.

We can find in history many very respected adherents of the Critical Text who taught that there is a Bible doctrine of preservation of the text, and that God employed **MIRACLES** in the preservation of His Word.

Dr. T. DeWitt Talmage (1832-1902) in his sermon, "The Splendors of Orthodoxy," ridiculed liberal ministers. He said they were in "a great London fog" because of their "advanced thought" in biblical interpretation. He said those liberals had philosophized, and guessed, and reasoned, and evolved their way right into a great continent of mud.

He then set forth his views on the preservation of the Bible:

> The Bible is not only divinely inspired, but it is divinely protected in its present shape. You could as easily, without detection, take *Hamlet* from the writings of Shakespeare and institute in place thereof Alexander Smith's drama as at any time during the last fifteen hundred years a man could have made any important change in the Bible without immediate detection.
>
> If there had been an element of weakness or of deception or of disintegration, the Book would long ago have fallen to pieces. If there had been one loose brick or cracked casement in this castellated truth, surely the bombardment of eight centuries would have discovered and broken through that imperfection.
>
> The fact that the Bible stands intact, notwithstanding all the furious assaults on all sides upon it, is proof to me that it is a miracle; and every miracle is of God.

Talmage would have rejected Central Seminary's position that the Bible's preservation was left to "natural processes." He believed that God **MIRACULOUSLY** took care of His Word and that we have it intact.

Lewis Sperry Chafer, president and professor of Systematic Theology at Dallas Theological Seminary (back in the days when it was a fundamental school), wrote in his *Systematic Theology*, in his section on Bible preservation:

> The preservation of the Scriptures, like the divine care over the writing of them and over the formation of them into the Canon, is neither accidental, incidental, nor fortuitous. It is the fulfillment of the divine promise....External endurance is predicated of the Bible; not that its message in all its parts will need ever be preached as it is now, but it is indestructible, being the Word of the eternal God. It is not that some one book out of the innumerable books men have written has been arbitrarily singled out for the highest honor. The Bible is eternal in its own right. It abides because of the fact that no word Jehovah has spoken can be removed or shaken...not one jot or tittle of the divine deposition can pass until all is fulfilled" [vol. I, pp. 124-125].

This statement by Chafer is a strong, good statement. He says that the preservation of the Word of God is in "fulfillment of the divine promise," something which Central Seminary does not believe as evidenced by the fact that Glenny "explains away" all of the promises of God concerning Bible preservation.

Chafer says God's care for the preservation of Scripture is the same care which God took about the original writing of them. This is far different from Central's position that preservation is done only through "natural processes," and therefore, the Bible is not preserved perfectly. Chafer never mentions the term "natural processes" anywhere in his discussion of Bible preservation. In fact, we have never read that term in any systematic theology by **ANY** writer. It is a new doctrine begun by Central writers to accommodate their view that we do not have any perfect Word of God today. Chafer says that the preservation of the Bible "is neither accidental, incidental, nor fortuitous." That does not sound like "natural processes," does it? That sounds like God was personally involved in overseeing the preservation of Scripture. That sounds like God **INTERVENED** whenever He, in His wisdom, decided to act to protect His Word.

Chafer says the Scriptures are "indestructible," "eternal," and says, "no word that Jehovah has spoken can be removed or shaken." That does not sound like God allows nature to take its course about the preservation of His Word. It does not sound like Chafer believed that some of the words of Scripture would be lost so that they could never be found; thus making imperfect the preservation of God's Word.

Chafer quotes or alludes to many Scriptures in setting forth his doctrine of preservation of Scripture. He wants us to know that this doctrine comes out of the Bible. By contrast, Brother Glenny does not mention or allude to a single verse of Scripture to prove his doctrine that God's Word was preserved "by natural processes" and that God has "not perfectly preserved His Word by miraculous, supernatural means." He does not even **REFER** to a verse of Scripture in pages 71–77, where he sets forth Central's strange position on preservation. He does not refer to any Scriptures in the end notes for these pages. The reason he does not point to any Scriptures is quite simple—**THERE**

ARE NO SCRIPTURES WHICH TEACH CENTRAL'S POSITION.

We refer our readers once again to what the Bible says in the Gospel of John. "If a man love me, he will keep my words....the Holy Ghost, whom the Father will send in my name, he shall teach you all things, and bring all things to your remembrance....the Spirit of truth, which proceedeth from the Father, he shall testify of me...when he, the Spirit of truth, is come, he will guide you into all truth...he shall receive of mine, and shall shew it unto you....All things that the Father hath are mine: therefore said I, that he shall take of mine, and shall show it unto you" (John 14:23, 26; 15:26; 16:13-15).

Surely the words of God are not to be excluded from "things which the Holy Spirit teaches." Surely the Holy Spirit has guided the true people of God through the centuries, so that they recognized as genuine the words of God. **GOD HAS NOT BEEN PASSIVE** in the preservtion of His Word.

Another well-known theologian who would differ with Central's doctrine of preservation is Arthur W. Pink. He wrote the widely used and much appreciated book, ***The Divine Inspiration of the Bible***. Chapter eleven of that book is titled "The Indestructibility of the Bible Is a Proof that its Author Is Divine."

> The survival of the Bible through the ages is very difficult to explain if it is not in truth the Word of God. Books are like men—dying creatures. A very small percentage of books survive more than twenty years, a yet smaller percentage last a hundred years and only a very insignificant fraction represent those which have lived a thousand years. Amid the wreck and ruin of ancient literature the Holy Scriptures stand

out like the last survivor of an otherwise extinct race, and the very fact of the Bible's continued existence is an indication that like its Author it is indestructible.

When we bear in mind the fact that the Bible has been the special object of never ending persecution the *wonder* of the Bible's survival is changed into a *miracle*. Not only has the Bible been the most intensely loved Book in all the world, but it has also been the most bitterly hated. Not only has the Bible received more veneration and adoration than any other book, but it has also been the object of more persecution and opposition. For two thousand years man's hatred of the Bible has been persistent, determined, relentless and murderous. Every possible effort has been made to undermine faith in the inspiration and authority of the Bible and innumerable enterprises have been undertaken with the determination to consign it to oblivion. Imperial edicts have been issued to the effect that every known copy of the Bible should be destroyed, and when this measure failed to exterminate and annihilate God's Word then commands were given that every person found with a copy of the Scriptures in his possession should be put to death. The very fact that the Bible has been so singled out for such relentless persecution causes us to wonder at such a unique phenomenon.

Although the Bible is the best Book in the world yet it has produced more enmity and opposition than has the combined contents of all our libraries. Why should this be? Clearly because the Scriptures convict men of their guilt and condemn them for their sins! Political and ecclesiastical powers have united in the attempt to put the Bible out of existence, yet their concentrated efforts have utterly failed. After all the persecution which has assailed the Bible, it is, humanly speaking, a wonder that there is any Bible left at all. Every engine of destruction which human philosophy, science, force, and hatred could bring against a book has been brought against the Bible, yet it stands unshaken and unharmed today. When we remember that no army has defended the Bible and no king has ever ordered its enemies to be extirpated, our wonderment increases. At times nearly all the wise and great of the earth have been pitted together against the Bible, while only a few despised ones have honored and revered it. The cities of the ancients were lighted with bonfires made of Bibles, and for centuries only those in hiding dare read it. How then, can we account for the survival of the Bible in the face of such bitter persecution? The only solution is to be found in the promises of God, "Heaven and earth shall pass away, but *My words shall not pass away.*"

Now suppose there was a man who had lived upon this earth for eighteen hundred years, that this man had oftentimes been thrown into the sea and yet could not be drowned; that he had frequently been cast before wild beasts who were unable to devour him; that he had many times been made to drink deadly poisons which never did him any harm; that he had often been bound in iron chains and locked in prison dungeons, yet he had always been able to throw off the chains and escape from his captivity; that he had repeatedly been hanged, till his enemies thought him dead, yet when his body was cut down he sprang to his feet and walked away as though nothing had happened; that hundreds of times he had been burned at the stake, till there seemed to be nothing left of him, yet as soon as the fires were out he leaped up from the ashes as well and as vigorous as ever—but we need not expand this idea any further: such a man would be super-human, a miracle of miracles.   Yet this is exactly how we should regard the Bible! This is practically the way in which the Bible has been treated. It has been burned, drowned, chained, put in prison, and torn to pieces, yet never destroyed!

No other book has provoked such fierce opposition as the Bible, and its preservation is perhaps the most startling miracle connected with it. But two thousand five years ago God declared, "The grass withereth the flower fadeth, *but the Word of our God shall abide for ever.*" Just as the three Hebrews passed safely through the fiery furnace of Nebuchadnezzar unharmed and unscorched, so the Bible has emerged from the furnace of satanic hatred and assault without even the smell of fire upon it! Just as an earthly parent treasures and lays by the letters received from his child, so our Heavenly Father has protected and preserved the Epistles of love written to His children. [pp. 113-117]

May we suggest that our readers go back now and read again this quotation from Arthur Pink. It is an exceedingly worthy and accurate statement on Bible preservation.

Notice that Pink believed that the Bible's preservation proves that God is its Author. And that statement may be reversed, i.e., if God authored the Bible (if it is inspired) that guarantees that it would be preserved by God. This is far from the teaching of Central Seminary that preservation is not a necessary corollary of inspiration. Glenny takes several pages to argue against the idea that preservation is a necessary corollary of inspiration (pp. 72-74).

Pink uses the word *miracle* with reference to the Bible's preservation. "A miracle of miracles," he says. He declares "its preservation is perhaps the most startling miracle connected with it." He says, "Our Heavenly Father has protected and preserved" the Word of God. None of this, of course, agrees with Central's doctrine that the Bible was preserved by "natural processes" in some haphazard, incidental, and impersonal manner which resulted in an imperfect Bible.

Pink's position on the preservation of Scripture is the historic, orthodox position. Central's position is a new, unscriptural, and dangerous position which should be rejected by Eclectic Text people and Traditional Text people alike.

When E. H. Bancroft wrote his *Christian Theology-- Systematic and Biblical*, in 1925, he quoted a portion of

Arthur Pink's article on preservation as his own position. See it in his book on page 360. Bancroft said nothing about the Bible being preserved by "natural processes." Such an idea is unworthy of true Bible scholarship.

Herbert Lockyer, in his book **_All the Miracles of the Bible_**, on pages 26 and 27, has a section titled, "The Miracle Book." In that article Lockyer discusses the "miracle of inspiration," the "miracle of its antiquity," the "miracle of its accuracy," the "miracle of its harmony," the "miracle of its abiding power," the "miracle of its circulation," etc. He also has a statement on the "miracle of its preservation."

Lockyer is correct when he says in this highly respected and helpful book,

> It is not only a Book relating credited miracles— everything associated with the Bible is miraculous, as one writer at least, Ada R. Habershon, indicates in her illuminating volume, **_The Study of Miracles_**. Everything about the Bible is supernatural, and in spite of all destructive criticism has done to weaken its authority, it remains an ever-present miracle....We could fill volumes with the divine preservation of the Bible through the centuries. Nothing man or devil has done has been sufficient to destroy it. "The Word of the Lord enduring forever."

Lockyer is correct about the Bible being a miraculously preserved Book. This has been the standard orthodox position on Bible preservation. Central Seminary is simply wrong in its position that preservation was through "natural processes" and not miraculous in any way.

Neither Talmadge, nor Chafer, nor Pink, nor Bancroft, nor Lockyer believed in the superiority of the Traditional Text nor in the King James Bible as their final authority. However, they were not so radical as to deny the miraculous preservation of Scripture, or to attribute an imperfect preservation to "natural processes."

Of course, we are not contending here for any "absolute miracles" (as theologians sometimes use the term) in the preservation of Scripture. By "absolute miracle" theologians mean a work of God brought about by unknown causes. It was an "absolute miracle" when our Lord fed the 5,000 with a small lunch of loaves and fishes, because loaves and fishes were made to appear mysteriously and instantaneously. But it was not an "absolute miracle" when the animals paired up and walked into Noah's ark, two by two. Not an "absolute miracle" because God did not instantaneously cause two of each animal, male and female, to materialize aboard the ark. But it was a type of miracle just the same when God caused the animals to walk to the ark and get on board.

By the same token, we are not arguing that God at any time in history caused a copy of the Scriptures matching the autographs to suddenly materialize out of thin air so that the Bible would be thus perfectly preserved. But, we believe it was a type of miracle each time God acted to guide His people to make decisions which resulted in the preservation of our perfect Bible.

A miracle in its simple sense is a work of God for His own purpose by means beyond the reach of man. Any time God acts instead of allowing nature to take its course un-interrupted (natural processes) it is a miracle. Miracles may be absolute or providential. Miracles and providence are not mutually exclusive. Whenever God intervenes in "natural processes" it is a miracle. A miracle is the "unresting activity" of God. A miracle is not necessarily contrary to nature; rather, it is above, beyond, or beside nature. A miracle occurs every time God exceeds the ordinary everyday workings of His world. For a fuller discussion of miracles the reader is referred to R. C. Trench's book, **_Notes on the Miracles of Our Lord_**. It is the "most comprehensive and penetrating study of the subject in the English language."

Central Baptist Theological Seminary downplays and minimizes the preservation of the Word of God. The faculty says, "God providentially, rather than miraculously, preserved the text...." [p. 14] "...We do not believe that God has preserved His Word perfectly and miraculously in any one manuscript or group of manuscripts, *or in all the manuscripts.*" [p. 131] The professors try to discredit and even denigrate the King James Bible in order to elevate their theological darling, modern textual criticism.

However, Central Seminary can not prove that God did not act (intervene) in the copying process so that we have in and among all the copies and ancient versions, all the words of God preserved. God promised such guidance and teaching and promised that the words of God would be protected and kept.

Nor can Glenny and his colleagues prove that God did not guide and teach Erasmus, Beza, and Stephanus, in their reconstruction and refining of the Greek Receptus so that we have the Word of God without omissions or additions.

Nor can Central professors prove that God did not give special guidance and wisdom to Tyndale and the translators of the other early English Bibles (Coverdale's, Matthew's, the "Great Bible," The Geneva Bible, and the Bishops Bible), helping them to prepare the way for the 1611 English Bible which would be used as the final authority among English-speaking Christians.

Nor can Central's teachers prove that God did not give special guidance and wisdom to the King James Bible translators so that our Bible is without any factual error. Central can **not** prove that God did nothing miraculous throughout the ages in copying, translating, keeping, collating, reconstructing, and translating into modern languages His Holy Word. The evidence favors the intervention of God. The orthodox position and the position of the best Christian minds has been that God did act (out of the ordinary) to keep His Word pure.

Finally, the authors of ***The Bible Version Debate*** can not prove that there are any factual errors in the King James Bible. Even though they seem desperate to find errors in the KJV, all they can come up with are the same old, tired, worn out, "hand-me-down" problems which have been answered many, many times. "Baptize," and "devils," the Johannine Comma, I Samuel 13:1, II Samuel 8:4, II Chronicles 22:2, and II Chronicles 36:9, and a few other such problems are all that Central or anyone else ever mentions; and adequate answers have been provided for these problems over and over again—adequate enough that no one should be caught accusing the KJV of being in error.

26. Glenny writes, "We do not believe that God has perfectly preserved His Word by miraculous, supernatural means *in any one manuscript*, version, or text-type." [p. 71]

Analysis: The problem here is that Glenny is being less than candid. Not only does Glenny and his seminary not believe that God perfectly preserved His Word "in any one manuscript, version or text-type," he does not believe God has perfectly preserved His Word *anywhere*, not even in the sum total of all of the witnesses. On page 99, Glenny quotes Rene Pache to define his own position, saying that the text is "essentially preserved in all, but perfectly preserved in none." Meaning, of course, that Glenny does not believe that the words of God are all perfectly preserved *anywhere* among all of the witnesses.

On page 131, Glenny admits that "we do not believe that God has preserved His Word perfectly and miraculously in any one manuscript or group of manuscripts, *or in all the manuscripts*."

When Glenny says that God has not preserved His Word perfectly "in all the manuscripts," he goes too far. He says that which he does not know, and could not possibly know.

Most "King James only" advocates would agree that God did not preserve all of His words, with no omissions, *in one manuscript,* and maybe not in one text-type or one group of manuscripts. However, we certainly do believe that God has perfectly preserved all of His words among all of the witnesses. We believe that all of the words of God were found by the translators of the King James Bible, so that the King James Bible has everything in it that God wanted in it.

However, it is not King James only advocates alone who believe God has preserved His Word perfectly in and among the words of *all of the witnesses*. This has been the standard position among Critical Text advocates, too. Of course, Critical Text defenders have disagreed with us about which manuscripts were the best, and hence, about which translation is the best. But, the standard Critical Text position has been that God has perfectly preserved all of His

124

words *somewhere* among all of the witnesses, *(if we could only find them!)*.

For example, John R. Rice, the famous evangelist and kindly soul winner, in his book, __Our__ __God-Breathed__ __Book—__ __The__ __Bible__, wrote a chapter titled, "God Preserves His Eternal Word." On page 360, this defender of the Critical Text quotes Matthew 5:17-18 and then makes this comment:

> The Lord here guarantees even the verbal accuracy of the translations and copies—not in one particular copy nor of one particular translation but of the inspired Word *in all of them together*....If we do not know how providence has overruled the wrath of men, the errors of copyists, the bias of translators, we can still know that He does overrule them. And *not altogether, perhaps, in one copy or in one translation, but in them all collectively* God has His perfect Word, never to be destroyed, never to pass away.

When Central professors teach that God has not perfectly preserved His Word, they do not teach the standard historical doctrine of preservation (even for Critical Text advocates). I do not believe it is the Scriptural position. When they teach that God did not perfectly preserve His Word, it makes us wonder, *what else do they think God did imperfectly*. God promised to preserve the Jews as a nation; will He not preserve them perfectly? God promised to preserve our souls; will He not do so perfectly? The very idea that God did something imperfectly is next to blasphemous. To say that God preserved His Word but that He did not do a very good job is to impugn the power and ability of God. However, *God is not inept*!

27. Glenny claims that verbal inspiration does not demand preservation. He denies that preservation is a necessary corollary of inspiration, calling this a "false assumption." [pp. 72-73, 83]

<u>*Analysis:*</u> The only reason for God to have His Word written down under inspiration of the Holy Spirit was so that it would be preserved for all future generations throughout the future ages. God could have (and often did) sent His word through *speaking* prophets (rather than writing prophets) when His word was for one person, one nation, or one generation only. But, when God desired for His exact words to be preserved, He had them written down under inspiration of the Holy Spirit.

Yes, indeed! The doctrine of verbal-plenary inspiration necessitates the doctrine of perfect preservation of the text. There is a necessary and logical linkage of these two doctrines. God did not lose His perfect words after taking special care in superintending the words as they were written, guaranteeing that the words written were His own words. He did not lose His perfect Word for eighteen centuries of church history after preparing the human penmen and giving to them His very words.

Dr. Edward Miller in his book, ***A Guide to the Textual Criticism of the New Testament*** [p. 66], testifies to the logic of the linkage of inspiration and preservation.

> The position of the Holy Scriptures as inspired by God the Holy Ghost must never be allowed to pass out of recollection. The great Inspirer of the writings is also Himself the great Guide of the Church. Accordingly, the overruling care exercised by Him according to promise is a factor all through the history which must ever be born in

mind. Not of course that evil has been excluded from co-
existing along with the good—such is the universal
experience: but nevertheless the Church, as the witness and
keeper of Holy Writ; has, under His direction, cast out the
evil from time to time....It can hardly be conceived that the
Holy Ghost, after communicating His Inspiration in the
composition of books, would in the midst of His
overruling care have allowed those books to be varied
according to changing winds of human opinion and human
action, without the maintenance throughout of a form mainly
at least free of error.

In the introduction to his book, ***The King James Version
Defended,*** Dr. Edward F. Hills shows that the doctrines of
inspiration and preservation of Scripture has formed a
corollary throughout history.

Since the doctrine of the *divine inspiration* of the New
Testament has in all ages stimulated the copying of these
sacred books, it is evident that this doctrine is important for
the history of the New Testament text, no matter whether it be
a true doctrine or only a belief of the Christian Church.
But what if it be a true doctrine? What if the original New
Testament manuscripts actually were inspired of God? If the
doctrine of the *divine inspiration* of the New Testament is a
true doctrine, then New Testament textual criticism is
different from the textual criticism of ordinary books.
    If the doctrine of the *divine inspiration* of the Old and
New Testament Scriptures is a true doctrine, the doctrine of
the *providential preservation* of the Scriptures must also be a
true doctrine. It must be that down through the centuries God
has exercised a special, providential control over the copying
of the Scriptures and the preservation and use of the copies,
so that trustworthy representatives of the original text have
been available to God's people in every age. God must have
done this, for if He gave the Scriptures to His Church by
inspiration as the perfect and final revelation of His will, then

it is obvious that He would not allow this revelation to disappear or undergo any alteration of its fundamental character.

Although this doctrine of the *providential preservation* of the Old and New Testament Scriptures has sometimes been misused, nevertheless, it also has always been held, either implicitly or explicitly, by all branches of the Christian Church as a necessary consequence of the *divine inspiration* of these Scriptures. Thus Origen in the third century was expressing the faith of all when he exclaimed to Africanus, "Are we to suppose that the Providence which in the sacred Scriptures has ministered to the edification of all the churches of Christ, had no thought for those bought with a price, for whom Christ died!"

If, now, the Christian Church has been correct down through the ages in her fundamental attitude toward the Old and New Testaments, if the doctrines of the *divine inspiration* and *providential preservation* of these Scriptures are true doctrines, then the textual criticism of the New Testament is different from that of the uninspired writings of antiquity. The textual criticism of any book must take into account the conditions under which the original manuscripts were written and also those under which the copies of these manuscripts were made and preserved. But if the doctrines of the divine inspiration and providential preservation of Scriptures are true, then THE ORIGINAL NEW TESTAMENT MANUSCRIPTS WERE WRITTEN UNDER SPECIAL CONDITIONS, UNDER THE INSPIRATION OF GOD, AND THE COPIES WERE MADE AND PRESERVED UNDER SPECIAL CONDITIONS, UNDER THE SINGULAR CARE AND PROVIDENCE OF GOD.

In the May, 1981, issue of ***Pillsbury Bulletin***, there appeared an article on the inspiration of the Bible. It was a good article. It said that preservation is a companion of inspiration.

...there is no need to doubt the trustworthiness of our present texts of Scripture. We believe God has preserved His Word so that the text we possess today is the very Word of God. **Since God took such care to reveal His inspired Word to man, He has, no doubt, preserved that Word through the ages** (cp. [sic.] Jeremiah 36:27ff) [emphasis mine]. God has not chosen to miraculously preserve the original autographs, but in His providence He has preserved His Word so that it has been kept pure in all ages....We have utmost confidence in the text of Scripture that God has preserved for us because of the doctrine of preservation and also because of the evidence of the biblical manuscripts themselves.

This good statement upholds the preservation of the Bible and makes that preservation consequential to the fact that God took care to reveal His inspired Word to man. The writer says that "since God took such care to reveal His inspired Word to man, he has, no doubt, preserved that Word through the ages."

We agree entirely with this writer when he makes the point that the logical result of inspiration is preservation. He makes the linkage between God revealing His inspired Word and the preservation of that Word. He knows preservation is the corollary, or result, or logical consequence of inspiration.

Who was the writer of that article in ***Pillsbury Bulletin***? **NONE OTHER THAN MR. ED. GLENNY!**

We can not help but wonder why Brother Glenny has changed his mind. What caused him to change his stand on preservation being a corollary of inspiration? Could it be that he could not handle the argument that inspiration is a strong evidence for the preservation of the words of God?

And did he change his position so that he could better oppose King James only advocates?

No matter what the reason for the change in Glenny's position, **HE WAS RIGHT THE FIRST TIME.** He had it right nineteen years ago! His current position is wrong.

As I penned this chapter, the *__Faith Pulpit__*, from Faith Baptist Theological Seminary, arrived. It has a monograph by Dr. Myron J. Houghton, Ph.D., Th.D., titled, "The Preservation of Scripture." Though we certainly do not agree with all that he says, we do agree with Houghton when he writes the following:

> To affirm the inspiration and inerrancy of the original writings while casting doubt on the authority of the Bible that is available to us is just plain silly. Can you really imagine someone seriously saying, "I have good news and I have bad news: the good news is that God wanted to give us a message and therefore caused a book to be written; the bad news is that He didn't possess the power to preserve it, and therefore we don't know what it said!" *A view of inspiration without a corresponding view of preservation is of no value.*

In making his disjunction of verbal inspiration from preservation, Professor Glenny copies Daniel B. Wallace's writings in the *__Grace Theological Journal__*. In so doing, he takes to task men like Dean Burgon, Wilber Pickering, Zane Hodges, and Theodore Letis. It is obvious that Glenny has bitten off more than he can chew. I say it kindly, but as theologians, neither Glenny nor Wallace are in the same class as those they choose as opponents on this issue. Perhaps on this particular issue, it would have been better had Glenny done a little more original thinking.

28. Glenny and Central Baptist Theological Seminary minimize the magnitude of their differences with the Traditional Text when he tries to put words in the mouths of King James Bible defenders. He says it is the position of King James Bible defenders that "if any portion of the New Testament is lost (no matter how small, even if only one word), then verbal-plenary inspiration is thereby falsified." [p. 72]

Analysis: The above quote is end-noted to Wallace. We believe it would be more honest if Glenny could actually cite a King James Bible defender who made such a statement, instead of quoting the opponents of such men. Any person knowledgeable of the subject knows that there are ***thousands of words*** which are in dispute in the Bible text issue. Why pretend that the issue might come down to "only one word"? Why debate over such an unrealistic hypothetical situation?

We would never say the words which Glenny tries to put in our mouth. We would ***never*** say, "If any portion of the New Testament is lost (no matter how small, even if only one word), then verbal-plenary inspiration is thereby falsified." Instead, we would say, *"**The doctrine of verbal-plenary inspiration is true**; therefore we know that God preserved His Word in the Traditional Text of Scripture and in the King James Bible because all other texts and versions have omitted and/or added **thousands of words**."*

We cannot allow Central Seminary to hide the magnitude of the falsity of her text behind such verbiage.

29. On page 74 of **_The Bible Version Debate_**, Dr. Glenny says the Traditional Text was not in the majority of manuscripts throughout history.

Analysis: In my copy of Glenny's book, I wrote in the margin, "How would you know?" Indeed, how would Glenny or anyone else know which text type was in the majority all through history? If, as we suspect, the early believers destroyed the most used and best copies when they became worn, then how would Glenny know how many there were? The question is not how many exemplars from various periods exist today, but **_how many copies were there in all periods throughout history_**?

Edward F. Hills in his book, **_The King James Bible Defended_**, pp. 185-186, reports on the conclusions of Kirsopp Lake regarding the numbers and types of manuscripts which existed at various times from the 4th through the 10th centuries.

As a result of these investigations, Lake found it "hard to resist the conclusion that the scribes usually destroyed their exemplars when they copied the sacred books." If Lake's hypothesis is correct, then the manuscripts most likely to be destroyed would be those containing the Traditional Text. For these were the ones which were copied most during the period between the 4th and 10th centuries, as is proved by the fact that the vast majority of the later Greek New Testament manuscripts are of the Traditional type. The Gothic version, moreover, was made about 350 A.D. from manuscripts of the Traditional type which are no longer extant. Perhaps Lake's hypothesis can account for their disappearance.

By the same token, the survival of old uncial manuscripts of the Alexandrian and Western type, such as _Aleph, B_ and

D, was due to the fact that they were rejected by the Church and not read or copied but allowed to rest relatively undisturbed on the library shelves of ancient monasteries. Burgon (1883) pointed this out long ago, and it is most significant that his observation was confirmed more than forty years later by the researches of Lake.

We repeat that Glenny could not possibly know that the Traditional Text was not in the majority throughout the Church Age. However, the real question that the Central professors should be asking themselves is not in regard to whether the Traditional Text was always in the majority before the Tenth Century, but is in regard to why the Traditional Text is the majority text *now*. Why has God in His providence made the Traditional Text the majority text for the last 1,000 years? Obviously, God is telling the world something.

30. Glenny claims, "there is no evidence that the majority/Byzantine text-type existed before the 4th century." [p. 74]

Analysis: What Glenny says is simply not true! It is almost unbelievable that he would make such a statement! I find myself exclaiming, "Surely he knows better!"

Scholars have found plenty of evidence that the majority text existed well before the Fourth Century. For example, Dr. Edward Miller in his book, _**A Guide to the Textual Criticism of the New Testament**_ (pp. 84-85), writes:

> But there is remaining even now to us sufficient demonstration of the existence and use of the Traditional Text in the first ages. The witness borne by the early Fathers

to controverted readings proves that they used Manuscripts belonging to the Traditional Class which were much older than any now in existence. Take, for example, fifteen passages which are at the present time under discussion, and the following Fathers are found to testify upon them to the Traditional readings: Ignatius (I), Papias (I), Justin Matyr (5), Ireaeus (6), Tertullian (7), Theophilus of Antioch (I), Hegesippus (I), Athenagora (I), Vincentius (I), Marcion (I), Clement of Alexandria (3), Hippolytus (6), Acta Apilati (2), Origen (II), Dionysius of Alexandria (3), Apostolical Constitions (6), Ps. Tatian (2), Cyprian (I), Macarius Magnes (2), Julius Africanus (I), Titus of Bostra (2), Archelaus with Manes (I), Ps. Justin (I), Clementine Homilies (I), Arius (I), Eusebius (9), Athanasius (8), Aphraates the Persian (4), Didymus (10), Epiphanius (II), Ephraem Syus (6), Ps. Ephraem (I), Gregory Nazianzen (9), Gregory of Nyssa (26), Basil (8), Cyril of Jerusalem (2), Lucifer (2), and Leontius (I). That is to say, in 165 places as relating to only 15 chance passages in Holy Scripture Ecclesiastical Writers living before the Era of St. Chrysostom are proved to have followed Manuscripts thus witnessing to the Traditional Text. It should be borne in mind that it was only at the close of this period that [Aleph] and B, the two oldest manuscripts now existing, were produced.

In a similar manner, the Peshito and Italic Versions – including under the latter class the best of the Old Latin Versions—were made two hundred years before those two Manuscripts, and—especially the former—support the Traditional Text. Nor is occasional evidence subsequently wanting in the Egyptian Versions which, as has been seen, came out later in the same period.

There is therefore, as these specimens show, no warrant for asserting that the Traditional Text is not traceable back as far as the earliest age of the Church.

Given the facts about the quotations in the early church fathers and the facts about the early versions, as presented by Miller, we find it astounding that Glenny would say that "there is no evidence that the Majority/Byzantine text-type existed before the 4ᵗʰ century."

31. Glenny charges, "The first version of Scripture which generally reflects the Majority text-type is the Gothic at the end of the 4ᵗʰ century." [p. 74]

Analysis: This is another false and reckless statement. Perhaps Glenny means that the first purely European translation supporting the Majority Text type was the Gothic version. Ulfilas, a missionary to Britania, produced this translation between A.D. 330 and A.D. 350 (not "at the *end* of the 4ᵗʰ century," as Glenny says), proving that he had access to the Traditional Text twenty or thirty years before the Sinaiticus and Vaticanus manuscripts were copied. There are eight surviving copies of the Gothic Bible.

Be that as it may, the first version of Scripture which reflects the Majority Text is the Italic Bible which was translated no later than about A.D. 160.

32. Professor Glenny complains that "there is no Majority text-type manuscript for the letters of Paul from before the 9ᵗʰ century." He calls this, "an 800 year leap of faith." [p. 75]

Analysis: The early manuscript evidence for the Pauline Epistles is very minuscule in *both* the Critical Text *and* the Traditional Text. Materials include P⁴⁶ (c. A.D. 200), B (A.D. 350), Aleph (A.D. 350), A (A.D. 425), and D (A.D. 560) as having all or most of Paul's epistles.

It should be noted that A is missing eight chapters of II Corinthians and B is missing the Pastoral Epistles and Hebrews 9:15-13:25. P^{46} is fragmentary and is missing most of Romans, most of I Thessalonians, all of II Thessalonians, and all of the Pastoral Epistles.

Only about eighty Greek manuscripts have been assigned a date earlier than the Sixth Century. Almost all of them are fragments, some containing a few words, some a few verses, and a small number have a few chapters. About half of these support the Traditional Text.

Only about 250 Greek manuscripts have been dated between the Fifth and Ninth Centuries. Almost all of these are fragments. All but about forty support the Traditional Text.

From century 4 through century 9 only eight manuscripts contain all four Gospels in their entirety. Only five contain all of Acts. Only five contain all of Romans. Only two contain the Book of Revelation.

So as anyone can clearly see, there is not much *early* Greek manuscript evidence for the Pauline Epistles in *any text type.*

Unfortunately for the Critical Text advocate, he has no evidence for *any part of the Bible* dated *later* than the Eighth Century because everyone recognized the inferiority of the Critical Text manuscripts and refused to copy them. Everyone at the time knew those manuscripts were corruptions.

The Traditional Text of the Gospels and some other parts of the New Testament (excluding the Pauline Epistles) are well preserved in some of the very early Greek manuscripts. Even P^{46} has some readings which agree with the Traditional Text against the Critical Text.

In fact, Branine, in his *The History of Bible Families and the English Bible*, quotes G. Zuntz [*The Text of the Epistles*] who says Traditional Text "readings previously discarded   as   late are in P^{46}...P^{46} and P^{45} support the Majority Text readings..." in many cases.

The entire Traditional Text of the New Testament is preserved in many ancient versions (especially Italic and Egyptian) of the 2nd and 3rd Centuries.

Also, the entire New Testament (with only a few lapses) is preserved in the Traditional Text by the writings of the early church fathers A.D. 150 – 350.

The lectionaries, all 2,143 of them, agree with the Traditional Text.

Of the 5,255 Greek manuscripts which are extant, 5,217 of them agree with the Traditional Text. Only about forty-five of them agree with the Critical Text.

Glenny seems to be worried about the "800 year leap of faith" for the Pauline Epistles. Why should this bother him? He must make a "leap of faith" of from 800 to 2,500 years, or more, for the entire Old Testament! There is very little Hebrew manuscript evidence for the Old Testament before A.D. 900 (with the exception of the Isaiah Dead Sea Scroll). That is at least a 2,400 year "leap of faith" for the Books of Moses, and probably a longer "leap" than that for the Book of Job! It is a 1,300 year "leap" for the Book of Malachi! Why stop "leaping" when you get to the New Testament? The simple fact is that you either believe God preserved His Word or you do not. Long periods of time with no manuscript evidence is no impediment to God. Of course, if you think the preservation of the Bible was all up to man and that it was all a matter of "natural processes," then you do have a problem.

33. Glenny quotes Bart Ehrman favorably and agrees that God gave the church only "theoretical" and not "actual" possession of the New Testament text. [p. 77]

<u>Analysis</u>: "Theoretical" possession of *anything* instead of "actual" possession of it will do no good at all! It reminds me of the news item which told about a man who received one of those letters from ***Reader's Digest*** which said, "You have won twelve million dollars." The man went all the way to Florida to collect his prize only to be told, "Well, you were only the *theoretical* winner of the twelve million dollars, not the *actual* winner." If all we have is "theoretical possession" of the New Testament, we have no New Testament at all.

Dear reader, can you imagine this? Here for 2,000 years God's people have believed they had the Word of God in their various languages. But wait! Now, seminary professors at a fundamental Baptist school are telling us, "No, you don't *actually* have it."

What does God say about Central's theoretical theory? Timothy had *actual* possession of the Scriptures, not some kind of *theoretical* possession (II Timothy 3:15-16). Theoretical Scriptures could make no one wise unto salvation.

Apollos had the *actual* possession of the Scriptures when he used them to mightily convince the Jews that Jesus was Christ (Acts 18:28). ***Theoretical*** possession of the Scriptures would have convinced no one of anything.

The Bereans had *actual* possession of the Scriptures when they searched the Scriptures daily (Acts 17:11). No one can search Scriptures which he only *theoretically* possesses.

When Jesus told the Jews to "search the scriptures" He was referring to Scriptures which they *actually* possessed (Matt. 5:39). No one can search Scriptures which he only *theoretically* possesses.

Philip had *actual* possession of the Scripture when he preached Jesus unto the Ethiopian eunuch (Acts 8:26-40). No one can read from Scripture which he only *theoretically* possesses.

34. Glenny quotes Ehrman favorably saying:

> Any claim that God preserved the New Testament text intact, giving His church actual, not theoretical, possession of it, must mean one of three things—either 1) God preserved it in all the extant manuscripts so that none of them contain[s] any textual corruptions, or 2) He preserved it in a group of manuscripts, none of which contain[s] any corruptions, or 3) He preserved it in a solitary manuscript which alone contains no corruptions. [p. 77]

Analysis: Glenny and Ehrman believe that the church has only theoretical possession of the New Testament, not actual possession of it, and that if any believes otherwise, he must believe one of three preposterous theories. But we can believe that we have actual possession of the New Testament and not believe any of those three theories. There is another possibility which Ehrman and Glenny failed to tell us about.

The truth is that God did preserve the New Testament text intact, giving His Church actual possession of it. God did this by preserving His Word in all of the witnesses. The Greek manuscripts, the ancient versions, the lectionaries, and the writings of the early church fathers all were witnesses to the text. Then God taught His people how to know the words of God. There **were** mistakes made in most, if not all, of the witnesses, but where a mistake was made God saw to it that it was corrected in other witnesses, and He gave guidance to His people to know the correct reading so that we have the Word of God today without errors of omission or addition (intact).

So when Glenny and Ehrman say "you must believe one of these views," we say, "None of the above."

35. Glenny says, "anyone who believes that God has preserved the New Testament text intact in the TR must argue for reinspiration of Scripture through the person who compiled the edition of the TR that perfectly preserves God's Word (whatever edition that is)." [p. 78]

**Analysis**: I do not know of a single Textus Receptus advocate who argues for the "reinspiration" of anything. No one "must argue" for reinspiration of anything.

If Erasmus, or Beza, or Stephanus, or Colinaeus, or Elzevir, or Luther, or Tyndale, or Calvin, or anyone else was able with God's help to find all of the correct readings and to reconstruct a Bible with those correct readings, he would have the perfectly preserved Word of God. That would be preservation, not inspiration. We should not call it inspiration every time God guides us or teaches us the truth.

The Word of God was inspired when it was first dictated by God to the original penmen. It did not lose its inspiration just because it was copied or translated. It did not **expire**. Therefore, whenever the right readings are found and put together properly, the result is that we have the inspired Word of God. And if that text is then correctly

PROBLEM # 36   CHAPTER FIVE

translated into a modern language, it is still the inspired Word of God.

So Erasmus, for example, was not used by God to "reinspire" the Word of God, because it was **already inspired** before Erasmus read it.

The King James Bible is the inspired and inerrant Word of God, not because of "double inspiration" or "reinspiration," but because God inspired His Word when He originally gave it, and because God helped the translators of the KJV to know all of the correct readings and to translate those words correctly.

36. Glenny cites Doug Kutilek who in turn gives *disinformation* about Erasmus. Kutilek says Erasmus was a "lifelong devoted Catholic" and had an "absolute undying loyalty to Roman Catholicism, its doctrine and its pope." He also says, "Erasmus consent[ed] to all that Rome stood for doctrinally, with its Mary-worship, veneration of the Saints, sacrifice of the mass, papal supremacy, ecclesiastical hierarchy, purgatory, sprinkling of infants, monastic vows and orders, and all else." While citing Kutilek's disinformation, Glenny says some TR supporters believe that Erasmus was "a writer of inspired Scripture." [pp. 78, 101]

<u>*Analysis*</u>: Professor Glenny here attempts to use Erasmus' "theological inclination" to discredit his work on the New Testament. This was exactly what Kutilek was saying should *not* be done (see the end note on p. 101 of the book from Central).

It is true that Erasmus never did leave the Catholic Church, though he did leave the active priesthood in 1492, the same year he was ordained. It is also true that he held to many Catholic heresies and that he was a compromiser. However, Glenny and Kutilek *go too far* when they say that Erasmus was a "life long devoted Catholic"; and when they say Erasmus had an "absolute undying loyalty to Roman Catholicism, its doctrine and its pope." Glenny and Kutilek also *go too far* when they say that Erasmus "consent[ed] to all that Rome stood for doctrinally." These are exaggerations.

Rather than our being too repetitious, we suggest that our readers go back to the preceding chapter and review our analysis of #24, where we discuss Glenny's comments about Erasmus. There we cite the ***Encyclopaedia Britannica*** which refutes Glenny and Kutilek when they say that Erasmus had undying loyalty to all Catholic doctrine. And we know Britannica is right about it and Glenny is wrong because we know that Erasmus wrote books and letters sharply critical of some Catholic doctrines and practices.

We also cite in our previous chapter such church historians as Hurlbut, Kuiper, and Durant, showing that Erasmus was never a good Catholic; that he never felt comfortable with the teachings nor the practice of his church; that he vociferously criticized his church, the popes, and the cardinals; that he joined the Brethren of the Common Life, an evangelical movement which attacked indulgences, rejected transubstantiation, and believed in justification by faith alone and salvation by grace alone.

If Erasmus was such a loyal Catholic, agreeing with all of the Roman church's doctrine, as Glenny says, then why was he branded as a heretic at the Council of Trent? Why was he called a "formenter of the revolt" (reformation)? Why were his books forbidden for Catholic readers? The fact is that Erasmus was always a controversial figure, even in his own day. The Catholics did not trust him because he had a lot of Protestant ideas, and the Lutherans (especially Luther himself) did not trust him in the later years because Erasmus was a moderate and refused to criticize Rome as harshly as Luther did. The ambiguity was made worse by the fact that Erasmus was known to have taken the stand that it was ethical for him to take two positions, one public, the other private. In public he gave lip service to the church, but in his private letters (of which he wrote approximately 40,000 in his lifetime), conversations, and classroom discussions he was a relentless critic of Rome. This divarication was not a strong point in his character.

Latourette, in volume II of his _**A History of Christianity**_, mentions:

> Reformers who, while they remained within the Roman Catholic Church, had strong spiritual kinship with the Protestants...who, repudiating the Roman Catholic Church, were never comfortable within any of the existing patterns of Protestantism but were pilgrims and strangers. Most of them bore the humanistic stamp and directly or indirectly were indebted to that great Christian humanist and individualist, Erasmus.

So obviously Kutilek and Glenny are wrong about Erasmus. There were many reformers in Europe who opposed much Roman Catholic doctrine; indeed, they had more in common with the Protestants than with the Catholics, but refused to leave Rome because they hoped to change her from the inside. And these reformers existed largely because of the teachings, the writings, and the influence of Erasmus.

Yes, it is true, as Glenny says, that Erasmus wrote a book championing the free will of man. This was probably the most humanistic thing he ever did. And, yes, it prompted Luther to write his book, ***The Bondage of the Will***, but we fail to see how this disqualifies Erasmus, or how it reflects badly upon his Greek text. And in any case, we do not believe Erasmus was "a writer of inspired Scripture" except in the sense that he *copied* the Scriptures as he reconstructed his Greek text.

It would also seem that Glenny's criticism of Erasmus is somewhat misplaced in as much as *the KJV was not based on Erasmus' text*, exactly; although his text did help Beza, Stephanus, Tyndale, and the translators of the KJV.

37. Glenny attacks the Majority Text position saying, "To argue that a numerical majority is an indication of God's providential blessing would mean that the Roman Catholic Church is correct and we should all become Roman Catholics!" [p. 79]

Analysis: The professor says this, following the logic that the minority is often right and the majority is often wrong. We will grant that the majority of people are often wrong. The Bible says, for example, that the road to heaven is a narrow road "and few there be that find it" (Matt. 7:14). What the Bible says about the "remnant" also addresses this same truth. However, what Glenny seems to have forgotten is that the Majority Text *is the text of God's remnant – a minority of people*.

The text of the majority (the Roman Catholic Church) was the text of Jerome which agrees with the Critical Text and with the Vatican manuscript. The text of the Waldensians, the Albigensians, and the Reformers was the Traditional Text. Those who held to that text, the true people of God, were always in the minority.

Again, we must point out that Glenny's remarks miss the mark and are misplaced, because while the King James translators (as well as "King James only" people) considered the majority reading to be a very important matter, they did not (and do not) believe it was the *only criteria* for determining the right reading. The KJV is not based in every single instance upon the majority reading, nor on the Textus Receptus.

However, among the true people of God (those who had the Holy Spirit's help) the Traditional Text was the text which was copied, read, and used. The way the Holy Spirit lead that little minority of people is an important factor which should not be so cavalierly dismissed. We as Baptists believe in congregational government in our churches for the same reason. We operate under the principle that God leads His people, and that a majority of the time they know what the will of God is. If we do not believe in this overruling providence of God, I do not say we should become Catholics, but I do say that we should stop calling ourselves Baptists! The doctrine of preservation of Scripture is wrapped up in the doctrine of the priesthood of all believers, a Baptist distinctive.

38. Glenny compares those who believe in the Traditional Text of Scripture to the supporters of Hitler and accuses them of playing God. He quotes M. James Sawyer who states that German Christians gave thanks for Adolf Hitler and were dedicated to the Fuhrer. Glenny then says that supporters of the Majority Text make the same kind of mistake because they presume to know what God is doing in history. [pp. 79-80]

Analysis: Glenny should be ashamed of himself for using such an illustration! For him to compare his Bible-believing brethren who differ with him about textual matters to the supporters of Adolf Hitler is almost unforgivable! Have we come to this in fundamentalism?

It is an outrage to even mention the name of Adolf Hitler in the context of this debate. It is offensive, and I take umbrage to it. The supporters of the Traditional Text of Scripture are not like the supporters of Adolf Hitler in any way, shape, or form! Anyone who would mention the two in the same context has absolutely no sensitivity for the feelings of his brethren.

This is the kind of crudeness and indecency we are accustomed to seeing in the muckraking liberal political scene in America where the name of Hitler is bandied about, where people call others Nazis just because they disagree. But, we have a right to expect better behavior from Christians.

Can we not have a discussion about the text of Scripture without making such comparisons, without name calling, without bringing the name of Hitler into it?

39. The Central Seminary book finds fault with TR/Majority text advocates for believing that the text of the Word of God must be "settled and certain" and that we have that text in the Traditional Text. We are faulted for thinking

that we have "absolute textual certainty." Glenny says
certainty is not identical with truth. [p.80]

Analysis: God wanted us to be absolutely certain that we
had the genuine Word of God. In fact, all that the Bible
says about itself presupposes that we should trust our Bible
in absolute certainty. Jesus said, for example, "Man shall
not live by bread alone, but by every word that proceedeth
out of the mouth of God" (Matt. 4:4). That takes for granted
that every generation of God's people would have all of the
words of God, and that they should have faith in them.

In Proverbs 1:23 we read, "I will pour out my spirit unto
you, I will make known my words unto you." And Hosea
6:3 says, "Then shall we know, if we follow on to know the
Lord." Yes, God wants us to be certain of what the Bible is
and of what it says.

All Critical Text advocates who are intelligent and
honest admit that *according to their theory* no one can be
certain about the text of the Bible; no one can know with
certainty exactly what the Bible says. They admit that they
can not absolutely know for sure which words are authentic
Scripture and which are spurious. No doubt, this is the
reason that Glenny berates us for our certainty on the text.

But uncertainty is not better than certainty when we
approach the Bible. "Faith cometh by hearing, and hearing
by the word of God" (Romans 10:17). That presupposes
that we **_know_** what the Word of God is. We do know this
because the Spirit of God has taught us.

Incidentally (or not so incidentally), Glenny does not use
a single verse of Scripture to try to prove his theory that we
can not have certainty about the text of Scripture. The

147

reason for this is obvious; the Bible does not teach Glenny's theory.

40. Glenny accuses those who differ with him about the text of being "simplistic." He says they "seek certainty by opting for a simplistic answer that does not have to face the complex facts involved in the issue." [pp. 81-82]

Analysis: Actually, it is not a question of simple vs. difficult. It is a question of believing what the Bible says about itself, about its own inspiration, preservation, and purpose.

Of course, some scholars tend to deplore anyone being able to understand anything without their scholarly expertise. Some seem to want to be the final authority in the same way that the Roman Catholic Church wants to be the final authority. They want believers to have to come to them to find out what the Bible is and what it says. However, God never intended for that to be the case.

On the other hand, the fact that God promised to preserve His Word and did so is still too "complex" for Central. They still don't "get it"!

41. Glenny accuses his opponents of defending the Traditional Text by using "ad hominem," "labeling," "question begging," and "guilt by association." [p. 81]

Analysis: There is enough of this to go around! Critical Text advocates are as guilty as anyone else of using the kind of arguments which Glenny describes. Glenny says his opponents use those arguments out of "psychological insecurity." That prompts us to ask, "What is Glenny's excuse?"

Right on the same page where he decries "labeling," etc., Glenny refers to some of his opponents as "cultic." He compares the supporters of the Traditional Text to the supporters of Hitler. Larry Pettegrew says a King James only person is "less of a fundamentalist." [p.13]   So, this is a clear case of the pot calling the kettle black!

42. Glenny says, "In our defense and propagation of the faith the key issue is not whether today we know the precise form of each of the words recorded in the autographs." He goes on to say that if anyone thinks that he has an infallible translation, that belief will move his focus away from God and Christ. [p. 82]

Analysis: The professor seems to be having some trouble with logic. How could it be that if we have an infallible translation and if we know the correct form of the words that our focus will be moved away from God and Christ? Being focused on Christ and God depends on having a true, accurate, and authoritative source of information about Christ and God. Having a fallible and erroneous source of information will not help us to grow in knowledge about the Lord Jesus Christ. If having a fallible translation could help us to focus on Christ, then why did God inspire the autographs? Why would not God just allow errors to be planted in the autographs, if that would help us to focus on Christ and God?

43. Another consequence of having certainty about the text, says Glenny, is that we would abandon "the search for a text or translation that better represents or gives a better understanding of the autographs." [p. 82]

Analysis: With this we agree. We do not believe there is any need today for what Miller calls "extreme textualism." We do not say that every word in the KJV is translated in the *only* possible way. In a few cases some modern words that have identical meaning *could* also be used. However, we do say that if all of the "extreme textualism" were to cease today, *we would not miss a thing*.

Yes, if all agreed that we certainly have the perfectly preserved Word of God in the KJV and its underlying texts that would cause critics to abandon their efforts to find a better text. It would also cause those critics to abandon their efforts to make a better English translation. The only disagreement we have with Central on this point is that we say *it would be a good thing* to abandon such efforts.

44. Glenny says, "What the world needs to hear is that God has spoken, not that we have the exact, perfectly-preserved text that Paul wrote in the first century." [p. 82]

Analysis: This is nonsense! It is not only important that God has spoken, but *what* God said is also important. It *is* important that God has spoken, but the world also needs to hear that what God said has been transmitted to us in an infallible, completely authoritative book. Glenny wants the *message* of God, but he does not believe we have the exact perfectly preserved *words*. But it is the *words* which God promised to preserve (Matt. 24:35).

45. Glenny defends using "mere conjecture" to emend all Hebrew manuscripts. He says these conjectures have been vindicated by the Dead Sea Scrolls. [p. 84]

**Analysis**: It is shocking to hear this kind of admission from Glenny. What is he saying? He is saying that the Hebrew text which we have in our possession should be corrected on the basis of man's guesswork. Since when are man's guesses better than what God preserved? Frankly, this is the kind of idea that started in liberalism. We do not say that Glenny is a liberal. He is not. However, he has been too much influenced by ideas that originated with liberals.

The professor says these conjectures have been vindicated by the Dead Sea Scrolls. Why then does he not give us some examples of emendations which have been vindicated by the Dead Sea Scrolls?

Our point is that we do not think that he has found any vindication of any emendations in the Dead Sea Scrolls.

The Central faculty refers several times to the Dead Sea Scrolls, as if it has studied them, and as if the scrolls support its position on the text and the "conjectures" which have emendated the Hebrew text.

But, we believe that CBTS, and many others, claim too much for the Dead Sea Scrolls. Except for the Book of Isaiah, there is very little in the Dead Sea Scrolls which has shed any light on the Old Testament text.

The Dead Sea Scrolls were discovered in eleven caves along the shore of the Dead Sea between the years of 1947 and 1956. The documents are numbered according to the caves from which they came. Only caves one and eleven have produced relatively intact manuscripts. The manuscripts found in cave one have proven to be the most valuable to determining the text of the Old Testament. Two scrolls of the Book of Isaiah were found in cave one. One of the Isaiah scrolls was complete. The other Isaiah scroll contained only some chapters of the Book. Also in cave one was a commentary on Habakkuk which contained the Hebrew text of two chapters of the book of Habakkuk.

Cave four had more manuscripts in it than any other cave (about 400). It was here that evidence was found that every Old Testament book except Esther had been placed in the jars in that cave. However, those manuscripts had all disintegrated into dust and small fragments. About 60,000 to 75,000 fragments were found in the jars. Most of the fragments were found to be the size of a finger nail or smaller. Some fragments contained part of a word, others contained a word or two. Much of the manuscript material found in cave four was in such bad condition that it has been described by scholars as "dust," "liquid," and "like ground coffee." It is doubtful that any of this material will ever be useful in determining anything about the Old Testament text.

There is evidence that there was a total of about 600 manuscripts in the eleven caves. However, most of the manuscripts (about 400) were not biblical manuscripts. Of the 200 manuscripts that were of Bible texts many of them were not in Hebrew, but in Aramaic or Greek. Some were in Egyptian.

Scholars try to reconstruct the texts in jigsaw puzzle fashion, but from cave four they have only small pieces of the puzzle to work with, and they are continually reassigning the pieces to different manuscripts. When they have put a few pieces together the way they think they should be, they take a picture of it. However, at least forty percent of the manuscripts from cave four have never been reconstructed *at all.*

Only about thirty-five percent of the DSS have been partly or wholly reconstructed. Only about twenty percent of the 600 manuscripts have been completely reconstructed, but most of these are either not Bible manuscripts, or not written in Hebrew.

Of the approximate 600 manuscripts known as the Dead Sea Scrolls about 257 have had *some part* of them reconstructed. These have been translated by several different scholars. The most complete translation of the available material was done by Michael Wise, Martin Abegg Jr., and Edward Cook. In their index, they list 131 works involving 157 manuscripts (more than one copy were found of some works). Only a few of these works are helpful in studying the text of the Old Testament. Some that might eventually be helpful are the commentaries which were written in Hebrew, including *A Commentary on Hosea, A Commentary on Nahum, Commentaries on Psalms, The Last Days: A Commentary on Selected Verses, A Commentary on Consoling Passages in Scripture,* and *A Collection of Messianic Proof Texts.* However, these scrolls are so fragmented and so incomplete that they are of very little help at the present time.

The only real help in a study of the Old Testament Hebrew text is from the scrolls of Isaiah taken from cave one along with *A Commentary of Habakkuk.* These are located in the Shrine of the Book, in Jerusalem.

When someone says that the Dead Sea Scrolls of "all of the Old Testament books except Esther" are available to inform us about the text of the Old Testament **he is wrong.** Some people who say that simply do not know the facts, and some who say that are, no doubt, intentionally trying to deceive others.

At a different location, about twelve miles from the Qumran Caves, at Wadi Murabba'at, a scroll was discovered which contained a Greek text of the Minor Prophets. This very valuable find is dated in the Second Century, A.D. Copied about 600 years after the prophets penned those books under inspiration, it still leaves a long "leap." And the copies are written in Greek, not Hebrew.

Nothing in the Dead Sea Scrolls or anywhere else argues against the Masoretic Hebrew text. As a matter of fact, the Isaiah scroll from cave one, and the Minor Prophets scroll from Wadi Murabba'at support the authenticity of the Masoretic Text and the King James Version. The Isaiah scroll is exactly the same as the Masoretic text, except for some of the spelling and grammar, even though 1,000 years separate the two. And the scroll of the minor prophets supports the Masoretic Hebrew text, even though 800 years separate the two.

Norton, writing in P. W. Comfort's book, *The Origin of the Bible* says, "The scholarly assessment of [The Dead Sea Scrolls] is, at present, far from complete...In a general sense, however, the Dead Sea Scrolls have affirmed the accuracy of the Masoretic Text that we use today."

The similarity of the Dead Sea Isaiah and the Wadi Murabba'at Minor Prophets scrolls to the Masoretic text is described by scholars with such words as "corresponds almost perfectly," "virtually identical," "almost identical," and "amazingly similar."

So when Glenny says that scholars have made emendations to the text and that their conjectures have been vindicated by the Dead Sea Scrolls, *I do not believe him*. I would challenge the professor to show us some of these emendations which have been vindicated by the Dead Sea Scrolls. He does not mention any in his book, and I do not believe they exist.

46. Glenny now sets out to show that there are mistakes in the KJV and in its underlying Masoretic Hebrew text. His first example of an error is I Samuel 13:1, which says, "Saul reigned one year; and when he had reigned two years over Israel." Glenny says "it makes no sense as it reads." [pp. 84-85]

Analysis: The verse makes sense to some people. Ellicott says "the usually accepted meaning is that Saul had reigned one year when the events related in the last chapter took place and after he had reigned two years he chose out the 3,000 men, and did what is related in this chapter."

Matthew Henry wrote, "We take it rather as our own translation has it, *Saul reigned one year*, and nothing happened that was considerable, it was a year of no action; but in his second year he did as follows:"

This is a matter of interpretation, of course, like many other things in the Bible. People can differ in their interpretations of what it means, but those who are reverent of the Word of God will not say that there is a mistake in the Bible. It is one thing to say, "I don't understand this verse" (which is perfectly acceptable), but it is an entirely different thing when a person says, "There are some wrong numbers in the Hebrew text. The numbers in I Samuel are untrustworthy." It does not represent a high view of Scripture when a person says there are mistakes in it.

Another possible interpretation for the verse is that it is a Hebrew idiom which literally says, "Saul was a son of a year in his reigning." Which is to say that "Saul reigned one year" means that he reigned in innocence as if he were a child of one year. Again this is a matter of interpretation, but the very fact that there are various interpretations proves that the verse does make sense to some people.

There are other possibilities than saying that God did not preserve His Word. Even if a person says, "I do not know what it means, but someday I hope to understand it better," that would be far better than saying that there are mistakes in the Bible.

47. Glenny's second example of a "mistake" in the Old Testament is found in II Samuel 8:4, which reads, "David took seven hundred horsemen." The professor says it is a mistake in the Hebrew text and that it should say "seven thousand horsemen" as it does in I Chronicles 18:4 and as the Septuagint has it in II Samuel 8:4. [p.85]

<u>*Analysis*</u>: Matthew Henry says the number 700 in II Samuel 8:4 refers to the captains of the companies of the horsemen, since it is probable that there were ten per company. This would mean that II Samuel 8:4 and I Chronicles 18:4 are both correct as they stand in the KJV since the former would refer to the captains only, whereas the latter would refer to all of the horsemen. There would be a company of ten horsemen and ten horses for each chariot, as seems to have been standard military practice (see and compare I Kings 4:26 and II Chronicles 9:25).

Again, this is a matter of interpretation and there are, no doubt, some interpretations that no one has yet thought of; but to say that there is a mistake in the Hebrew text and in the KJV just because there *appears* to be a contradiction is to concede that the liberals have been right all along.

48. Glenny's third example of a mistake in the Hebrew text is found in II Chronicles 22:2 where it tells us that Ahaziah began to reign at the age of forty-two. I Kings 8:26 says that Ahaziah was twenty–two when he began to reign. [p.85]

Analysis: The evidence is overwhelming that II Chronicles 22:2 should read "forty-two," just as it does in the KJV. *All* of the Hebrew manuscripts say "forty-two." The Septuagint says neither "twenty-two" nor "forty-two"; it says "twenty." A few ancient *versions* say "twenty-two," but this was an obvious attempt (by those who made those versions) to reconcile the two passages, probably thinking that they were correcting a copyist's error.

The usual explanation is to attribute the "forty-two" to copyist's errors. I do not accept this explanation because there are many other good possibilities.

John Gill believed (to his discredit) that a copyist's errors were the best explanation for the "forty-two" in II Chronicles 22:2; however, he mentions *four other possible explanations* which have been put forth by various writers; (1) that the "forty-two" referred to Ahaziah's mother's age; (2) that it referred to his father's age; (3) that there was a co-regency for twenty years before Ahaziah came to power fully, publicly, and independently; and (4) that the "forty-two" refers to the forty-second year of the Omri dynasty (family rule).

I do not know for sure that any of the four explanations is the right one (although I do favor one of them). The right explanation might be one no one has even thought of yet. However, with so many different credible, or semi-credible, explanations (at least Gill thought they had enough merit to mention them), I would not want to be caught in a position of accusing the King James Bible *and* its underlying Hebrew text of having a mistake.

The word "was" in II Chronicles 22:2 is in italics (which means the word was added by the editors to attempt to make things clearer, but it is not part of the sacred text since no Hebrew word supports it). This leaves open the possibility that the verse is not saying that Ahaziah was forty-two years old, but that in someone else's forty-second year he began to reign. The idiom is literally "a son of the forty-second year," which could refer to his *mother's* forty-second year of life, or to his *father's* forty-second year.

It is likely that the meaning of II Chronicles 21:18-20 is that Jehoram lived to the age of forty-two; i.e., he was thirty-two when he began to reign, he reigned for eight years, and he was deposed and lived for two years as a sick man and then died. If this is true, then Ahaziah began to reign in Jehoram's forty-second year.

If Ahaziah was king in a co-regency with his mother, with his father, or with someone else, then he could have ascended to the throne at age twenty-two but could have come into full and independent power at age forty-two. Some believe this co-regency view, and add to the theory that Ahaziah may not have been the actual blood relative of Jehoram, but maybe a step-son, a son-in-law, or an

158

adopted son thus allowing Ahaziah to be about the same age as Jehoram.

Adam Clarke is unfriendly to the "forty-two" in II Chronicles 22:2 and to all explanations to try to harmonize it with II Kings 8:26. He believes the "forty-two" is a copyist's error. However, Clarke quotes Lightfoot (whom we take to be John Lightfoot, the venerable old British divine) saying,

The original meaneth thus: *Ahaziah was the son of two and forty years,* namely of the house of Omri, of whose seed he was by the mother's side, and he walked in the ways of that house, and came to ruin at the same time with it. This the text directs us to look after, when it calleth his mother the *daughter of Omri,* who indeed was the daughter of *Ahab.* Now these forty-two years are easily reckoned by any that will count back in the chronicle to the second of Omri, such an other reckoning there is about Jechoniah, or Jehoiachin, (II Kings 24:8): *Jehoiachin was eighteen years old when he began to reign.* But, II Chronicles 36:9 [says] *Jehoiachin, the son of eight years*; that is that the beginning of his reign fell in the eighth year of Nebuchadnezzar, and of Judah's first captivity.

Matthew Henry wrote that

Many good expositors [He never does say exactly what his own view is!] are ready to allow that this, with some few more such difficulties, arises from the mistake of some transcriber, who put forty-two for twenty-two.

But he also says,

Some make this forty-two to be the age of his mother, Athaliah, for in the original it is *he was the son of forty-two years*, that is, the son of a mother that was of that age.

159

With all of the above mentioned positions and possibilities it can not be said that an error has been found in the KJV. No errors have *ever* been **proven**. The critics have been looking for errors for the past four hundred years (come A.D. 2011), **and they have not been able to find one yet!** Today, critics of the KJV, such as the Central Baptist Theological Seminary faculty, are desperate to find an error in it, but all they can come up with are these same old, worn out, warmed-over charges which have been answered many times.

There are certain problems in the Bible that I can not answer and can not find a solution for, but that means absolutely nothing to the discussion of Bible infallibility. Just because I do not know the answer does not mean that it is a mistake in the Bible. I do not know everything; so, no surprise that I can not solve all problems presented to me. However, I do not believe that there are any mistakes in the Bible. I have faith in what God said about preserving His Word (Ps. 12:6-7; Ps. 78:1-8; Ps. 105:8; Ps. 119:89; Ps. 119:111; Ps. 119:152; Ps. 119:160; Prov. 22:20-21; Ecc. 3:14; Matt. 4:4; Matt.5:17-18; Matt. 24:35; John 10:35; Col. 1:17; I Pet. 1:23-25). God said He would preserve all of His words *perfectly*. I believe He did that. I do not believe God intended that we should come down here to the last days of the last days and **not know where the Bible is**. I do not believe that God kept His Word *imperfectly*. He used His people through all the ages to keep His Word pure (John 14:21 and 23-24 and 26; John 16:13-15).

Therefore, when I face a "problem" in the Bible, something that looks like a contradiction, my first reaction is not, "Well, I guess there are mistakes in the Bible." Rather, my first reaction is, "This is God's Holy Word, and

160

there are no mistakes in it. I may not be able to solve this 'problem,' but I will wait for further enlightenment. Until such time as I receive greater enlightenment, I will give God the benefit of the doubt."

Everyone has "problems" about the Bible. I would not trade my problems for the problems of the Critical Text person. Those who believe the Critical Text do not believe that there is an inspired, infallible book anywhere on earth! They have been trying to reconstruct the Bible for 150 years, and they know they still do not have it! All of the English Bibles which have been produced from the Critical Text (including the NASB) are gross corruptions. Those who believe in the Critical Text have no final authority. They do not have a God who is sovereign because they think He could not preserve His Word perfectly, *after promising He would*. And they find themselves embracing the text which the faithful people of God (including Anabaptists, Waldensians, Albiginsians, Luther, Calvin, Knox, and Tyndale) have stood against all through the centuries. *Now, those are problems!*

49. Glenny says II Chronicles 36:9 is one of the "obvious discrepancies" in the Hebrew text and in the KJV. [p. 85]   He says Jehoiachin was not eight when he began to reign since he had wives at that time.

Analysis: One possible solution to this problem has already been mentioned here in the analysis of problem # 48. Lightfoot is quoted by Adam Clarke as saying that the verse means that the beginning of Jehoiachin's reign fell in the eighth year of Nebuchadnezzar's and Judah's first captivity.

Another possibility (and a more likely one) is that Jehoiachin did begin to reign when he was eight years old and that his was a *joint regency with his mother*. There *was* a queen in Judah at the time (see Jeremiah 13:18-19), and there is little doubt that one of two things was true, (1) the queen was Jehoiachin's mother, or (2) Jehoiachin had wives.

Glenny cites II Kings 24:15 to show that it is ridiculous to assert that Jehoiachin was only eight years old "since he had wives at that time." However, the Bible does not say that he had wives when he was eight. He had wives (plural!) when he was carried away into Babylon. No doubt the wives were some kind of political arrangement executed by his mother.

The most likely solution is that Jehoiachin began to reign at age eight in a *co-regency* with his mother (and that is why she is mentioned with him in II Kings 24:8, 12, and 15). At age eighteen he began to reign *independently* of his mother and in his own right.

Some time later, he was carried away into Babylonian captivity. This happened, probably in 597 B.C.

If this explanation is the correct one, then both the Hebrew text and the KJV are correct as they stand in all of the passages that deal with the subject.

In any case, there are good possibilities other than concluding that this is a mistake in the Hebrew text and in the KJV.

Glenny and Central Seminary are frantic to find an error in the KJV and/or in the underlying Hebrew and Greek texts. Only by discrediting the KJV can they show a need for modern, naturalistic textual criticism and for the modern new versions.

50. Glenny says, "proponents of the doctrine of perfect providential preservation do not grapple with these kinds of textual issues [the apparent discrepancies]. They cover them up or inconsistently avoid them rather than deal with the biblical evidence." [p. 85]

**Analysis**: The professor is wrong. Those of us who believe in perfect providential preservation do study these issues. We are always defending the Bible against attacks by modern textual critics, and therefore, we study the passages in which Glenny thinks there are errors. Just because we come to different conclusions than he does, it is not reason that Glenny should accuse us of not studying. The conclusions we come to are very legitimate ones; usually they are conclusions long held by scholars for hundreds of years.

The difference between critical/eclectic text advocates and those who defend the King James Bible has nothing to do with how much they study. It has everything to do with the attitude each group has when it approaches the Book. The critical/eclectic text advocate, such as Glenny, approaches the Bible with the attitude that there are errors in it and that it his job to correct it.

On the other hand, the attitude of the King James Bible defender as he approaches the Book is that there are no errors in it and that he must believe it.

51. Glenny makes the strange suggestion that advocates of perfect providential preservation should "take the Old Testament out of their Bibles" because the text is often uncertain, and because the correct reading can not be determined by "counting noses" or by following the same methods used on the New Testament text. [p. 85]

Analysis: The text of the Old Testament is not "often uncertain." It is not even occasionally uncertain. In fact, it is not uncertain at all, in any place.

God preserved His Word in the Masoretic Hebrew text. In the few instances where Old Testament manuscripts have been discovered, copied between 100 B.C. and A.D. 200, they agree exactly with the Masoretic text of A.D. 900 – A.D. 1000. The Book of Isaiah and the two chapters of Habakkuk found in cave one at Qumran are in amazing agreement with the Masoretic text. The Greek manuscripts of the minor prophets found at Wadi Marabba'at are also in exact agreement with the words of the Masoretic text of 800 years later.

Since there are no other readable or translatable Old Testament Hebrew manuscripts from cave four, or from anywhere else, we do not understand Glenny's statement that the correct reading is often "not found in the majority of Hebrew manuscripts."

What is he talking about? He is talking about his conjectures. Since his mere conjectures are not found in the Hebrew text, he thinks the Hebrew text is incorrect.

Why would those of us who believe that the Hebrew text is perfect want to throw the Old Testament out of our Bible? If anyone should want to throw the Old Testament out of his Bible, it should be he who thinks it is **_often uncertain and incorrect_**.

52. Brother Glenny says, "The doctrine of preservation was not a doctrine of the ancient church." [p. 86]

Analysis: This he says, quoting Wallace, apparently a very unreliable man. The statement goes beyond any rational thought. Wallace and Glenny would have us believe that the ancient church taught nothing about the reliability and authenticity of the Old and New Testaments. They would have us believe that the ancient church taught nothing at all about Matt. 5:17-18 and I Peter 1:23-25. They would have us believe that no one in the church took sides against the early corrupters of Scripture; that no one taught that the church must help to preserve Scripture by seeing to it that only good, accurate copies were used; and that no one made sure that only accurate and true Scriptures were copied.

NONSENSE!

The very fact that there is a doctrine of the Canon proves that the ancient church had a doctrine of preservation of Scripture. It is obvious that the ancient church believed God had preserved the thirty-nine books of the Old Testament and the twenty-seven books of the New Testament.

In the Fifth Century, the Roman Catholic Church believed the Latin Vulgate was the preserved Word of God, but the independent Bible-believing churches believed that it was preserved elsewhere. That is the doctrine of preservation in the ancient church.

53. Glenny is now ready to explain away all the verses which have the doctrine of preservation, saying that it "is not taught in the verses they use to support it." [p. 86] His first attack is on *Matt. 5:18*, which he says means only that "Jesus did not come to destroy but to fulfill...[It is] not speaking about the exact words...does not even refer to the

165

New Testament text, let alone speak of its perfect, supernatural preservation." [p. 87]

Analysis: Yes, the words of Jesus in this passage refer to the Old Testament Law. And yes, the words refer to the prophecies of the Old Testament. But, the promises of Jesus in this passage must not be limited to the Old Testament Scriptures nor to Old Testament prophecies alone. If God preserved every jot and tittle of Old Testament Law until all of the prophecies in it were fulfilled, then why would He not do the same for the poetry of the Old Testament? Why would He not do the same for **all** of the Old Testament? Why would He not do the same for the New Testament prophecies? Why would He not do the same for New Testament history and New Testament epistles?

Matthew 5:17-18 reveals the mind of God; that He intended to preserve His words. The Old Testament prophecies will not all be fulfilled until we are in the New Heaven and New Earth! In other words, God will preserve His words forever. Even the smallest and least significant part of the Bible will be preserved.

Matthew Henry comments on the passage,

> He asserts the perpetuity of it; that not only he designed not the abrogation of it but that it would never be abrogated...Heaven and earth shall come together, and all the fullness thereof be wrapped up in ruin and confusion, rather than **any word of God** shall fall to the ground, or be in vain. The word of the Lord endures forever, **both that of the law and that of the gospel.** Observe, the care of God concerning his law extends itself even to those things that seem to be of least account in it, the iotas and the tittles; for whatever

belongs to God, and bears his stamp, be it ever so little, shall be preserved.

Matthew Henry is correct in his comments about the meaning of Matthew 5:18. Glenny is incorrect, unreasonable, and illogical in what he says about the passage.

54. Matthew 24:35, says Glenny, "refers to fulfillment, not textual preservation." [p. 87] It does not, says he, "guarantee that every word of the autographs of Scripture will be preserved...Instead, they teach that the Word of God is true...." [p. 88]

Analysis: "Heaven and earth shall pass away, but my words shall not pass away." These words refer to fulfillment _and_ textual preservation. Those words guarantee that every word of our Scriptures will be preserved _and_ they teach that the Word of God is true.

Lewis Sperry Chafer cites Matthew 24:35 in his discussion of preservation in Volume I of his _Systematic Theology_ and then says,

> The Bible is eternal in its own right. It abides because of the fact that no word Jehovah has spoken can be removed or shaken. In fact, it is by means of His written Oracles that God announces His binding declarations concerning the 'all things' which can not be shaken. The Scriptures are the legal instrument by which God obligates Himself to execute every detail of His eternal covenants and to fulfill every prediction His prophets have made. The legal instrument which secures this vast consummation must continue, and shall continue, until the last promise, for which it stands as surety, has been realized.

Not one jot or tittle of the divine deposition can pass until all is fulfilled.

Not only does Chafer cite Matthew 24:35 in support of the doctrine of preservation of Scripture, he also cites Psalms 119:89 and 152, I Peter 1:23, and Matthew 5:18. These are all verses which Glenny tries to explain away as having nothing to do with the preservation of the words of Scripture.

Matthew Henry says of Matthew 24:35,

> The word of Christ is more sure and lasting than heaven and earth. Hath he spoken? And shall he not do it? We may build with more assurance upon the word of Christ than we can upon the pillars of Heaven; or the strong foundations of the Earth; for, when they shall be made to tremble and totter, and shall be no more, the word of Christ shall remain, and be in full force, power, and virtue. See I Peter 1:24-25. It is easier for heaven and earth to pass, than the word of Christ...Every word of Christ is very pure, and therefore very sure.

Countless students and expositors of Scripture have taught that Matthew 24:35 means that God would preserve the words of the Bible. Many of these commentators do not hold our view of the Traditional Text nor of the KJV, but they dealt with the verses on preservation honestly and fairly.

John R. Rice, for example, wrote in his book ***Our God-Breadth Book-The Bible***, citing Matthew 24:35; Mark 13:31; and Luke 21:33,

> Here thrice repeated is the promise of Christ, "My words shall not pass away." Here the Scriptures in their eternal nature are contrasted with the earth and the heavens about it, which are under a curse and which must be purged by fire and,

in their present state, pass away.   Not so the Word of
God...When Jesus says, "My words shall not pass away," He
refers to all the Scriptures.   All the words of the Bible are the
words of Christ, and they shall never pass away!

We are surprised and saddened to see Professor Glenny
say that Matthew 24:35 can not refer to all of Jesus' words
being perfectly preserved in the text of Scripture "since all
of His words were not recorded in the text of Scripture." I
say that we are surprised at this poor way of arguing the
issue. No one is contending that all of Jesus' *spoken* words
were preserved according to any promise. No, when Jesus
says, "my words shall not pass away" he means all of *the
Bible* will be preserved in as much as the entire Bible
consists of *His words.*

Chafer, Matthew Henry, and Rice are correct in their
comments about the meaning of Matthew 24:35. Glenny is
incorrect, unreasonable, and illogical in what he says about
the passage.

55. Next the professor turns his attention to Psalm
119:89. He denies that the verse has anything to do with
Bible preservation. According to him, it only means that
"God's word is infallible and it holds the universe in place."
He further states that "if this verse did teach the preservation
of the text of God's Word, it would   mean   the   text is
preserved in Heaven, which is no help to those who want to
argue for preservation in the KJV, TR, or Majority Text."
[p. 88]

Analysis: Psalms 119:89, "For ever, O Lord, thy word is
settled in heaven," is cited as evidence that God has
preserved His word (*on the Earth!*) by Chafer, Pink, Rod

Bell, Ian R. K. Paisley, Charles Spurgeon, John Phillips, W.A. Criswell, John Rice, and thousands of other commentators. But, Glenny says all of those who thus use Psalm 119:89 as a proof text are in error. He is right about the meaning of it and others are all wrong, he thinks.

Settled means set, like concrete. It means established or appointed. The reason it is said to be "settled in heaven" is that that is where the Setter is located. He is in Heaven, but that which He set is on Earth. That which was set in Heaven and by Heaven can not be unsettled on Earth. It is beyond the reach of man or the devil to unsettle it because God, who is in Heaven, preserves it.

John Phillips says God's Word is settled "On this Globe" as the very next verse clearly says: "Thy faithfulness [trustworthiness in the Bible] is unto all generations: thou hast established the earth, and it abideth."

Spurgeon says the verse means that "Jehovah's word is not fickle nor uncertain; it is settled, determined, fixed, sure, immovable."

56. "...Everyone of thy righteous judgments endureth forever" does not mean, says Professor Glenny, "that the text of God's Word will remain intact centuries after [David] dies." This is the way he explains away any Bible preservation in Psalm 119:160. [p. 89]

Analysis: "Righteous judgments" is a designation for the Bible.

John Rice wrote of this verse: "I think there can be no doubt that this promise refers to the Word of God on earth and among men and it is not only true from the beginning, but 'every one of thy righteous judgments endureth forever.'" [*Our God-Breathed Book-The Bible*, p. 358]

Adam Clark says, "For it 'endures forever.' All other things wear out or decay; lose their testimony, and become obsolete. But God will ever bear testimony to His own word, and continue to support its veracity by fulfilling it *to all successive generations*."

57. Isaiah 40:8 and I Peter 1:23-25, says Glenny, have "nothing to do with the words of Scripture being preserved perfectly, but instead it has everything to do with the lasting and life-changing effect of God's Word in the lives of believers." [p. 89]

Analysis: Of course the passage does have to do with how the Word of God changes lives, saves souls, delivers His people, as Glenny says. *But that is not all that* it means.

"The grass withereth, the flower fadeth: but the word of our God shall stand forever" (Isaiah 40:8). "Being born again, not of corruptible seed, but of incorruptible, by the word of God, which liveth and abideth forever. For all flesh is as grass, and all the glory of man as the flower of grass. The grass withereth, and the flower thereof falleth away: But the word of the Lord endureth for ever. And this is the word which by the gospel is preached unto you" (I Peter 1:23-24).

In his dealing with these two passages (and time and time again in dealing with the other passages which we have looked at), Glenny is saying that the verses are only about the truthfulness of the Word of God and have nothing to do with having a preserved text. In other words, he is saying that the *message* of the Bible is true, but the actual physical text of the Bible is not even under discussion and that there is no promise to preserve the *words* of the text. I would submit that it is not an "either, or" situation. It is not that the Bible is saying that the promises of God are true *instead* of saying that the Bible text is preserved. God is saying *both* that His promises are true *and* that the text will always be accurate, authoritative, enduring, preserved. How could Israel *know* or *believe* God's promises of His future deliverance of them from Babylonian Captivity *unless they had the promises accurately preserved for them in the text of Scripture*?

People could not be born again by the words of Scripture, nor could the words of the Gospel be "preached unto you," as Peter said, unless the words of Scripture were preserved in the text.

You could not know about any of God's promises, nor could you believe God's word about anything, unless His Word is preserved in a text for us. So, it is not just the *messages* of the Bible which are preserved, nor is it only that the words of God are *true* which is important. You could not know or trust what anybody said or wrote about God's promises unless you have those promises in a preserved text of Scripture, inspired, inerrant, and authoritative.

When Glenny says that the verses in question are "speaking of the infallibility and incorruptible nature of the Word of God not of the preservation of the text of Scripture," [p. 89] he is using doublespeak, Clinton-ese, something similar to neo-orthodox descriptions of the Bible. He tries to separate the Word of God from the text of Scripture, a divarication which we can not and must not

172

allow him to make because *if we do not have the text of Scripture, we also do not have the Word of God.* In his book, <u>*Why I Preach that the Bible is Literally True*</u>, Dr. W.A. Criswell wrote,

> The reason that Isaiah 40:8 is my favorite verse is because it includes the entire revelation of God. We would not know God without the Book. We would not know Jesus Christ without the Book. We would have no assurance of salvation or of heaven without the Book. Our eternal hope lies in the promise, assurance and revelation of the Lord God written in His Book....The Lord God preserved the life of the incarnate Word, Jesus Christ, from the sword of Herod when He was born in Bethlehem. The Lord God preserved the body, the incarnate Word of Jesus from corruption when He died and was laid in Joseph's tomb. The same Lord God preserved His true believers so that they some day will appear in Heaven, justified and redeemed. It is the same Lord God who preserves His Word incorruptible through the present and continuing generations. The Holy Spirit wrote and keeps the Word incorruptible.
>
> How does God do that? How does He keep out corruption and error from the Word of God? The way God accomplished that was by the multiplying of the text....That is the way He keeps His Word incorruptible....God's Word can not be corrupted nor written with error. It cannot be continued with emendations, because God sees to it that any discrepancies in copies are pointed out, corrected, and removed.

Criswell does not hold my position on many things. I do not approve of his neo-evangelicalism nor of his position on staying in the Convention. And he does not hold the right view entirely on the text type nor of the KJV. He believes in modern textual criticism and the Eclectic Text. However, his view of Bible preservation and of all the verses mentioned by Glenny is the standard historical position held by Eclectic and Critical Text people. Criswell would agree with other Eclectic/Critical Text people on these issues; people like Pink, Bancroft, Chafer, J.R. Rice, Lockyer, A.H. Strong, and many others.

However, neither Criswell, nor any of the others that we have just listed would agree with Central Baptist Seminary's position on the matter of preservation, nor would they agree with Central's position on Matthew 5:18; Matthew 24:35; Luke 16:17; Psalm 119:89; Psalm 119:152; Psalm 119:160; Isaiah 40:8; I Peter 1:23-25; and Psalm 12:5-8.

The position of Central Seminary is unorthodox, even *within the Critical Text position*. Glenny and his school are out of step, not with Traditional Text and KJV advocates only, but also out of step with Critical Text advocates. Glenny's view is a new, novel view, dreamed up apparently to help answer Traditional Text and KJV advocates. The views expressed in ***The Bible Version Debate***, views on the doctrine of preservation and on the preservation verses, should be rejected by Critical Text advocates and Traditional Text advocates alike. The historic, standard Critical Text advocates would never say that God preserved His Word after a fashion "through natural processes." Nor would they say that the preservation verses cited "have nothing to do with the words of Scripture being perfectly preserved." Nor would they say, "These passages do not guarantee that every word of the autographs of Scripture will be preserved intact..."

58. Glenny is opposed to our using Psalm 12:5-8 "to support the doctrine of the supernatural preservation of God's Word," a doctrine he denies, believing instead his doctrine of "natural processes." He holds that verse seven "does not refer to the doctrine of the preservation of God's Word." He says it only means that God is keeping and preserving the righteous. He says the context, the grammar, and the textual evidence requires his interpretation of the passage. [pp. 90-92]

Analysis: The verses say, (5) "For the oppression of the poor, for the sighing of the needy, now will I arise, saith the Lord; I will set him in safety from him that puffeth at him. (6) The words of the Lord are pure words: as silver tried in a furnace of earth, purified seven times. (7) Thou shalt keep them, O Lord, thou shalt preserve them from this generation for ever."

Verses 6 and 7 are a very strong, clear statement on the preservation of the words of God as found in the Holy Bible. We can understand why Critical Text people would level their guns against this verse. They must try to explain it away some how if they are to teach that God has not been personally involved in the preservation of the Bible, and if they are going to teach that all of the words of God have not been available to every generation of man. They must get rid of this verse. But, it will not work! Why? Because of the very truth stated in the verses! The words of the Lord are pure words, and God will keep them, preserve them forever!

Peter VanKleek, writing in his lecture on Central's book, [_A 16th and 17th Century Exegetical and Theological Assessment of Central Baptist Theological Seminary's Perspective of the Bible Version Debate_] shows that the historic position of Bible believers before the 18th Century revealed no consensus for the interpretation of "them" in Psalm 12:7. "The evidence shows that the churchly tradition allows 'them' the breadth to include both people and God's words in its interpretation."

Glenny's modern sectarian approach, says Van Kleek, has "limited the scope of his exegesis."

In so far as the context is concerned, we should point out the "them" of verse 7 is in the context of the "words" of verse 6.

Verse 5 is not in the doctrinal "context" of verses 6 and 7 just because it is found in the immediate vicinity in the text. "Context" may be doctrinal, or historical; near, or far. Every verse in the Bible must be located next to something, even if the subject is being changed completely. There are **MANY** places where the subject of a verse is totally unrelated to the verse next to it. Read I Thessalonians 5 and Hebrews 13 for examples of this.

In so far as the grammar is concerned, the closest antecedent to the pronoun "them" is "words." According to Van Kleek, any writer or version which has "you" or "him" in verse 7 is following the Greek-Latin exegetical tradition to the exclusion of the Hebrew.

In the Hebrew, "them" is masculine. The first "them" is plural. The second "them" is singular, not because it refers to a person, but because it refers to each word of God. "Words" is in the feminine gender, but genders do not have to match in **EVERY** case.

Those who think that gender agreement is decisive in Psalm 12:6-7 should be consistent enough to admit that I John 5:7-8 makes no sense without the Johanine comma. They should also remember that the Holy Spirit is referred to as "it," and Jesus is referred to as "it" and "that holy thing" (Romans 8:16; 8:26; Genesis 3:15; Luke 1:35).

Psalm 12:7 means exactly what it says: God keeps His words – **ALL OF THEM**. He preserves His words for every generation. Every generation has had **ALL** of the words of the Bible. Thank God, we have **ALL** of the words of God today.

59. Psalm 105:8, says Brother Glenny, speaks only of "God's faithfulness to His covenant with Abraham. The emphasis here is clearly on infallibility and eternal authority of God's Word." [p. 92]

Analysis: The verse says, "He hath remembered his covenant for ever, the word which he commanded to a thousand generations."

While we do not believe that this is one of the strongest verses in the Bible on the subject of the preservation of Scripture, we do believe that "his covenant" can refer to all of Scripture. We believe Glenny is correct when he says the verse refers to the covenant of Abraham, but if it is true of that part of the Word of God then why would it not be true of the entire Word of God? Yes, God preserved the text of His covenant with Israel, and if He preserved that part He also preserves the whole of the Bible unto a thousand generations.

60. Glenny defines his doctrine of preservation of Scripture saying, "It is a belief that God has providentially preserved His Word in and through all the extant manuscripts, versions, and other copies of Scripture."[p. 93]

Analysis: The reader must read this definition carefully, and note what is *not* said. 1) He does not say *how well* God preserved His Word. In many other places he says God did not do it *perfectly*.

2) He does not say what he believes the Word of God to be. Does he mean that God preserved the *words of Scripture* or only the *message*? We know from reading other pages of the book that he does not mean the words. If he believed that God preserved all of the words of Scripture, then he would also believe that God preserved His Word perfectly. Alas, Glenny believes neither of these truths.

3) He does not tell us that by "preserved" he means *not completely preserved*. He does not believe the Bible is preserved as to the entire text. He thinks the text was only "essentially" preserved. [p. 131]

4) He does not say what he means by "providential." We know from reading other pages of the book that he does not mean *special providence* and certainly not *miraculous providence*, in any sense. He means "natural processes," which is no providence at all.

5) When he says, "God preserved His Word in and through all the extant manuscripts..." and "in the multiplicity of manuscripts that exist today" (p. 131), he does not bother to tell us that the "multiplicity of manuscripts" do not agree with his Critical Text. More than 5,200 manuscripts agree with the KJV text and only about forty or forty-five agree with the Critical Text/NASV. Most of those are fragments.

A clearer statement of what Central believes on the issue is this one found on page 131: "We do not believe that God has preserved His Word perfectly and miraculously in any one manuscript or group of manuscripts *or in all the manuscripts*" [emphasis mine].

61. Glenny and Central Seminary get their doctrine of preservation of Scripture from history, not from the Bible. "No passage of Scripture promises this, but *the evidence of history* leaves no doubt that such is the case." [p. 93]

<u>**Analysis**</u>: It is dangerous, unscriptural, and man-centered to get doctrine from history instead of from the Bible. *All of our doctrine should come from the Bible.* If the Bible does not say it, then we should not teach it! Charles Hodge said "The Scriptures contain all the facts of theology" [<u>*Systematic Theology*</u>, p. 15].

We ask the reader to be awake to what Central Seminary is doing here. It is very dangerous! Glenny is admitting that he could not find his doctrine of preservation in the Bible! He had to look to history for the evidence for his doctrine.

Dozens of times in chapter 5, and throughout the book, Glenny, appeals to "the evidence of history," "the historical evidence," or "the facts of history." He says, "this conviction is not based on a verse of Scripture; it is based on the evidence of history. Therefore, we need to use that evidence of history and all of the evidence of history when we make decisions concerning the text of Scripture." [p. 95]

God never intended that we should get our doctrine from history or from man's experience. History is the story of man's experience as interpreted by someone and written down.

History is not authoritative. History is open to interpretation. History must be interpreted by the Bible.

History, properly interpreted, will never contradict the Bible. The Bible is a "more sure word of prophecy" than history (see II Peter 1:15-21).

There is nothing wrong with history or with the proper study of it. We can learn much from it to cause us to praise God. However, history must be interpreted in the light of God's Word. We are not to go to history to try to formulate doctrines about which we think the Bible does not speak. To do so is no better than the practice of the modern charismatics who get their doctrines from man's experience, either their own or someone else's experience in history.

The Scriptures are "profitable for doctrine"; history is not (II Timothy 3:16).

We are forced to question Central's doctrine of the sufficiency of Scripture. Apparently Glenny does not believe that the Scriptures contain enough revelation from God to provide all we need for a rule of faith and practice. He thinks we must depend on history to teach us the doctrine of preservation.

The Roman Catholic Church has always held that "some doctrines which all Christians are bound to believe, are only imperfectly revealed in the Scriptures; that others are only obscurely intimated; and that others are not therein contained at all." [Charles Hodge, Ibid. p. 105] However, Bible-believing Baptists have always held that the Scriptures are complete and sufficient in all matters of faith and doctrine.

It is both strange and dangerous to find a fundamental Baptist seminary saying that the Bible has nothing to say about the important matter of the preservation of the Bible. It is strange and dangerous to find that Seminary getting doctrine from history and man's experience.

There is nothing in either the Bible *or* history to teach Central's doctrine of preservation. Central can not find in history *or* in the Bible any evidence that God preserved His Word *imperfectly*. Nor can she show from history or the Bible that God preserved His Word through *natural processes*.

This is one of the most serious errors in a very error-ridden book.

62. Glenny says, "Our earliest manuscript of the N.T. is only one generation after the originals were written." [p. 96]

Analysis: He wants us to believe that he has a manuscript of the New Testament written only one generation after the originals, *and* that it agrees with his Critical Text and with the NASV. He is wrong on every point. According to an obscure endnote, he is talking about P^{52}, which he dates at A.D. 125.

First, it is not even certain that P^{52} should be dated at A.D. 125. It is a Second Century fragment, but P^{32}, P^{46}, P^{64}, P^{66}, and P^{77} are all Second Century documents, also. Scholars are not at all agreed about which of them is the oldest. Many believe P^{66} is the oldest papyrus in the world. P^{66} has predominantly KJV readings. Many others believe P^{46} is the oldest Greek New Testament document. It also supports the Traditional Text, at least in many disputed passages. P^{46} is much longer than P^{52}, containing portions of Romans, I Corinthians, II Corinthians, Galatians, Ephesians, Colossians, I Thessalonians, and Hebrews.

P^{52} is not a "manuscript of the N.T." It is a **FRAGMENT** containing about eleven words, or parts of words, from John 18.

A small early fragment, containing a few words of the New Testament is interesting, a conversation piece for scholars, and valuable as a rare antique; but it is not much help in determining the text of the New Testament.

It is rather dishonest for a textual critic or a scholar to pretend that P^{52} is profoundly important to knowing the text of the New Testament. It is dishonest to mislead people who do not know about such things. It is dishonest to claim more for the fragment than it can deliver.

The truth is that P^{52} does not settle anything about the text of the New Testament. We would be no worse off if the fragment had never been discovered in so far as knowing the text of the New Testament is concerned. The text of John 18 was preserved in many manuscripts, ancient versions, and in the writings of the church fathers. There was never any question about the text of John 18.

How could a little fragment containing a few words and portions of a few words help settle anything?

The text of the Bible will never be settled by early manuscripts nor by scholars. We do not have the early manuscripts, and God never said that scholars should determine the text of the Bible. The text of the Bible has always been settled and certain. This was accomplished by God the Holy Spirit and by what the Bible says about itself.

Central Seminary does not believe that the Bible says anything about its own preservation. That is why Central can not be trusted regarding anything she says on the subject.

CHAPTER SIX

Professor Glenny of Central Baptist Theological Seminary continues in this chapter, giving his opinion about English translations and translating. It is important for us to keep in mind that almost everything he says in this chapter is just that—*an opinion.* An opinion is not a demonstrable fact. Everybody is entitled to an opinion. But, no one else is obligated to accept it as fact. If a person's position is based on the Word of God, then it is not just an opinion; it is a conviction and a fact. When a professor puts forth an opinion about English translations, and he has already been found to be wrong about many important related matters, no one should take his words for more than what they are – personal opinion. His opinion is no better than anyone else's.

Glenny has already shown that he gets his doctrine of Bible preservation, not from the Bible, but from history. This is a grave error.

He has already given his opinion that the Bible nowhere speaks of its own preservation – not in any of the verses which thousands of others have cited as proof of the preservation of the words and texts of Scripture. This is a grave error.

He has already ventured the opinion that the words of God have not been perfectly preserved in any or all of the manuscripts. This is a grave error.

Glenny and Pettegrew have already put forth the opinion that there are many errors in the King James Bible. In fact, they seem desperate to find errors in it. This is a grave error.

Glenny's book finds fault with the Massoretic Hebrew Text, gives inaccurate and misleading manuscript evidence, and says that it is good to emend the original language texts on the basis of mere conjectures. These opinions are filled with error.

He holds the opinion that those who strongly defend the King James Bible are less than fundamentalists, that they are cultic, and that they should be compared to Hitler's supporters. These opinions are filled with error.

He has the opinion that any preservation of the Bible which did occur (and he thinks that was far less than perfect) was accomplished through "natural processes," and that God was not greatly involved personally in the preservation of His Word. This opinion is a grave error.

Since he holds all of these erroneous opinions, why should we trust Brother Glenny's opinion about English translations? As we shall see, his opinions about translations and translating are no better than his other opinions.

63. The professor begins his discussion of translations by saying, "From the standpoint of preservation, the Latin

Vulgate has more claim to be the providentially preserved Word of God than the TR or the KJV do." [p. 108]

Analysis: What does Glenny mean by this? We presume that he means that because the Vulgate is older than Erasmus' receptus and older than the KJV that that proves it has more claim to being the providentially preserved Word of God. However, this is an erroneous opinion. Just because the Catholic Vulgate is older than the KJV does not mean it preserves the Word of God. Nor does it mean that it is accurate.

The Vulgate is correct in many of its readings and wrong in many others.

Unlike the KJV, the Vulgate intersperses the Apocrypha throughout the Old Testament *as Scripture*.

The Vulgate, like the Vatican manuscript, has many corrupted readings agreed to by only one or two manuscripts and a few fragments.

The *readings* of the Textus Receptus and the KJV are older than the Latin Vulgate. The Old Italic Bibles (A.D. 150-400) agree with the King James readings. It was recognized from the beginning (A.D. 400) that Jerome included many corrupt readings in his work, corrupt readings which he got from Origen through Eusebius. As such, the Latin Vulgate is like the other Catholic productions, Vaticanus and Siniaticus—corrupted.

The Latin Vulgate of Jerome was rejected by the Waldenses (the Vaudais), the Albigenses, all of the reformers including Luther and Calvin, and almost everybody else in history who were pronounced heretics by Rome. Why? Because the Latin Vulgate of Jerome did

NOT HAVE MORE LEGITIMATE CLAIM TO BEING THE PROVIDENTIALLY PRESERVED WORD OF GOD THAN DID THE TR OR THE KJV.
If Glenny believes what he wrote, he should have been teaching from the Douay Version through all of these years. His *opinion* that the Latin Vulgate has more claim to being the providentially preserved Word of God than the TR or the KJV is an *opinion* that is erroneous and should be rejected.

64. Glenny says "another objection to the KJV was the inclusion of the Apocrypha between the testaments." [p. 111]

Analysis: The problem with this statement is that Glenny seems to want to draw the inference that the translators of the KJV believed that the Apocrypha was Scripture. This would be an absolutely false inference. The Apocrypha was put between the testaments and was marked in the index as the Apocrypha, separate from either the Old Testament or the New Testament. Many people believed, perhaps correctly, that the Apocrypha was good to read but should not be accepted as Scripture. This was the position of Luther, for example. The Puritans and the Calvinists were probably right in wanting the Apocrypha removed from the Book altogether, since there is always the possibility that some people will make the mistake of thinking that it is inspired. While we contend that the KJV is the Word of God, we do not defend anyone's study notes, marginal notes, or any other articles or materials that might have been included in any edition of the KJV. On the other hand, just because somebody makes the mistake of thinking that the Apocrypha is inspired does not mean that we should declare it without value, worthless. So far in my life I have not even met one man who thought that Scofield's notes were inspired! That does not mean that they are worthless. It is a mistaken *opinion* when Glenny infers that the translators of the KJV thought that the Apocrypha should be in the canon of Scripture.

65. Professor Glenny says, "There have been several editions and revisions of the KJV." [p.111]

Analysis: He is half right. There have indeed been many *editions* of the KJV. But there has never been a *revision* of the KJV. Spelling and printing errors being corrected does not rise to the level of a revision. Taking the Apocrypha out, or putting it in, does not a revision make! Using different forms of the same words, "burned" instead of "burnt," for example, is of no real consequence and does not constitute a revision. The word "revision" in book publishing, and especially as it pertains to Bible publishing indicates a far more pervasive and extensive change or addition of material than anything that has happened to the text of the KJV. Opponents of the King James Bible like to say it has been "revised" because they want to have uninformed people think that if the KJV has been revised, then it is okay to revise and revise and revise again. This justifies, they think, the new versions of the Bible. It is an erroneous *opinion*.

66. Central's favorite translation seems to be the NASB, which Glenny refers to as "a careful 'word for word' translation, which is very trustworthy." [p. 113]

<u>Analysis</u>: The NASB (also designated as NASV) is an inferior translation made from a minuscule number of inferior manuscripts. Its New Testament is based on an unreliable form of the Greek text which was popularized by liberals (Griesbach, Lachmann, Westcott and Hort, Schaff, Goodspeed, Moffatt, Nida, Aland, Barclay, Bruce, Kenyon, Driver, Kittel, VonSoden, and others) over the past 150 years.

The Greek manuscript evidence for the NASV is very slim. There are only about forty to forty-five pieces of manuscript evidence supporting that version. Most of those pieces of evidence are only fragments containing a few words or a few verses. Fewer than ten of those manuscripts contain any whole books of the Bible. Only three of those manuscripts contain most of the New Testament; however, these three also contain various types of pseudepigrapha in the New Testament. So the manuscript evidence which sides with the NASV against the KJV is very scant, indeed.

By contrast, there are more than 5,200 Greek manuscripts which favor the KJV against the NASV. The Greek church and the independent churches through the ages copied the Traditional Text which underlies the KJV because they recognized it as superior. No one bothered much to copy the Critical Text underlying the NASV after the sixth century because it was known to be inferior.

In addition to the Greek manuscript evidence, the ancient versions favor the KJV as do the writings of the early church fathers.

Of course, the text of the NASV survived through the centuries in the Roman Catholic Latin Vulgate of Jerome.

The NASV weakens several great doctrines of the Faith. We will list ten great doctrines with a few verses for each doctrine so that the reader may make the comparisons.

THE DEITY OF JESUS CHRIST IS WEAKENED IN THE NASB.

KJV	*NASB*
But seek ye first the kingdom of God, and his righteousness; and all these things shall be added unto you. (Matthew 6:33)	But seek first His kingdom, and His righteousness; and all these things shall be added to you. (Matthew 6:33)

It is the righteousness of Christ and the Kingdom of Christ which is under discussion in Matthew 6:33, but the NASB refuses to call Him God in the verse.

KJV	*NASB*
Jesus heard that they had cast him out; and when he had found him, he said unto him, Dost thou believe on the Son of God? (John 9:35)	Jesus heard that they had put him out; and finding him, He said, "Do you believe in the Son of Man?" (John 9:35)

Son of man is the name for Jesus in His humanity. Son of God is a name for Christ in His deity. To change this verse, as the NASB does, is to weaken the doctrine of Christ's deity.

KJV	*NASB*
The God of Abraham, and of Isaac, and of Jacob, the God of our fathers, hath glorified his Son Jesus; whom ye delivered up, and denied him in the presence of Pilate, when he was determined to let him go. (Acts 3:13)	The God of Abraham, Isaac, and Jacob, the God of our fathers, has glorified His Servant Jesus, the one whom you delivered up, and disowned in the presence of Pilate, when he had decided to release Him. (Acts 3:13)

Augustus Strong, the Baptist theologian wrote, "His Sonship is inseparable from His Godhood."

Loraine Boettner wrote, "Wherever the Scriptures call Christ the 'Son of God' they assert His true and proper deity."

John Calvin wrote in his ***Institutes***, Vol. 1, p. 442, "I contend that He is denominated 'The Son of God' on account of His deity and eternal existence."

Liberals and cultists have a long history of putting "Servant" in Acts 3:13 instead of "Son." The liberal commentator, Ellicott argues for "Servant." The Jehovah's Witnesses want it to say "servant" not "Son."

The Greek word translated "Son" is the word "Pais." It is one of those words which can be translated in various ways depending on the context. It can be translated "boy," "slave," "servant," "minister," "young man," "child," or "son." The key element is the matter of being in subjection to another.

The context of Acts 3:13 demands that the word "Pais" be translated as "Son," because it is the deity of Christ which Peter is discussing. The question is, "How did the Jews treat the Son of God?"

Adam Clarke, on Acts 3:13, wrote, "This was wisely introduced to show them that He whom they called their God had acknowledged Jesus Christ for his Son, and wrought this miracle in his name; and, by thus honoring Jesus whom they slew, he had charged home the guilt of that murder upon them."

Matthew Henry comments upon the verse, "He preaches Christ, as the true Messiah promised to the fathers; for (1.) He is Jesus the Son of God; though they had lately condemned Christ as a blasphemer for saying that he was the Son of God, yet Peter avows it: he is his Son Jesus; to him dear as a Son; to us Jesus, a Saviour."

The new versions, including the NASB, make the same error in Acts 3:26, 4:27, and 4:30. In the last two references the KJV translates "Pais" as "child" because a child is a son of a younger age and because the context has to do with Christ as a baby Son of God, i.e., Holy Child.

And finally, here is the clincher. How does the NASB translate "Pais" in John 4:51? It is "Son." The deity of Jesus Christ is an issue in Acts 3:13; Acts 3:26; Acts 4:27; and Acts 4:30 where the NASB says "servant." But the deity of Jesus Christ is *not* an issue in John 4:51 where it is translated "Son." I think I smell a rat – or more accurately, I think I see the hand of the devil!

> *"Contrary to what the president of Central thinks, almost all fundamentalists have been KJV-only people." [p. 31]*

KJV	*NASB*
Unto you first God, having raised up his Son Jesus, sent him to bless you, in turning away every one of you from his iniquities. (Acts 3:26)	"For you first, God raised up His Servant, and sent Him to bless you by turning every one of you from your wicked ways." (Acts 3:26)

It is tragic that the NASB has weakened the deity of Christ in this verse.

KJV	*NASB*
For of a truth against thy holy child Jesus, whom thou hast anointed, both Herod, and Pontius Pilate, with the Gentiles, and the people of Israel, were gathered together. (Acts 4:27)	For truly in this city there were gathered together against Thy holy Servant Jesus, whom Thou didst anoint, both Herod and Pontius Pilate, along with the Gentiles and the peoples of Israel. (Acts 4:27)

"Thy holy child Jesus" is changed to "Thy holy Servant Jesus." This weakens the deity of Christ.

KJV	*NASB*
By stretching forth thine hand to heal; and that signs and wonders may be done by the name of thy holy child Jesus. (Acts 4:30)	while Thou dost extend Thy hand to heal, and signs and wonders take place through the name of Thy holy Servant Jesus. (Acts 4:30)

"Holy child" emphasizes the incarnation and deity of the Lord Jesus Christ. "Servant" weakens the incarnation and deity of Christ.

KJV

And Philip said, If thou believest with all thine heart, thou mayest. And he answered and said, I believe that Jesus Christ is the Son of God. (Acts 8:37)

NASB

[The NASB leaves this verse out completely and has a footnote which says, "Late mss. Insert verse 37."]

The verse was eliminated by Vaticanus, probably because it teaches the baptism of believers only. The NASB, by following one or two corrupt manuscripts, weakened the doctrine of the deity of Christ as well as the doctrine of believer's baptism.

KJV

But why dost thou judge thy brother? Or why dost thou set at nought thy brother? For we shall all stand before the judgment seat of Christ. For it is written, As I live, saith the Lord, every knee shall bow to me, and every tongue shall confess to God. So then every one of us shall give account of himself to God.
(Romans 14:10-12)

NASB

But you, why do you judge your brother? Or you again, why do you regard your brother with contempt? For we shall all stand before the judgment-seat of God. For it is written, "As I LIVE, SAYS THE LORD, EVERY KNEE SHALL BOW TO ME, AND EVERY TONGUE SHALL GIVE PRAISE TO GOD." So then each one of us shall give account of himself to God.
(Romans 14:10-12)

193

The Word of God here says we shall all stand before the Judgment Seat of Christ. And then immediately identifies (twice) as God this one before whom we shall stand. But the NASB changes "Christ" to "God" and thus muddles and weakens the deity of Christ.

**KJV**	_**NASB**_
And without controversy great is the mystery of godliness: God was manifest in the flesh, . . . (I Timothy 3:16)	And by common confession great is the mystery of godliness: He who was revealed in the flesh, . . . (I Timothy 3:16)

By substituting "He" for "God" the NASB greatly weakens the doctrine of the deity of Christ.

**KJV**	_**NASB**_
And I saw the dead, small and great, stand before God, . . . (Revelation 20:12)	And I saw the dead, the great and the small, standing before the throne, . . . (Revelation 20:12)

It is Christ who is on the throne and the Word of God says to stand before Him is to stand before God. But the NASB, by substituting "throne" for "God" greatly weakens the deity of Christ.

> "I believe that our version is the correct one, but the fiercest battlings have been held over this sentence. . . . We believe that, if criticism should grind the text in a mill, it would get out of it no more and no less than the sense expressed by our grand old Version. God Himself was manifest in the flesh."
> - C. H. Spurgeon
> From his sermon "The Hexapla of Mystery"

THE DOCTRINE OF THE SUBSTITUTIONARY BLOOD ATONEMENT IS WEAKENED IN THE NASB.

KJV	NASB
And the scripture was fulfilled, which saith, And he was numbered with the transgressors. (Mark 15:28)	[The NASB leaves this verse out completely and has a footnote which says, "Later mss. add verse 28."]

The substitutionary aspect of Christ's blood atonement is weakened by leaving this verse out of the NASB.

KJV	NASB
Purge out therefore the old leaven, that ye may be a new lump, as ye are unleavened. For even Christ our passover is sacrificed for us. (I Corinthians 5:7)	Clean out the old leaven, that you may be a new lump, just as you are *in fact* unleavened. For Christ our Passover also has been sacrificed. (I Corinthians 5:7)

By leaving out "for us" the NASB weakens the substitutionary aspect of Christ's blood atonement.

KJV	NASB
In whom we have redemption through his blood, even the forgiveness of sins. (Colossians 1:14)	in whom we have redemption, the forgiveness of sins. (Colossians 1:14)

The eliminating of the Blood of Christ by the NASB greatly weakens the doctrine of the Blood atonement.

**KJV**	_**NASB**_
Forasmuch then as Christ hath suffered for us in the flesh, arm yourselves likewise with the same mind: for he that hath suffered in the flesh hath ceased from sin. (I Peter 4:1)	Therefore, since Christ has suffered in the flesh, arm yourselves also with the same purpose, because he who has suffered in the flesh has ceased from sin, (I Peter 4:1)

When the NASB leaves out "for us," it weakens the substitutionary aspect of the blood atonement. Christ suffered *for us*, just as the KJV says.

THE RESURRECTION OF CHRIST IS WEAKENED IN THE NASB.

**KJV**	_**NASB**_
Now when Jesus was risen early the first day of the week, he appeared first to Mary Magdalene, out of whom he had cast seven devils. (Mark 16:9)	[The NASB calls into question this verse and all of the next eleven verses. The passage is placed in brackets and a footnote says "Some of the oldest mss. omit from verse 9 through 20.]

On very flimsy manuscript evidence, the New American Standard Bible calls into question the genuineness of these verses and weakens thereby the doctrine of the resurrection of Christ. In the entire twelve verses there is a great deal of evidence for the resurrection, including the account of a post-resurrection appearance of Christ to the eleven. But the NASB would weaken the resurrection of Christ by questioning the authenticity of these verses!

Burgon and Miller wrote the definitive material on Mark 16:9-20. They proved beyond any shadow of a doubt that the verses belong in the Word of God.

Not only the resurrection, but also several other doctrines are also weakened (including the doctrine of the ascension of Christ) by those who would knock the passage out of the Bible.

KJV	*NASB*
Then arose Peter, and ran unto the sepulchre; and stooping down, he beheld the linen clothes laid by themselves, and departed, wondering in himself at that which was come to pass. (Luke 24:12)	[The NASB puts this entire verse in brackets with a footnote saying, "Some ancient mss. omit verse 12"]

Again the New American Standard Bible plants the seeds of doubt about an important verse on the resurrection of Christ.

KJV	*NASB*
And when he had thus spoken, he shewed them his hands and his feet. (Luke 24:40)	[The NASB leaves this verse out completely and has a footnote which says, "Some mss. add verse 40" etc.]

Again the New American Standard Bible questions the authenticity of a verse which gives important information about the resurrection of Christ. Again the doctrine of the resurrection of Christ is weakened.

KJV	**_NASB_**
To whom also he shewed himself alive after his passion by many infallible proofs. . . .	To these He also presented Himself alive, after His suffering, by many convincing proofs. . . .
(Acts 1:3)	(Acts 1:3)

There is a huge difference between "many infallible proofs" and "many convincing proofs." The evidence for the resurrection of Christ is *infallible*, being proof which is in the very Word of the living God. The NASB weakens the doctrine of the resurrection in this verse.

KJV	**_NASB_**
Therefore being a prophet, and knowing that God had sworn with an oath to him, that of the fruit of his loins, according to the flesh, he would raise up Christ to sit on his throne.	And so, because he was a prophet, and knew that God had sworn to him with an oath to seat *one* of his descendants upon his throne.
(Acts 2:30)	(Acts 2:30)

Peter quotes Psalm 132:11 where the Lord swears to David that the fruit of his body will sit upon David's throne. The Holy Spirit in Acts 2:30 tells us that Christ is the fulfillment of that promise and that God would raise Him up. The NASB is extremely weak in several respects because it does not say that Christ is the fulfillment of the promise and *it does not say that Christ was raised up*. So the NASB weakens the doctrine of the bodily resurrection of Christ again.

"The textual criticism which supports the Critical Text says that MAN preserved the Scriptures, and man's own wisdom and scientific procedure will determine what the Bible is." [p. 93]

THE INCARNATION AND VIRGIN BIRTH OF CHRIST IS WEAKENED IN THE NASB.

KJV	*NASB*
And Joseph and his mother marvelled at those things which were spoken of him. (Luke 2:33)	And His father and mother were amazed at the things which were being said about Him. (Luke 2:33)

The King James version does not call Joseph the father of Jesus in this verse. The NASB weakens the doctrine of the Virgin Birth of Christ when it calls Joseph the father of Jesus.

KJV	*NASB*
And when they had fulfilled the days, as they returned, the child Jesus tarried behind in Jerusalem; and Joseph and his mother knew not of it. (Luke 2:43)	and as they were returning, after spending the full number of days, the boy Jesus stayed behind in Jerusalem. And His parents were unaware of it. (Luke 2:43)

The KJV preserves the doctrine of the Virgin Birth in this verse. The NASB weakens that doctrine.

KJV	*NASB*
No man hath seen God at any time; the only begotten Son, which is in the bosom of the Father, he hath declared him. (John 1:18)	No man has seen God at any time; the only begotten God, who is in the bosom of the Father, He has explained Him. (John 1:18)

"Only begotten Son" speaks of the Virgin Birth of Christ. He was begotten of God in the womb of the Virgin. The NASB destroys the idea of Jesus being the "only begotten Son." "Only begotten God" as the NASB has it, is an impossible translation since God is not begotten. The Jehovah's Witnesses like the NASB's translation of John 1:18 because they believe God created another god. The Incarnation and Virgin Birth of Christ is weakened in the NASB.

KJV	*NASB*
And every spirit that confesseth not that Jesus Christ is come in the flesh is not of God: . . . (I John 4:3)	and every spirit that does not confess Jesus is not from God; . . . (I John 4:3)

The NASB weakens the doctrine of the Incarnation of Christ in this verse because it says nothing about false teachers who do not confess that Jesus Christ is come in the flesh.

THE LORDSHIP OF CHRIST IS WEAKENED IN THE NASB IN THE FOLLOWING VERSES:

Titus 1:4; Mark 11:10; Luke 23:42; Mark 9:24; Acts 9:5-6; Hebrews 10:30; Acts 7:30; II Corinthians 4:10; Ephesians 3:14; and Colossians 1:2.

> *"Surely no corollary of inspiration is more logical than the preservation of God's Word which lives and abides forever."*
> - Dr. Manfred E. Kober. Th.D.

THE ASCENSION OF CHRIST IS
WEAKENED IN THE NASB.

There are only three actual accounts of the ascension of our Lord. In the NASB, two of these narratives are destroyed. Only the account in Acts 1 is still intact. The direct statements of the ascension in Mark 16 and in Luke 24 are destroyed. Additionally, there are several places in Scripture where the ascension is implied. Several of these are destroyed in the NASB.

KJV	*NASB*
So then, after the Lord had spoken unto them, he was received up into heaven, and sat on the right hand of God. (Mark 16:19)	[The NASB calls into question this verse and all of the last twelve verses in Mark's Gospel. The verses are placed in brackets and a footnote says, "Some of the oldest mss. omit from verse 9 through 20"] (Mark 16:19)

On very flimsy evidence, the New American Standard Bible calls into question the genuineness of these verses and weakens the doctrine of the ascension of Christ.

KJV	*NASB*
And it came to pass, while he blessed them, he was parted from them, and carried up into heaven. (Luke 24:51)	And it came about that while He was blessing them, He parted from them. (Luke 24:51)

The rest of the verse "and [was] carried up into heaven" is completely out of the NASB. A footnote says, *"Some mss. add, and was carried up into heaven."*

In one chapter, Luke 24, the NASB manages to mutilate and weaken three major doctrines: The Resurrection of Christ, The Ascension of Christ, and The Deity of Christ.

KJV	*NASB*
And no man hath ascended up to heaven, but he that came down from heaven, even the Son of man which is in heaven. (John 3:13)	And no one has ascended into heaven, but He who descended from heaven, *even* the Son of Man. (John 3:13)

The NASB does not say in this verse that Jesus is in heaven now. This weakens the doctrine of the ascension, especially when the verse is linked to other verses in the NASB wherein the doctrine of the ascension is undermined.

KJV	*NASB*
A little while, and ye shall not see me: and again, a little while, and ye shall see me, because I go to the Father. (John 16:16)	A little while, and you will no longer behold Me; and again a little while, and you *will* see Me. (John 16:16)

The New American Standard Version weakens the doctrine of the ascension in this verse because it does not have Jesus saying, "I go to the Father." Someone will say, "But the disciples ask a question about it in the very next verse and say that Jesus had said, 'Because I go to the Father?'" But the disciples asking a question about what

Jesus had said is far different than Jesus saying it! Every single time a doctrine is removed from a verse, or partially removed from a verse that doctrine is weakened.

KJV	*NASB*
Seeing then that we have a great high priest, that is passed into the heavens, Jesus the Son of God, let us hold fast our profession. (Hebrews 4:14)	Since then we have a great high priest who has passed through the heavens, Jesus the Son of God, let us hold fast our confession. (Hebrews 4:14)

There is a big difference between Jesus having "passed into the heavens," and Jesus has "passed through the heavens." Again it has to do with where Jesus is today. Did He only "pass through" the heavens, or did He pass "into the heavens" and stay there to intercede for us?

THE PRE-EXISTENCE AND THE ETERNALITY OF CHRIST IS WEAKENED BY THE NASB.

KJV	*NASB*
(For those priests were made without an oath; but this with an oath by him that said unto him, The Lord sware and will not repent, Thou art a priest for ever after the order of Melchisedec): (Hebrews 7:21)	(for they indeed became priests without an oath, but he with an oath through the one who said to Him, "THE LORD HATH SWORN AND WILL NOT CHANGE HIS MIND, 'THOU ART A PRIEST FOREVER'"); (Hebrews 7:21)

Melchisedec is a preincarnate appearance of Jesus Christ, and He existed in the days of Abraham and was without lineage. But the NASB does not even mention Melchisedec in this verse. Of course, Melchisedec is mentioned in other verses in the same chapter, but the doctrines of pre-existence and eternality of Christ are weakened whenever a verse leaves it out.

KJV	*NASB*
I am Alpha and Omega, the beginning and the ending, saith the Lord, which is, and which was, and which is to come, the Almighty. (Revelation 1:8)	"I am the Alpha and the Omega," says the Lord God, "who is and who was and who is to come, the Almighty." (Revelation 1:8)

"The beginning and the ending" is left out. This weakens the doctrines of the pre-existence and the eternality of the Lord Jesus Christ.

KJV	*NASB*
Saying, I am Alpha and Omega, the first and the last: and, What thou seest, write in a book, and send it unto the seven churches which are in Asia; ... (Revelation 1:11 A & B)	saying, "Write in a book what you see, and send it to the seven churches: . . . (Revelation 1:11 A & B)

"Saying, I am Alpha and Omega, the first and the last" is all left out of the verse in the NASB. This weakens the doctrines of the pre-existence and incarnation of Christ.

KJV	*NASB*
And the four beasts said, Amen. And the four and twenty elders fell down and worshipped him that liveth for ever and ever. (Revelation 5:14)	And the four living creatures kept saying, "Amen." And the elders fell down and worshiped. (Revelation 5:14)

The NASB does not say they worshipped *Him*, thus weakening the deity of Christ; and it does not say "him that liveth for ever and ever," thus weakening the doctrines of the pre-existence and eternality of the Lord Jesus Christ.

THE SECOND COMING OF CHRIST IS WEAKENED IN THE NASB.

KJV	*NASB*
Watch therefore, for ye know neither the day nor the hour wherein the Son of man cometh. (Matthew 25:13)	Be on the alert then, for you do not know the day nor the hour. (Matthew 25:13)

The day nor the hour of what? The NASB does not say. And so the Coming of Christ is weakened.

KJV	*NASB*
Saying, We give thee thanks, O Lord God Almighty, which art, and wast, and art to come; because thou hast taken to thee thy great power, and hast reigned. (Revelation 11:17)	saying, "We give Thee thanks, O Lord God, the Almighty, who art and who wast, because Thou hast taken Thy great power and hast begun to reign." (Revelation 11:17)

The NASB, without an explanation whatsoever, leaves out the words "who art to come." The verse speaks of the Coming of the Lord to take power and reign. This doctrine is weakened in the NASB.

THE DOCTRINE OF SALVATION IS WEAKENED IN THE NASB.

KJV	NASB
For the Son of man is come to save that which was lost. (Matthew 18:11)	[For the Son of Man has come to save that which was lost.] (Matthew 18:11)

The NASB calls the genuineness of this verse into question by putting the verse in brackets and having a footnote which reads, "most ancient mss. omit this verse." The verse does not appear in the Vatican manuscript. However, Edward Miller, in discussing the work of the "Extreme Textualists" lists the verse along with several others, which he says have "all the appearance of being intrinsically genuine." Indeed, the verse has very strong manuscript evidence. And yet, the NASB translators decided to question the verse, thus weakening this important salvation passage.

KJV	NASB
That whosoever believeth in him should not perish, but have eternal life. (John 3:15)	that whosoever believes may in Him have eternal life. (John 3:15)

The NASB has a footnote which says, "Some mss. read, *believe in Him may have eternal life.*"

The change from the KJV reading is inexcusable. The New American Standard Version does not say *who* or *what* is to be believed in order to have eternal life. It also does not say what will happen to those who do not believe (perish). The NASB weakens the doctrine of salvation in this verse.

KJV	***NASB***
Verily, verily, I say unto you, He that believeth on me hath everlasting life. (John 6:47)	Truly, truly, I say to you, he who believes has eternal life. (John 6:47)

Again the NASB does not say *in whom* or *what* a person is to believe in order to be saved. A person may *believe* on religion, self, church, the Golden Rule, The Ten Commandments, and doing "the best that I know how" and be lost forever. The NASB weakens the doctrine of salvation in this verse.

KJV	***NASB***
By whom also we have access by faith into this grace wherein we stand, and rejoice in hope of the glory of God. (Romans 5:2)	through whom also we have obtained our introduction by faith into this grace in which we stand; and we exult in hope of the glory of God. (Romans 5:2)

"Obtained our introduction?" What is this? We have not simply been introduced to the subject. We have entered into the grace of God by faith. An "access" is for entering in. Those who have faith in Christ have entered into God's grace. A person may be introduced to something without actually experiencing it for himself. The verse is more accurate *and clearer* in the KJV. The NASB weakens the doctrine of salvation in this verse.

KJV	*NASB*
And if by grace, then is it no more of works: otherwise grace is no more grace. But if it be of works, then is it no more grace: otherwise work is no more work. (Romans 11:6)	But if it is by grace, it is no longer on the basis of works, otherwise grace is no longer grace. (Romans 11:6)

I have always loved this verse in the KJV because it is so emphatic. It makes it clear that there can be no admixture of works for salvation. However, the NASB has made the truth less emphatic, and therefore it has weakened the doctrine of salvation in this verse.

KJV	*NASB*
Christ is become of no effect unto you, whosoever of you are justified by the law; ye are fallen from grace. (Galatians 5:4)	You have been severed from Christ, you who are seeking to be justified by law; you have fallen from grace. (Galatians 5:4)

The NASB has given the verse a decided Armenian translation, making it possible for a Christian to be "severed from Christ." The verse actually means that Christ and His saving work has been set aside by those who attempt to keep their salvation by law-keeping. This means that the full result of Christ and His saving work is not being realized by those who have fallen away from the *doctrine* of grace.

The NASB translators have made their version acceptable to the Armenians by saying that it is possible for a believer to be severed from Christ. This is not a possibility according to Romans 8:35-39.

Again the NASB weakened the doctrine of salvation.

KJV	*NASB*
And the nations of them which are saved shall walk in the light of it: and the kings of the earth do bring their glory and honour into it. (Revelation 21:24)	And the nations shall walk by its light, and the kings of the earth shall bring their glory into it. (Revelation 21:24)

The NASB has a universalist translation in this verse since it does not limit admission to the New Jerusalem and Heaven to "them which are saved." This weakens the doctrine of salvation.

THE DOCTRINE OF JUDGMENT AND HELL ARE WEAKENED IN THE NASB.

KJV	*NASB*
They say unto him, Because no man hath hired us. He saith unto them, Go ye also into the vineyard; and whatsoever is right, that shall ye receive. (Matthew 20:7)	"They said unto him, 'Because no one hired us.' He said to them, 'You too go into the vineyard.'" (Matthew 20:7)

By leaving out the words "and whatsoever is right, that shall ye receive," the NASB avoids the fact that believers will be judged at the Judgment Seat of Christ.

There is no explanation for leaving out these words. The NASB has weakened one of the future judgment events in this verse.

KJV	*NASB*
And whosoever shall not receive you, nor hear you, when ye depart thence, shake off the dust under your feet for a testimony against them. Verily I say unto you, It shall be more tolerable for Sodom and Gomorrha in the day of judgment, than for that city. (Mark 6:11)	And any place that does not receive you or listen to you, as you go out from there, shake off the dust from the soles of your feet for a testimony against them. (Mark 6:11)

The NASB has removed the judgment and Hell from this verse.   Sodom and Gomorrha were judged in fire and brimstone! But there is a judgment worse than Sodom and Gomorrah—Hell! In a day when Hell is being minimized, along come the new Bible versions which try to make the Bible more polite and acceptable. The verse says if people reject the Gospel message they are doomed to a Hell of fire! The NASB has weakened the doctrines of Judgment and Hell in this verse.

KJV	*NASB*
Where their worm dieth not, and the fire is not quenched. (Mark 9:44 and 46)	[These two verses are out completely.] (Mark 9:44 and 46)

The two verses are identical and they are also identical to verse 48.

The statement is repeated three times for emphasis. God has a reason for everything He says. Sometimes He repeats things for poetic reasons in various places, and often He repeats things for emphasis. The NASB has a footnote saying, "verses 44 and 46, which are identical with verse 48, are not found in the best ancient mss."

By "best ancient mss." is meant the Vatican manuscript. However, Vaticanus is not a trustworthy witness. It was set aside, never copied, and was finally lost in the Vatican Library where it lay for centuries. It was not used because it was inferior.

Edward Miller says the verses in question are genuine.

The verses give emphasis to the matter of hell-fire and conscious torment of the doomed.

The NASB weakens the doctrines of judgment and Hell by eliminating the verse.

**KJV**	_**NASB**_
These are wells without water, clouds that are carried with a tempest; to whom the mist of darkness is reserved for ever. (II Peter 2:17)	These are springs without water, and mists driven by a storm, for whom the black darkness has been reserved. (II Peter 2:17)

What happened to the "forever"? Hell is *eternal* punishment for all of the lost who will go there, including all liberal preachers who are described in II Peter, chapter 2. The doctrines of Judgment and Hell are weakened in this verse in the NASB.

KJV	**_NASB_**
and fire came down from God out of heaven, and devoured them....And I saw the dead, small and great, stand before God;... (Revelation 20:9 and 12)	and fire came down from heaven and devoured them.... And I saw the dead, the great and the small, standing before the throne. . . (Revelation 20:9 and 12)

God is taken out of both verses, but it is God who administers the judgment, and it is God who is the judge. Judgment would not be much of a judgment without God. It is a necessary and terrifying part of the judgment that the unsaved will stand before the Lord God. The doctrines of Judgment and Hell are weakened in these verses in the NASB.

Not only does the NASV weaken the above mentioned ten doctrines, it also plays fast and loose with the titles of God. *The title "Lord" is taken out of* Mark 9:24; Mark 11:10; Luke 23:42; Acts 7:30; Acts 9:5-6; I Corinthians 11:29; I Corinthians 15:47; II Corinthians 4:10; Ephesians 3:14; Col. 1:2; Titus 1:4; Hebrews 10:30, and many other places. *The names "Jesus," "Christ," "The Lord Jesus Christ," and "God" are taken out or changed* in Matthew 6:33; Matthew 8:29; Matthew 13:51; Matthew 16:20; Matthew 19:17; Luke 4:41; John 4:42; Acts 16:31; Acts 20:25; Romans 16:24; I Corinthians 16:22; I Corinthians 16:23; II Corinthians 4:6; Galatians 6:15; Ephesians 3:9; Ephesians 3:14; Colossians 1:2; I Thessalonians 3:11; II Thessalonians 1:8; I Timothy 3:16; II Timothy 4:22; I Peter 5:10; I John 1:7; I John 4:3; Revelation 12:17; Revelation 20:12, and several other places. Additionally, Christ's designations "the beginning and the end," and "I am the

Alpha and Omega the first and the last" has been taken out of Revelation 1:8-11.

The NASV leaves out the strongest proof in all the Bible for the Trinity (I John 5:7-8). It is the only passage in the Bible which directly *states* the Trinity. The Trinity is *implied* in other passages but not *stated.*

The NASV weakens the Doctrine of Repentance in Matthew 9:13 and Mark 2:17.

The NASV gives Catholic readings in Matthew 1:25 and Matthew 12:47 where the translators apparently try to make their version more ecumenically acceptable by hiding the fact that Mary, the mother of Jesus, had other children (by taking out the word "firstborn," or by removing a whole verse which speaks of Jesus' brothers).

The NASV weakens the Doctrine of Separation from sinning brethren (neo-evangelicals) in I Timothy 6:5 ("from such withdraw thyself" is left out) and II Thessalonians 3:6 ("keep aloof from" in the NASV is much weaker than the KJV's "withdraw thyself").

The NASV weakens the authorship of the Book of Daniel in Mark 13:14, a critical issue in our day because the liberals dispute that Daniel wrote the book.

The NASV weakens the Doctrine of the Inspiration and Preservation of Scripture in Luke 4:4, where "but by every word of God" is eliminated.

The NASV has a very poor translation in John 1:18, where it says "God" is begotten instead of the "Son" (The verse is a reference to the incarnation of the Son when He was begotten of the Holy Spirit, and perhaps to the Resurrection of the Son when He was begotten from among the dead.); of course, the Jehovah's Witnesses love to read that God is begotten since they believe that God created another god.

In addition to all of the above, the NASV has many, many verses which are not as clear as they are in the KJV. The new version has phrasing which is almost unintelligible and substitutes difficult words for easily understood ones, and leaves out words essential to understanding. Consider the following:

KJV	*NASV*
For ye had compassion of me in my bonds, and took joyfully the spoiling of your goods, knowing in yourselves that ye have in heaven a better and an enduring substance.	For you showed sympathy to prisoners, and accepted joyfully the seizure of your property, knowing that you have for yourselves a better possession and an abiding one.
(Hebrews 10:34)	(Hebrews 10:34)

Without the words "in heaven" it appears that the saints did not give out of their poverty but out of an abundance of earthly riches. Their goods were not *seized*, as the NASV says, but were *given* to help the author of Hebrews who was in prison. It is not clear in the NASV that the saints were being compassionate *to the writer of Hebrews.* As it stands in the NASV, the verse is confusing and not as clear as the KJV.

> "The providential preservation of the Scriptures is also a necessary consequence of their divine inspiration. The God who inspired the Scriptures and gave them to His people. . . cannot allow this perfect and final revelation of His will to perish."
> - Dr. Edward F. Hills

Consider another passage:

KJV	**_NASV_**
Being justified freely by his grace through the redemption that is in Christ Jesus: Whom God hath set forth to be a propitiation through faith in his blood... (Romans 3:24 and 25A)	being justified as a gift by His grace through the redemption which is in Christ Jesus; whom God displayed publicly as a propitiation in His blood through faith.... (Romans 3:24 and 25A)

The verse in the NASV is clumsy and obscured in its meaning. It is much clearer in the King James Version.

All of the following verses are clearer (what God is saying is more easily understood) in the KJV. Look them up and read them in both versions and you will, no doubt, agree. Luke 7:31; Luke 23:17; Luke 23:38; Luke 24:49; John 5:3-4; Acts 2:30; Acts 23:9; Acts 24:6-8; Romans 15:29; I Corinthians 10:28; I Corinthians 15:47; I Corinthians 16:22; Galatians 3:1; and Galatians 4:7.

The New American Standard Version is Central Baptist Theological Seminary's favorite version of the Bible. Glenny says it "is a careful 'word for word' translation, which is very trustworthy."

However, we have just shown the reader at least 100 verses that have been mutilated in the NASB. More than ten major doctrines are weakened in this remake of the American Standard Version of 1901. The cumulative error in these verses is a matter of grave concern, especially when more and more fundamentalists are promoting this dangerous version.

The usual response of NASB defenders and of Central Seminary is that all of the doctrines can still be found in the NASB somewhere, so it does not matter that verses are changed or eliminated. This attitude is a strange, cavalier view which denigrates the Word of God. All of the doctrines can be found in any version of the Bible, even in those Central thinks are the worst versions. Central's *opinion* of the NASB is in error.

67. The New International Version seems to be accepted as a reasonably good translation by Glenny and the Central Baptist Seminary faculty. He says, "The translation team of 115 scholars from many different denominations was designed to insure there was no 'sectarian bias.'" And Glenny likes it that the NIV "is based on the critical Greek text and best available OT manuscripts." He has no criticism of the fact that the NIV is a "thought for thought" translation, saying it is "very smooth, readable, and consistent." [p. 113]

Analysis: We find it both sad and strange that Glenny has no criticism of the NIV but attacks the KJV. He accuses the KJV of having mistakes but seems to find no mistakes in the NIV.

The NIV is a poor translation made from the same inferior manuscripts which gave us the NASB. Furthermore, the NIV was produced by men who have a highly defective philosophy of translating. It was produced from a thought for thought technique rather than a word for word technique. If we believe in verbal inspiration, then we should believe in verbal translation. Thought translation negates verbal inspiration, makes verbal inspiration of no effect insofar as promulgating the Word of God in translations is concerned.

The NIV has all of the problems of the NASB, and many more! We will cover the same ten doctrines which we pointed out in discussing the NASB and show how the NIV weakens those doctrines.

THE DOCTRINE OF CHRIST'S DEITY IS WEAKENED IN THE NIV

KJV	*NIV*
But seek ye first the kingdom of God, and his righteousness; and all these things shall be added unto you. (Matthew 6:33)	But seek first his kingdom and his righteousness, and all these things will be given to you as well. (Matthew 6:33)

It is Christ's kingdom which is under discussion. The KJV calls him God. The NIV takes the word "God" out of the verse.

KJV	*NIV*
Jesus heard that they had cast him out; and when he had found him, he said unto him, Dost thou believe on the Son of God? (John 9:35)	Jesus heard that they had thrown him out, and when he found him, he said, "Do you believe in the Son of Man?" (John 9:35)

"Son of God" is a title for deity. The NIV changes this title for deity to "Son of Man," Christ's title for humanity. The NIV weakens the Doctrine of Christ's deity in this verse.

KJV	*NIV*
And Philip said, If thou believest with all thine heart, thou mayest. And he answered and said, I believe that Jesus Christ is the Son of God. (Acts 8:37)	[Acts 8:37 is left out of the NIV altogether.]

Not only does the verse have a title for deity—"Son of God," it also teaches that only believers should be baptized. This tremendously important doctrinal verse is left out of the NIV with a footnote which says that some late manuscripts have verse 37. Actually the verse is found in some Sixth or Seventh Century manuscripts. It is also found in the Old Latin A.D. 200 and the Latin Vulgate of A.D. 400, and it is quoted by Irenaeus in A.D. 180 and by Cyprian in A.D. 250. So, there is no excuse for taking this verse out of the New Testament. The NIV weakens important doctrines by removing this verse.

KJV	*NIV*
And without controversy great is the mystery of godliness: God was manifest in the flesh, justified in the Spirit, seen of angels, preached unto the Gentiles, believed on in the world, received up into glory. (I Timothy 3:16)	Beyond all question, the mystery of godliness is great: He appeared in a body, was vindicated by the Spirit, was seen by angels, was preached among the nations, was believed on in the world, was taken up in glory. (I Timothy 3:16)

"God was manifest in the flesh" is changed to "He appeared in a body" in the NIV. This strong verse on the deity of Christ is mutilated, weakening the deity of Christ in the NIV. Edward Miller lists the overwhelming evidence for "God" in this verse (see the appendix, *A Guide to the Textual Criticism of the New Testament*).

KJV	*NIV*
And I saw the dead, small and great, stand before God;... (Revelation 20:12)	And I saw the dead, great and small, standing before the throne,... (Revelation 20:12)

It is the Lord Jesus Christ who is seated on the throne, and the KJV rightly calls Him "God"; but the NIV takes out the word "God," thus weakening the doctrine of the deity of Christ.

THE DOCTRINE OF THE SUBSTITUTIONARY BLOOD ATONEMENT IS WEAKENED IN THE NIV.

KJV	*NIV*
And the scripture was fulfilled, which saith, And he was numbered with the transgressors. (Mark 15:28)	[Mark 15:28 is left out of the NIV completely.]

This verse emphasizes the substitutionary nature of Christ's cross work. The fact that the NIV leaves out the verse weakens the doctrine of the substitutionary blood atonement.

> "The providence of God hath manifested itself as no less concerned in the preservation of the writings than of the doctrine contained in them...."
> -Dr. John Owen

KJV	**_NIV_**
For even Christ our passover is sacrificed for us. (I Corinthians 5:7)	For Christ, our Passover lamb, has been sacrificed. (I Corinthians 5:7)

By removing "for us" from the verse, the NIV weakens the doctrine of the substitutionary blood atonement.

KJV	**_NIV_**
In whom we have redemption through his blood, even the forgiveness of sins. (Colossians 1:14)	in whom we have redemption, the forgiveness of sins. (Colossians 1:14)

The blood of Jesus Christ is omitted from the verse in the NIV.

KJV	**_NIV_**
when he had by himself purged our sins. . . (Hebrews 1:3)	After he had provided purification for sins, . . . (Hebrews 1:3)

The King James makes it clear that all of the work of our salvation was done by the Lord Jesus—He did it "by himself." The NIV says Christ made purification for sins, but does not say that Christ purged *all* of our sins; rather it leaves open the possibility that some sins may be purged by someone or something else. The doctrine of the substitutionary blood atonement is weakened by the NIV.

> *"The verbal Inspiration of the Scriptures demands the verbal Preservation of the Scriptures."*
> - Ian R. K. Paisley

KJV	*NIV*
Forasmuch then as Christ hath suffered for us in the flesh. . . (I Peter 4:1)	Therefore, since Christ suffered in his body. . . (I Peter 4:1)

The KJV clearly shows the substitutionary element of Christ's suffering—it was done "for us." By leaving out "for us," the NIV destroys the substitutionary aspect of Christ's atonement. The doctrine of the substitutionary blood atonement is weakened in the NIV.

THE DOCTRINE OF THE RESURRECTION OF CHRIST IS WEAKENED IN THE NIV.

KJV	*NIV*
Now when Jesus was risen early the first day of the week, . . . (Mark 16:9)	The NIV publishes Mark 16:9-20 but has a footnote which says, "[The two most reliable early manuscripts do not have Mark 16:9-20.]"

The Vatican manuscript and the Sinai manuscript do not have Mark 16:9-20. Those manuscripts are **NOT** "the two most reliable early manuscripts." They are utterly unreliable. Both were copied from the same corrupt source. The Vatican manuscript leaves a blank column long enough that the twelve verses could have been copied there—the only blank column in the whole volume. The evidence for the authenticity of the passage is so great that the passage should never be questioned by anyone.

The resurrection and several other important doctrines are mentioned in the passage. Some post-resurrection appearances of Christ are mentioned.

When the NIV omits the passage, it weakens the doctrine of the resurrection of our Lord.

KJV	*NIV*
Therefore being a prophet, and knowing that God had sworn with an oath to him, that of the fruit of his loins, according to the flesh, he would raise up Christ to sit on his throne. (Acts 2:30)	But he was a prophet and knew that God had promised with an oath that he would place one of his descendants on his throne. (Acts 2:30)

There is no reference to Christ being "raised up" in the NIV in this verse. The resurrection of Christ is lost in the NIV, thus weakening the doctrine of the resurrection of Christ.

KJV	*NIV*
To whom also he shewed himself alive after his passion by many infallible proofs, . . . (Acts 1:3)	After his suffering, he showed himself to these men and gave many convincing proofs that he was alive. (Acts 1:3)

"Infallible proofs" is much stronger than "convincing proofs," thus is the doctrine of the resurrection of Christ weakened in the NIV. "Infallible" speaks of the absolutely indisputable and authoritative nature of the proof, whereas "convincing" only speaks of the result of this proof on most people. Whether most people are convinced or not, the proof stands as infallible.

THE INCARNATION AND VIRGIN BIRTH OF CHIRST IS WEAKENED IN THE NIV.

KJV	**_NIV_**
And Joseph and his mother marvelled at those things which were spoken of him. (Luke 2:33)	The child's father and mother marveled at what was said about him. (Luke 2:33)

The King James, following the Greek text, is careful to not call Joseph Jesus' father, holding forth in an unambiguous way the virgin birth of our Lord. But the NIV, for some unknown reason, destroys the safeguard which the Holy Spirit placed into the text, weakening the doctrine of the virgin birth.

KJV	**_NIV_**
. . .the child Jesus tarried behind in Jerusalem; and Joseph and his mother knew not of it. (Luke 2:43)	. . .while his parents were returning home, the boy Jesus stayed behind in Jerusalem, but they were unaware of it. (Luke 2:43)

We see once again that the NIV has failed to follow the Greek text, destroying the virgin birth of Christ in this verse by making Joseph the father of Jesus. This weakens the doctrine of the virgin birth in the NIV.

KJV	**_NIV_**
And every spirit that confesseth not that Jesus Christ is come in the flesh is not of God: . . . (I John 4:3)	but every spirit that does not acknowledge Jesus is not from God. (I John 4:3)

The incarnation and virgin birth of Christ is clearly in the verse, as the Greek text and the context (see verse 2) show. And yet, the NIV knocks out of the verse anything having to do with Christ coming in the flesh and dilutes it down to simply acknowledging Jesus. A teacher, motivated by a spirit, is not from God simply because he "acknowledges Jesus" in some way. If he is a teacher from God, he must teach "Jesus Christ is come in the flesh." This verse in the NIV weakens the doctrine of the incarnation and virgin birth of Christ.

KJV	*NIV*
No man hath seen God at any time; the only begotten Son, which is in the bosom of the Father, he hath declared him. (John 1:18)	No man has ever seen God, but God the only ₁Son₁, who is at the Father's side, has made him known. (John 1:18)

Note that the NIV has removed the word "begotten." This word is in the Greek text. The purpose of the word "begotten" is threefold: A) It states the virgin birth of Christ (He was begotten of the Father physically when He was incarnated). B) It states the resurrection of Christ, begotten from among the dead (life from God when He came out of the tomb). C) It states the eternal generation of the Son (He is eternally progressing from the Father and is the eternal Son of the Father).

> *"The NIV is not worthy of becoming the standard version of the English-speaking world. Its accuracy is suspect in too many ways.*
>
> -Dr. R. P. Martin

More verses must be compared in this regard:

KJV

And the Word was made flesh, and dwelt among us, (and we beheld his glory, the glory as of the only begotten of the Father,) full of grace and truth.
(John 1:14)

NIV

The Word became flesh and lived for a while among us. We have seen his glory, the glory of the one and only [Son], who came from the Father, full of grace and truth.
(John 1:14)

KJV

For God so loved the world, that he gave his only begotten Son, . . .
(John 3:16)

NIV

For God so loved the world that he gave his one and only Son, . . .
(John 3:16)

KJV

. . .but he that believeth not is condemned already, because he hath not believed in the name of the only begotten Son of God.
(John 3:18)

NIV

. . .but whoever does not believe stands condemned already because he has not believed in the name of God's one and only Son.
(John 3:18)

KJV

. . .God sent his only begotten Son into the world, that we might live through him.
(I John 4:9)

NIV

. . .He sent his one and only Son into the world that we might live through him.
(I John 4:9)

In every case, there are footnotes in the NIV that say "or his only begotten Son," as if it is a remote possibility, but also as if "one and only Son" is preferred. But this ignores the fact that the Greek word "*gennao*," means "beget." Jesus is not the "one and only" Son of God. He is the only begotten Son of God.

Both the holy angels and born again believers are the sons of God. So it is simply not true that Jesus is the one and only Son of God (see Genesis 6:2,4; Job 1:6; 2:1; 38:7; John 1:12; Romans 8:14; I John 3:1-2).

The doctrine of the virgin birth of Christ is weakened when the NIV refuses to acknowledge Him as the begotten Son of God.

To study the word *begotten* as it relates to the resurrection of Christ the reader should look up and read Romans 8:29 and Revelation 1:5. The NIV mutilates these verses, obscuring the truth that Christ is the firstfruits of the resurrection.

To study the word *begotten* as it relates to the eternal generation of Christ (i.e., that He is the eternal Son, eternally proceeding from the Father), the reader should look up and read Psalm 2:7; Acts 13:33; Colossians 1:15; Hebrews 1:5-6; and Hebrews 5:5. The NIV mistranslates these verses, obscuring the eternal generation of the Son.

THE LORDSHIP OF CHRIST IS WEAKENED IN THE NIV.

The title *Lord* is deleted from Matthew 13:51; Mark 9:24; Mark 11:10; Luke 7:31; Luke 23:42; Acts 9:6; I Corinthians 15:47; II Corinthians 4:10; Galatians 6:17;

Ephesians 3:14; Colossians 1:2; II Timothy 4:1; and Titus 1:4, and other places.

The concept of Christ as Lord is a very important one. And yet, the NIV leaves this important word out in many, many places. No wonder that many modern, professing Christians know nothing of His lordship.

Many other titles such as *Christ* and *God* are also deleted or changed in the NIV.

THE DOCTRINE OF THE ASCENSION OF CHRIST IS WEAKENED IN THE NIV.

KJV	*NIV*
So then, after the Lord had spoken unto them, he was received up into heaven, and sat on the right hand of God. (Mark 16:19)	A footnote says "The two most reliable early manuscripts do not have Mark 16:9-20."

On the basis of only two inferior manuscripts the NIV puts a question over the last twelve verses of Mark. Hundreds of manuscripts, ancient versions, and lectionaries have the passage, but on the basis of only two manuscripts, the genuineness of the passage is questioned.

The NIV weakens the doctrine of the ascension of Christ in its footnotes.

KJV	*NIV*
A little while, and ye shall not see me: and again, a little while, and ye shall see me, because I go to the Father. (John 16:16)	In a little while you will see me no more, and then after a little while you will see me. (John 16:16)

227

The words, "because I go to the Father" are left out of the NIV. This is a reference to the ascension of our Lord. It is a weakening of the doctrine when the NIV leaves it out.

KJV	*NIV*
Seeing then that we have a great high priest, that is passed into the heavens, Jesus the Son of God, . . . (Hebrews 4:14)	Therefore, since we have a great high priest who has gone through the heavens, Jesus the Son of God, . . . (Hebrews 4:14)

"Gone through the heavens" does not mean the same thing as "passed into the heavens." Going "through the heavens" sounds very transitory, as if Christ just passed through the atmosphere. When He went "into the heavens," He stayed there for 2000 years. He did not just pass through. The NIV weakens the doctrine of the ascension of Christ in this verse.

Interestingly, in the first edition of the NIV it said, "who has gone into heaven," which was much better than the later editions which say, "who has gone through the heavens." We wonder why such a deliberate attack on the ascension was devised.

> *"The KJV is the best we have and the best we will ever have, so it is time to stop finding fault with it and to begin to more earnestly believe it and obey it."*
>
> - pg. 25

THE PRE-EXISTENCE AND ETERNALITY OF CHRIST IS WEAKENED IN THE NIV.

KJV	NIV
I am Alpha and Omega, the beginning and the ending, saith the Lord, which is, and which was, and which is to come, the Almighty. (Revelation 1:8)	"I am the Alpha and the Omega," says the Lord God, "who is, and who was, and who is to come, the Almighty." (Revelation 1:8)

The New International Version omits "the beginning and the ending," a title for Christ's eternity. He is the **BEGINNING** in the sense that He began everything. And He is the **ENDING** in the sense that He will bring everything to a consummation. The NIV weakens the doctrine of the pre-existence of Christ in this verse.

KJV	NIV
Saying, I am Alpha and Omega, the first and the last: and, What thou seest, write in a book, . . . (Revelation 1:11)	which said: "Write on a scroll what you see. . . . (Revelation 1:11)

The phrase, "I am Alpha and Omega, the first and the last" is deleted from the NIV. The NIV has the "I am the Alpha and the Omega" in verse eight, but deletes it in verse eleven. The phrase, "the first and the last" is deleted even though it is not repeated elsewhere in the chapter.

"The Alpha and Omega, the first and the last" is an indication of the eternity of Christ. An attack on His eternality is also an attack upon His deity. If Christ did not exist from eternity to eternity, He could not possibly be

God.   So, when the NIV leaves out **ANY WORDS** pertaining to Christ's pre-existence and eternality, it weakens those doctrines.

KJV	*NIV*
And the four beasts said, Amen. And the four and twenty elders fell down and worshipped him that liveth for ever and ever. (Revelation 5:14)	The four living creatures said, "Amen," and the elders fell down and worshiped. (Revelation 5:14)

The weakness of the NIV on the doctrines of the pre-existence and eternality of Christ in this verse is obvious. What may not appear so obvious to some readers is the attack on the deity of Christ. That attack is accomplished by deleting the pronoun "him." The verse says that the elders worshipped but **DOES NOT SAY WHO OR WHAT** they worshipped. This robs the Lord Jesus Christ of the proper worship that belongs **TO HIM.**

KJV	*NIV*
Saying, We give thee thanks, O Lord God Almighty, which art, and wast, and art to come; because thou hast taken to thee thy great power, . . . (Revelation 11:17)	saying: "We give thanks to you, Lord God Almighty, who is and who was, because you have taken your great power. . . . (Revelation 11:17)

The words "and art to come" are out of the verse. Does Christ have **ONLY** a past and present? Does He have no eternal **FUTURE**? The passage is about the eternity of

Christ, eternity past to eternity future, and to drop the words which the NIV deletes is to weaken that doctrine.

THE DOCTRINE OF THE SECOND COMING OF CHRIST IS WEAKENED IN THE NIV.

KJV	*NIV*
Watch therefore, for ye know neither the day nor the hour wherein the Son of man cometh. (Matthew 25:13)	Therefore keep watch, because you do not know the day or the hour. (Matthew 25:13)

The day or the hour of what?! The NIV drops from the verse any reference to the coming of the Lord. This is translating? The doctrine of the second coming of Christ is weakened in this verse.

The verse which we discussed above (Revelation 11:17) in regard to the eternity of Christ also weakens the doctrine of His coming since His coming is a part of His eternal future.

THE DOCTRINE OF SALVATION IS WEAKENED IN THE NIV.

KJV	*NIV*
For the Son of man is come to save that which was lost. (Matthew 18:11)	[Has a footnote which says that "some manuscripts" have the verse] deletes the verse. (Matthew 18:11)

231

There is no excuse for the NIV omitting this verse. Doing so weakens the doctrine of salvation.

KJV	**_NIV_**
Verily, verily, I say unto you, He that believeth on me hath everlasting life. (John 6:47)	I tell you the truth, he who believes has everlasting life. (John 6:47)

"On me" is omitted from the NIV. This obscures the nature of true saving faith. The object of faith is crucial in salvation. No one is saved because he believes! To be saved one must believe **ON THE LORD JESUS CHRIST**. The NIV weakens the doctrine of salvation in this verse.

KJV	**_NIV_**
Then Peter said unto them, Repent, and be baptized every one of you in the name of Jesus Christ for the remission of sins, and ye shall receive the gift of the Holy Ghost. (Acts 2:38)	Peter replied: "Repent and be baptized, every one of you, in the name of Jesus Christ so that your sins may be forgiven. And you will receive the gift of the Holy Spirit." (Acts 2:38)

The NIV has people being forgiven of their sins because they have been baptized. The Greek New Testament does not say that, nor does the King James Bible. The Greek word *eis* translates into an English preposition. It could be one of several prepositions depending on the context. It could be "over," "under," "for," "because of," etc. However, it can never be "so that," as the NIV has it.

232

In the KJV "for" means "because of." That is, be baptized because of the forgiveness of sins.

The NIV teaches salvation by baptism. This weakens the doctrine of salvation in the NIV.

KJV	*NIV*
And if by grace, then it is no more of works: otherwise grace is no more grace. But if it be of works, then is it no more grace: otherwise work is no more work. (Romans 11:6)	And if by grace, then it is no longer by works; if it were, grace would no longer be · grace. (Romans 11:6)

The King James is much more emphatic. Therefore, it must be said that the NIV weakens the doctrine of salvation in this verse.

KJV	*NIV*
And the nations of them which are saved shall walk in the light of it: and the kings of the earth do bring their glory and honour into it. (Revelation 21:24)	The nations will walk by its light, and the kings of the earth will bring their splendor into it. (Revelation 21:24)

The NIV gives a universalist reading to the verse by omitting the words, "them which are saved." The passage speaks of the heavenly city, and to have all the nations walking by its light, without regard to whether or not they have been saved is a perversion of Scripture.

233

THE DOCTRINES OF JUDGMENT AND HELL
ARE WEAKENED IN THE NIV.

KJV	NIV
They say unto him, Because no man hath hired us. He saith unto them, Go ye also into the vineyard; and whatsoever is right, that shall ye receive. (Matthew 20:7)	"'because no man has hired us,' they answered. "He said to them, 'You also go and work in my vineyard.' (Matthew 20:7)

By omitting the last phrase, the NIV obscures the righteous judgment of God. God says, "Go work in my vineyard," but He also says that He will reward in righteousness those who serve Him.

KJV	NIV
Verily I say unto you, It shall be more tolerable for Sodom and Gomorrha in the day of judgment, than for that city. (Mark 6:11)	[The entire phrase is omitted from the NIV, with no explanation.] (Mark 6:11)

The subject of the verse is the preaching of the Word of God in various cities. If the message of God is rejected, it will result in punishment in a Hell of fire. The NIV weakens the doctrines of judgment and Hell in this verse.

KJV	NIV
Where their worm dieth not, and the fire is not quenched. (Mark 9:44 and Mark 9:46)	[The two verses are omitted in their entirety.] (Mark 9:44 and Mark 9:46)

The passage is about hell fire. Three times God makes the same statement (v. 48). He says it three times for emphasis, but the NIV omits two of the verses. There will be conscious, everlasting torment of the doomed in a fire that is never extinguished! This cannot be said too often, nor can the warning be repeated too often. The NIV weakens the doctrines of judgment and Hell in this passage.

KJV	*NIV*
That whosoever believeth in him should not perish, but have eternal life. (John 3:15)	that everyone who believes in him may have eternal life. (John 3:15)

The NIV says nothing about the believer not perishing. The obvious meaning is that the unbeliever **WILL PERISH**. This is an obvious attempt to take as much hell and damnation out of the Bible as possible.

KJV	*NIV*
These are wells without water, clouds that are carried with a tempest; to whom the mist of darkness is reserved for ever. (II Peter 2:17)	These men are springs without water and mists driven by a storm. Blackest darkness is reserved for them. (II Peter 2:17)

The NIV expunges the word **FOREVER**. The word **FOREVER** is a very important word in any discussion of Hell. False teachers and false prophets will be banished to an **EVERLASTING** Hell. The NIV weakens the doctrine of Hell in this verse.

In addition to all of the above stated doctrinal problems, there are *many missing verses* from the NIV. Altogether these missing verses would fill about five full pages in most Bibles. In other words, the amount of Scripture omitted in the total of the whole missing verses would equal about the same amount of God's Word as we have in the book of I Peter or I Timothy. In addition to that, there are many partial verses which have been omitted. This should not be a small concern to Bible believers.

There are *outright mistakes* of a very obvious nature in the NIV. For example:

KJV	*NIV*
But made himself of no reputation, and took upon him the form of a servant,. . . (Philippians 2:7)	but made himself nothing, taking the very nature of a servant, being made in human likeness. (Philippians 2:7)

Christ did not make Himself **NOTHING**! Jesus did not cease to exist!

Another example of an obvious mistake is found in Mark 1:2 where the NIV says an Old Testament quotation comes from Isaiah. But, half of the quotation comes from Malachi 3:1. The KJV says the quotation comes from "the prophets."

Still another mistake in the NIV is found in Hebrews 11:11. The KJV correctly translates that Sara was "past age" to have a child. The NIV, however, says that it was Abraham who was "past age."

Still another error in the NIV is found in I Corinthians 5:5. The KJV reads, "deliver such an one unto Satan for the destruction of the flesh." But, the NIV, apparently wishing to give a "holiness" interpretation to the verse says, "hand this man over to Satan that the sinful nature may be destroyed." This is a serious theological error, since the sinful nature is never destroyed in this life.

There is a monumental blunder in the NIV when it robs a title of Christ and gives it to Satan. Note the following:

KJV	*NIV*
How art thou fallen from heaven, O Lucifer, son of the morning! (Isaiah 14:12)	How you have fallen from heaven, O morning star, son of the dawn! (Isaiah 14:12)

There is no doubt at all that the passage in Isaiah 14 refers to Satan, the Devil. It is blasphemous to put one of Christ's titles there as if the passage referred to Him.

Christ is the "day star" (II Peter 1:19), and "the morning star" (Revelation 2:28). He is "the bright and morning star" (Revelation 22:16). It is a gross twisting of the Scriptures to steal a title for the Lord Jesus Christ and attribute it to Satan.

The Luciferians love the NIV translation of Isaiah 14:12, and have used it to try to persuade people of the truth of their doctrine, that Satan should be worshipped.

Still another obvious error in the NIV is found in II Samuel 21:19 where it says Elhanan killed Goliath. The KJV says Elhanan killed Goliath's brother. Everyone knows that this is a mistake but the NIV tries to justify its error by appealing to Hebrew and the Septuagint. Ridiculous!

In addition to the above mentioned obvious errors, there are some morally unworthy **INTERPRETATIONS** in the NIV. For example, in Titus 1:2, the NIV says, "God who does not lie" instead of the KJV's "God that cannot lie." The NIV interprets that God could lie if He wanted to, but He does not. The KJV is correct; God cannot lie. God cannot sin, and He cannot do that which violates His own nature.

Another morally unworthy **INTERPRETATION** in the NIV is found in I Corinthians 7:1 where the NIV says, "It is good for a man not to marry." However, getting married is not under discussion in the passage. Immorality is being discussed, and the KJV is correct when it says, "It is good for a man not to touch a woman."

In the same chapter, in I Corinthians 7:36, the NIV has yet another morally unworthy **INTERPRETATION** by adding words. The NIV makes the passage refer to a man and his fiancée. Actually, the passage refers to a man and his daughter. Note the following:

KJV	*NIV*
But if any man think that he behaveth himself uncomely toward his virgin, if she pass the flower of her age, and need so require, let him do what he will, he sinneth not: let them marry. (I Corinthians 7:36)	If anyone thinks he is acting improperly toward the virgin he is engaged to, and if she is getting along in years and he feels he ought to marry, he should do as he wants. He is not sinning. They should get married. (I Corinthians 7:36)

The NIV pulls the words "he is engaged to" out of thin air! In doing so, according to Stewart Custer [**Which Translation?**], "This interprets the passage to refer to a strange and questionable custom. In some sections of the early church, it was customary for an unmarried man and

238

woman to travel together to serve God; they lived as though they were brother and sister."

This interpretation, says Custer, is "uncalled for" and "morally unworthy."

Still another morally unworthy interpretation has Jesus getting saved. This we find in the NIV in Hebrews 2:10.

KJV	*NIV*
For it became him, for whom are all things, and by whom are all things, in bringing many sons unto glory, to make the captain of their salvation perfect through sufferings. (Hebrews 2:10)	In bringing many sons to glory, it was fitting that God, for whom and through whom everything exists, should make the Pioneer of their salvation perfect through suffering. (Hebrews 2:10)

A pioneer is one who does something first, blazes a trail and has others follow him. But Jesus did not get saved! To call Him "the Pioneer of their salvation" is to make him a sinner **WHO GOT SAVED** by blazing a trail to God.

We are glad to see that in later editions the NIV was changed to say "author" instead of "Pioneer." However, the very fact that the translators said "Pioneer" in the beginning goes to the issue of trust. Can we trust people who commit *textual abuse* against the Word of God? A *textual abuser* is never cured and cannot be trusted.

Finally, we must point out with regard to the New International Version, that the publishers are committed to eventually replacing the current edition with an Inclusive Language Edition. That means that a gender neutral version is coming! In fact, the NIV published in England is already gender neutral. The only reason that the Inclusive Language Edition has not already been published in America is that **_World Magazine_** revealed Zondervan's surreptitious publishing plan in 1997, and the Southern Baptist Convention threatened to boycott the NIV if the publisher proceeded with its plan. Real Bible believers need to ask themselves if they can afford to trust people with such a lack of convictions as is seen in the publishers of the NIV! Should we be using a Bible whose publisher **_WANTS_** to bring out a unisex edition ("Our father-mother, who art in heaven..." or "For God so loved the world that God gave God's only child...")? We think not!

In 1973, when the NIV New Testament first appeared, I wrote to the Executive Secretary of the New York Bible Society International who sponsored the project and asked him for a list of the names of the translators. Dr. Edwin H. Palmer wrote me, sending a copy of a prepared list of all of the translators, including the governing committee. We are going to list here all of those who were on that translation committee. Remember that over the last twenty-six years some have been taken off this committee and have been replaced by others. But these are the men who did the first and most complete work on the NIV New Testament. And please note on this list that there is **_NOT A SINGLE FUNDAMENTALIST_**.

GOVERNING COMMITTEE
Ralph Earle, Nazarene Theological Seminary
Burton L. Goddard, Gordon-Conwell Theological Seminary
R. Laird Harris, Covenant Theological Seminary
Earl S. Kalland, Conservative Baptist Theological Seminary
Youngve R. Kindberg, New York Bible Society International

Richard N. Longenecker, Wycliffe College, Toronto
William J. Martin, Regent College, Vancouver
Stephen W. Paine, Houghton College
Charles F. Pfeiffer, Central Michigan University
Robert Preus, Concordia Theological Seminary
Charles C. Ryrie, Dallas Theological Seminary
John H. Stek, Calvin Theological Seminary
Larry L. Walker, Southwestern Baptist Theological Seminary
J. C. Wenger, Goshen Biblical Seminary
Marten H. Woudstra, Calvin Theological Seminary

TRANSLATORS AND EDITORS

Robert L. Alden, Conservative Baptist Theological Seminary
Gleason L. Archer, Trinity Evangelical Divinity School
Carl E. Armerding, Regent College, Vancouver
Glenn W. Barker, Fuller Theological Seminary
Kenneth Barker, Dallas Theological Seminary
S. Herbert Bess, Grace Theological Seminary
Edward M. Blaiklock, University of Auckland, New Zealand
Harvey J. S. Blaney, Eastern Nazarene College
Frederic E. Blume, Wisconsin Lutheran Seminary
W. Gordon Brown, Central Baptist Seminary, Toronto
Donald W. Burdick, Conservative Baptist Theological
    Seminary
Frederic W. Bush, Fuller Theological Seminary
Philip S. Clapp, Western Evangelical Seminary
Edmunc Clowney, Westminster Theological Seminary
Ralph R. Covell, Conservative Baptist Theological Seminary
Leo G. Cox, Barlesville Wesleyan College
John J. Davis, Grace Theological Seminary
Wilber T. Dayton, Houghton College
Howard M. Ervin, Oral Roberts University
Lewis A. Foster, Cincinnati Bible Seminary
Francis Foulkes, St. Andrew's Hall, Victoria, Australia

Clyde T. Francisco, Southern Baptist Theological Seminary
Frank E. Gaebelein, Arlington, Virginia
Richard B. Gaffin, Westminster Theological Seminary
Wesley L. Gerig, Fort Wayne Bible College
Donald Glen, Dallas Theological Seminary
Louis Goldberg, Moody Bible Institute
J. Kenneth Grider, Nazarene Theological Seminary
Vernon C. Grounds, Conservative Baptist Theological
    Seminary
Clarence B. Hale, Wheaton College
Murray J. Harris, Trinity Evangelical Divinity School
Everett Harrison, Fuller Theological Seminary
Roland K. Harrison, Wycliffe College, Toronto
Gerald F. Hawthorne, Wheaton College
Roy E. Hayden, Oral Roberts University
William Hendriksen, Boca Raton, Florida
D. Edmond Hiebert, Mennonite Brethren Biblical Seminary
Mark E. Hillmer, Northwestern Lutheran Theological
    Seminary
F. B. Huey, Southwestern Baptist Theological Seminary
Charles Hummel, Barrington College
S. Lewis Johnson, Dallas Theological Seminary
Walter C. Kaiser, Trinity Evangelical Divinity School
Kenneth S. Kantzer, Trinity Evangelical Divinity School
Homer A. Kent, Grace Theological Seminary
F. Derek Kidner, Tyndale House, Cambridge, England
Dennis F. Kinlaw, Asbury Theological Seminary
Simon Kistemaker, Reformed Theological Seminary
Meredith G. Kline, Gordon-Conwell Theological Seminary
Fred C. Kuehner, Reformed Episcopal Seminary
William L. Lane, Gordon-Conwell Theological Seminary
G. Irvin Lehman, Eastern Mennonite College
Elisabeth E. Leitch, South Hamilton, Massachusetts
Paul E. Lenonard, Trinity Evangelical Divinity School

Arthur H. Lewis, Bethel Theological Seminary
Walter L. Liefeld, Trinity Evangelical Divinity School
G. Herbert Livingston, Asbury Theological Seminary
Kathryn Ludwigson, The King's College
Allan A. MacRae, Biblical School of Theology
Donald H. Madvig, North Park Theological Seminary
W. Harold Mare, Covenant Theological Seminary
Alvin Martin, Canadian Bible College, Regina
Thomas E. McComiskey, Trinity Evangelical Divinity School
J. Ramsey Michaels, Gordon-Conwell Theological Seminary
A. R. Millard, University of Liverpool, England
Virginia Mollenkott, Paterson State College
Leon Morris, Ridley College, Melbourne, Australia
Robert Mounce, Western Kentucky University
Roger Nicole, Gordon-Conwell Theological Seminary
J. Barton Payne, Covenant Theological Seminary
Stephen M. Reynolds, Faith Theological Seminary
Walter R. Roehrs, Concordia Theological Seminary
Robert P. Roth, Northwestern Lutheran Seminary
Theron F. Schlabach, Goshen College
Samuel J. Schultz, Wheaton College
Jack B. Scott, Reformed Theological Seminary
Bruce L. Shelley, Conservative Baptist Theological Seminary
Elmer B. Smick, Gordon-Conwell Theological Seminary
Francis Steele, Upper Darby, Pennsylvania
Marvin E. Tate, Southern Baptist Theological Seminary
Willard Taylor, Nazarene Theological Seminary
Merrill C. Tenney, Wheaton College
John J. Timmerman, Calvin Colege
Gerard Van Groningen, Reformed Theological Seminary
Wilber B. Wallis, Covenant Theological Seminary
Bruce K. Waltke, Dallas Theological Seminary
G. Henry Waterman, Wheaton College
Walter W. Wessel, Bethel College

David J. Williams, Ridley College, Melbourne, Australia
Marvin R. Wilson, Gordon College
Donald J. Wiseman, University of London, England
Herbert M. Wolf, Wheaton College
Leon J. Wood, Grand Rapids Baptist Bible Seminary
Seird Woudstra, Geelong Theological Seminary
Ronald Youngblood, Bethel Theological Seminary
John M. Zinkand, Dordt College

Again we say, there is not a single fundamentalist in the whole bunch! There are neo-evangelicals on the list. There are neo-orthodox leaders on the list. There are charismatics on the list. There are outright liberals on this list. But, there are no fundamentalists on the list!

There are no fundamentalist schools represented among the NIV translators. There are neo-evangelical schools represented. There are neo-orthodox and liberal schools on this list. But there is not a single fundamentalist school on the list. There are "conservatives" on the list, but no fundamentalists.

Someone will, no doubt, object, "But what about Wood, MacRae, Kent, Goldberg, Archer, Ryrie, or Harris? Are not any of these fundamentalists?" No! They are more conservative than some of the others, but they are not fundamentalists. The schools where these men taught are neo-evangelical schools, and teachers cannot be fundamentalists and stay at such neo-evangelical schools. Furthermore, no true fundamentalist would cooperate on a translation committee with neo-evangelical, neo-orthodox, and liberal scholars!

It should be remembered that a fundamentalist is not simply someone who believes five, six, or seven fundamentals of the faith. A fundamentalist is one who believes the affirmations of the Bible and is willing to militantly defend those affirmations. In his fight for the fundamentals of the faith, the fundamentalist *SEPARATES* from those who hold non-biblical positions.

The NIV is a neo-evangelical production. Liberal, neo-orthodox, neo-evangelical, and conservative scholars worked together to produce a Bible which they hoped would be acceptable to all groups. No surprise then that the doctrines are weakened, watered down, and withered.

It is no surprise, given what we know of the translators positions, that the doctrine of separation is omitted from some passages. Consider the following:

KJV	*NIV*
Perverse disputings of men of corrupt minds, and destitute of the truth, supposing that gain is godliness: from such withdraw thyself. I Timothy 6:5	and constant friction between men of corrupt mind, who have been robbed of the truth and who think that godliness is a means to financial gain. I Timothy 6:5

We will bypass the several lesser weaknesses of the NIV in dealing with this verse and come right to the most important issue—what happened to *"FROM SUCH WITHDRAW THYSELF"*? This translation shows the neo-evangelical bias of the NIV! It was produced by (in the case of those who were saved) disobedient men who do not want to separate from those who teach error.

245

Note also the following:

KJV	*NIV*
Now we command you, brethren, in the name of our Lord Jesus Christ, that ye withdraw yourselves from every brother that walketh disorderly, and not after the tradition which he received of us. II Thessalonians 3:6	In the name of the Lord Jesus Christ, we command you, brothers, to keep away from every brother who is idle and does not live according to the teaching you received from us. II Thessalonians 3:6

In the above verse the NIV *INTERPRETS* into the verse the idea that Christians should "keep away from" every brother who is idle and will not work. This is the standard neo-evangelical commentary on this verse, (i.e., that it refers only to being idle and not working, and not to any other form of disobedience, such as holding to false doctrines or holding to unscriptural fellowship).

The context of II Thessalonians 3:6 is not being idle *ONLY*. The context is also that of being delivered from unreasonable and wicked men who do not have biblical faith (cf. v. 2).

Once again the neo-evangelical prejudices of the translators are showing.

This has been a very brief review of the NIV. There are many other problems with it.

When fundamentalists promote the NIV, they are promoting a neo-evangelical work, one that weakens doctrine to make it acceptable to liberalism and neo-orthodoxy. It is a version that has many errors in translation. It is a version that is unworthy of the support of Bible-believers.

Dr. Stuart Custer, Bible and Theology professor at Bob Jones University, does not totally reject all new versions; however, he calls the NIV, "The result of 'new evangelical' efforts." He further says it is "highly interpretive," and has interpretations which are "morally unworthy," and some which are "High-handed and arbitrary," or "liberal." He concludes by calling the NIV "an unreliable translation." [*Which Translation?*, pp. 12-16] I agree!

The *opinion* of Central Baptist Seminary that the NIV should be criticized very little and that the KJV should come in for lots of criticism is an *opinion* filled with error.

68. Professor Glenny says The New Living Translation has a 6.3 reading level, and that the reading levels of other popular translations are KJV–12.0; The Living Bible–8.3; NKJV–7.0; and NIV–7.8. [p. 115]

Analysis: In his endnote, Glenny says the information for the New Living Translation comes from its publisher. He also says, "Some of this information is also in the introduction to The New Living Translation. The endnote is rather obscure and does not say exactly what information came from which source. His purpose seems to be to tell us that the KJV is not readable, that it is too difficult. This is false.

According to Waite [*Defending the King James Bible*, p. 50] the various chapters of the KJV vary as to readability. Genesis 1 is on an 8.1 readability level (eighth grade, first month). Exodus 1 is 7.9; Romans 1 is 9.7; Romans 3 is 5.6; Romans 8 is 7.7; and Jude 1 is 10.1.

The above is according to "Right Writer" readability index, a computer program. Various methods of analysis report differently on the readability of the KJV. However, because of its beauty of style, its rhythm, its cadence, and its flowing smoothness, the KJV is easier to read than any other version. The new versions are difficult to read (especially the NASB) as anyone can know who has listened to someone trying to read it. Even professional speakers, such as radio people, stumble all over themselves trying to read the LB or the NIV. The new versions are awkward, disjointed, and lacking in smoothness, and therefore difficult to read, no matter how easy or difficult the individual words might be.

Furthermore, if a version has great readability but does not say exactly what God said, the readability means nothing. It is of no value.

Always in the past, Christians have taken the position that people be educated up to the Bible. Now, unfortunately, many people seem to believe that we should dumb the Bible down to where people are. But, you will never be able to dumb it down that far, because "the natural man receiveth not the things of the Spirit of God,...neither can he know them" (I Corinthians 2:14).

Perhaps this is a good place to review the words of Dr. Martyn Lloyd-Jones. This English preacher-physician, successor to G. Campbell Morgan at Westminster Chapel, spoke in 1961, at a rally at Royal Albert Hall:

> "I suppose that the most popular of all the proposals at the present moment is to have a new translation of the Bible....The argument is that people are not reading the Bible any longer because they do not understand its language—particularly the

248

archaic terms—what does your modern man...know about justification, sanctification, and all these Biblical terms? And so we are told the one thing that is necessary is to have a translation that Tom, Dick and Harry will understand, and I began to feel about six months ago that we had almost reached the stage in which the Authorized Version was being dismissed, to be thrown into the limbo of things forgotten, no longer of any value. Need I apologise for saying a word in favour of the Authorised Version in this gathering?.....

"It is a basic proposition laid down by the Protestant Reformers, that we must have a Bible 'understanded of the people.' That is common sense...we must never be obscurantists. We must never approach the Bible in a mere antiquarian spirit...but it does seem to me that there is a very grave danger incipient in so much of the argument that is being presented today for these new translations. There is a danger, I say, of our surrendering something that is vital and essential....

"Take this argument that the modern man does not understand such terms as justification, sanctification and so on. I want to ask a question. When did the ordinary man ever understand those terms?....Did the colliers to whom John Wesley and George Whitefield preached in the 19th century understand? They had not even been to a day school...they could not read, they could not write. Yet these were the terms that were used. This was the version that was used – the Authorised Version. The common people have never understood these terms....We are concerned here with something that is spiritual; something which does not belong to this world at all; which, as the Apostle Paul reminds us, the princes of this world do not know. Human wisdom is of no value here – it is a spiritual truth. This is truth about God primarily, and because of that it is a mystery....

"Yet we are told – it must be put in such simple terms and language that anybody taking it up and reading it is going to understand all about it. My friends, this is sheer nonsense. What we must do is to educate the masses of the people up to

249

the Bible, not bring the Bible down to their level. One of the greatest troubles today is that everything is being brought down to the same level, everything is cheapened. The common man is made the standard of authority; he decides everything, and everything has to be brought down to him....

"Are we to do that with the Word of God? I say No! What has happened in the past has been this—ignorant, illiterate people, in this country and in foreign countries, coming into salvation have been educated up to the Book and have begun to understand it, to glory in it, and to praise God for it, and I say that we need to do the same at this present time. What we need is therefore, not to replace the Authorised Version...we need rather to reach and train people up to the standard and the language, the dignity and the glory of the old Authorised Version."

The above statement by Dr. Martyn Lloyd-Jones was cited in ***The Old is Better***, by Alfred Levell, published by the Trinitarian Bible Society, London, England. It is an exceedingly sensible and spiritual statement.

The *opinion* of Central Baptist Seminary that the KJV is difficult to read and that therefore new versions of the Bible are needed is an *opinion* filled with error.

69. Glenny says, "What should our response be to such a large number of translations in our native language? Certainly it should first be one of thanksgiving if we are seeking God and His truth." [p. 115]

Analysis: I cannot be thankful for the mistranslation and perversion of Scripture. If one of the new versions is the Word of God, then the KJV is not. If, on the other hand, the KJV is the Word of God, then the new versions are not.

They cannot both be the Word of God when they differ so greatly from one another. Things different are not the same. It is because I seek God and truth, and because I want others to seek God and truth, that I am not thankful for all of these new versions. The new versions, and the promotion of them, have caused confusion and division in churches, in camps, and in the publishing of Sunday school and youth programs. How can we be thankful for that? The mutilating of old standard Bible terms; the flippant and irreverent language; the weakening of doctrine; and the weakening of the faith of man in the Bible; how can we be thankful for this?

This is another of Glenny's *opinions* which is erroneous.

70. After arbitrarily setting up three criteria for determining if a translation is the Word of God, Glenny says, "We can be confident that any nonsectarian translation of manuscripts of the original languages is the Word of God." [p. 119]

Analysis: This is an extremely low standard of what constitutes the Word of God in English! This means that the RSV, Good News for Modern Man, The New English Bible, Moffatt's, Phillips', Berkeley's, and many other liberal versions are the Word of God!

The statement by Glenny shows the very low standard that Central has set up for Bible versions. The Seminary is almost completely open-minded and accepting of new versions, rejecting only such versions as the Jehovah's Witness Bible and the Living Bible.

Central's *opinion* is in error when Glenny states that, "We can be confident that any nonsectarian translation of manuscripts of the original languages is the Word of God."

71. Glenny says that in order to be the Word of God, a translation must be translated from original language manuscripts. We presume he says this in order to put down the practice of translating the King James into various foreign languages on the mission field.

<u>*Analysis*</u>: We do not believe that a translation *must* be translated from the KJV in order to be a good translation. We believe that translations should be made from the same original language manuscripts and sources which gave us the KJV whenever possible. However, Glenny has gone too far in declaring that a Bible cannot be the Word of God unless it is translated from original language documents.

Often missionaries do not have the tools or knowledge of the original language texts, and can make a better translation by translating from the King James Bible. **IT HAS BEEN DONE BETWEEN 600 AND 700 TIMES**. Let us not find fault with this and go around the world telling various peoples that they do not have the Word of God!

I would rather see the King James Bible translated into a tribal language than to see the Critical Text (which for all practical purposes equals the Vatican manuscript) translated into that language. The translation of the KJV would result in a much more accurate Bible. Glenny's *opinion* on this should be ignored.

72. Professor Glenny compares the differences in translations to the differences in the sermons of various preachers. He says, "Should we be afraid of occasionally hearing sermons which conflict with each other in some minor detail?" [pp. 120-121]

Analysis The accuracy of the Bible we use should never be compared to the accuracy of a sermon. The Bible is the Word of God; sermons are not! The Bible is inspired; sermons are not! The Bible is without any error; sermons are not! It does matter whether the Bible is correct or not, much *much* more than whether a sermon is correct or not. To say that it makes no more difference whether the Bible has it right than if a sermon has it right is to denigrate the Bible. With an attitude like this no wonder Central has put the bar so low on Bible translations. This is another *opinion* which should be rejected.

73. The Central professor says, "the Hebrew, Aramaic and Greek sources upon which our translations are based have a higher degree of authority because they are one step closer to the original manuscripts, the autographa." [p. 121]

Analysis: Here we come to one of the real cruxes in the whole debate. Central thinks if we read the reconstructed Greek, Hebrew, and Aramaic texts that we are one step closer to the autographs. No, not necessarily so! If he is reading the Critical Text, he is not nearer to the autographs. He has taken several steps away from the autographs.

Glenny's premise is only true if he is reading the Traditional Text. A person who is reading the King James Bible is reading a more accurate representation of the autographs than is a person who is reading the Vatican manuscript! Since the King James Bible is a more accurate representation of the autographs, it is also more authoritative.

Actually, of course, very few people can read the Hebrew, Greek, and Aramaic well enough to claim it as any authority. This includes most seminary professors. I've known only two or three people who could read Hebrew, Greek, and Aramaic well enough so that they could honestly say that the Hebrew Old Testament, the Greek New Testament, and the Aramaic parts of the Bible were their final authority. In-so-far as the vast majority of English speaking people are concerned, an English translation is going to be their final authority. The question is still, "Which Bible?"

I would much rather have my final authority be the King James Bible than a seminary professor, a church, or any of the new translations.

It is a mistaken *opinion* when Glenny says that "the Hebrew, Aramaic, and Greek sources upon which our translations [such as the NASB and the NIV] are based have a higher degree of authority because they are one step closer to the original manuscripts, the autographs."

74. Glenny has recommendations to help churches avoid the confusion and trouble that comes when new versions come in, recommendations to help the church with public "Bible reading and memorization." His recommendations include choosing a preaching Bible to be used consistently for all preaching services, putting copies of this Bible in the "hymn racks" [sic] for visitors, and not making the Bible a church uses a test of fellowship. [p. 123]

Analysis: The new versions have worked havoc with public Bible readings and with memorization. They have also proved to be very distracting in preaching, because often congregants cannot follow the preacher when he uses a new version, and they think more about the differences in the texts than they do about what is being preached.

Many churches will run into some practical problems trying to carry out Glenny's recommendations. They may have to add hymnal racks, for example. The cost of purchasing six or eight new Bibles for each pew could also be a problem. Of course, these are minor problems compared to the horrific spiritual and theological problem of a church throwing out the KJV for the inaccurate, irreverent, flippant, confusing new versions.

Glenny does not address the problem of what to do about camps. Many parents and pastors do not want their children being confused by being forced to listen to preaching from a new version. These parents and pastors also do not want their young people doing their Bible memorization from a new version.

The professor's recommendation about never allowing "the use or non-use of a particular version to become the basis of personal and ecclesiastical fellowship" is not realistic. The King James Bible is the basis of our personal and ecclesiastical fellowship at First Baptist Church of LaSalle, just as it has been for the past 160 years. It will

255

continue to be so. The KJV is our final authority. It has been written into our church constitution. We are perfectly happy with the King James Bible. We do not see anything wrong with it.

I suppose Glenny means that we should never **SEPARATE** from people over Bible versions. This is also unrealistic and wrong.

I do not separate, nor does First Baptist Church separate, from a Christian brother or a preacher just because he believes the Critical Text theory of Westcott and Hort. However, we do not want a preacher preaching from a new version here in our church. We do not want a preacher in our pulpit who corrects the King James Bible and says that it is a poor translation or that it has mistakes in it. If a preacher insists on doing these things, there is going to be a parting of the ways in our fellowship.

We will separate from camps where new versions of the Bible are promoted and used. We will separate from Sunday school and youth literature publishers who insist on using new versions as their Bible text.

If a person is moving to a new neighborhood and is looking for a church, we would certainly suggest that he go to a Bible-believing church where the preacher believes that the KJV is the Word of God and preaches from it. I personally would not stay in a church that begins using a new translation of the Bible in Sunday school or from the pulpit.

We do not care how many new versions a preacher has in his library. I have many translations in my own library. I study and compare them. But they are not my standard, or final authority. New translations may be used as commentaries, and judged as good or bad on any particular verse, just as we judge Adam Clarke's commentary or **_Barnes_ _Notes_**. But new translations are not the Word of God. Therefore, I do not carry one into the pulpit instead of my Bible. I would never suggest that my church members lay aside their Bible and read a new translation instead. My advice to my hearers has been that where any new translation differs from their King James Bible they should just ignore the new translation and believe the KJV.

Now I have a recommendation of my own for Central Seminary and for all who hold her position on the Bible text and on Bible versions: **IF THE DIFFERENCES BE- TWEEN THE NEW TRANSLATIONS AND THE KJV ARE AS MINOR AS YOU SAY** (when you are trying to convince people that the new translations are not dangerous and should be used) **WHY DON'T YOU JUST STICK WITH THE KJV AND AVOID ALL THE CON- FUSION AND TROUBLE?**

In this chapter we have looked at some of Professor Glenny's *opinions*. Any view which is not backed up with Scripture is just an *opinion*. Glenny does not prove with Scripture anything he says in this chapter. Some of his *opinions* are "far out," and "beyond the beyonds" (as they say in Ireland). His *opinions* are hurtful and dangerous because he is a professor and because his *opinions* are erroneous.

CHAPTER SEVEN

Chapter 7, of Central Baptist Theological Seminary's book, ***The Bible Version Debate***, is a summary and conclusion. It was written by Dr. W. Edward Glenny. It repeats many of the same problems and errors which are found in the previous six chapters.

He repeats the statement that, "We do not believe that the KJV was supernaturally reinspired at the time of its translation." We do not believe that either, and we do not know anyone who does.

He repeats the position that, "We reject the idea that the KJV is inerrant...." Of course, this means that he believes the KJV (and all other Bibles, including those in Hebrew and Greek as well as English) has errors. If there are errors in the Bible then you can not trust anything that it says because you will not know what is error and what is truth. This weakens the Bible's authority.

He repeats the teaching that, "we also reject the idea that the Word of God can be found only in the KJV." We agree with Glenny that **SOME** of the Word of God can be found

259

in the new versions. The new translations are not the Word of God, but they do **CONTAIN** the Word of God. **SOME** of the verses are translated correctly in every version, and therefore those verses are the words of God. But none of the new translations can be honestly called the Word of God, because they have too many errors in them. We can not say the NASB **IS** the Word of God, we can only say that it **CONTAINS** the Word of God. The KJV, on the other hand, **IS** the Word of God because there are no errors in it.

Glenny also repeats his ideas that the KJV has been revised; that inspiration does not necessitate the doctrine of providential preservation; that the doctrine of preservation of Scripture comes from history rather than from the Bible; and that the Bible has no explicit statement that God will preserve His Word. We have dealt with all of these errors before. None of Glenny's ideas are improved by repetition; and we will not take time to comment on them further.

75. The last statement that we **WILL** comment upon is the professor's assertion that, "We work with all the manuscripts to compile a text closer to the original than any one manuscript or group of manuscripts." [p. 131]

Analysis: We can not think of any statement which better summarizes the evils of modern textual criticism. This "extreme textualism" exalts man's own mind. The very idea that every textual critic can make his own Bible and that it will be a better Bible than any that has come before should be repugnant to every person who has any reverence for God and His Word. This humanistic naturalistic approach to the Bible makes man himself the final authority. It is the idea that some men are so smart that they can "shoot in the dark" and come closer to what God said than that which the Holy Spirit has preserved. This is equivalent to every man doing that which is right in his own eyes even if it means making a Bible of his own choosing. **THE RESULT IS THAT EVERY MAN IS HIS OWN FINAL AUTHORITY.**

So we come to the end of our review of ***The Bible Version Debate***, ***The Perspective of Central Baptist Theological Seminary***. It is the most error-ridden, the most dangerous, and the most unscriptural book on the subject of Bibliology to be written "on Planet Earth in this post-modern era" (to quote McLachlan's cutesy clichés). It is a book which has ideas which should be soundly rejected by advocates of the Critical Text and the Traditional Text alike.

APPENDIX 1

Adding to the Problems

A Review of:
One Bible Only? Examining Exclusive Claims for the King James Bible

Roy E. Beacham and Kevin T. Bauder are the general editors of this 238 page book, which has a 2001 copyright date. It is published by Kregel Publications, Grand Rapids.

To save time and space we will hereafter refer to *One Bible Only?* as OBO, and we will refer to Central's 1995 book, *The Bible Version Debate*, as TBVD.

The Writers

There are seven contributors to OBO, all of them connected to Central Baptist Theological Seminary, Plymouth, Minnesota. The writers are Kevin T. Bauder, Roy E. Beacham, W. Edward Glenny, Douglas K. Kutilek, Douglas R. McLachlan, Robert W. Milliman, and Larry D.

Pettegrew.   Four of these writers, Beacham, Glenny, McLachlan, and Pettegrew, were the authors of Central's previous book, TBVD.

Both Glenny and Pettegrew have now left Central Seminary and have gone to teach at neo-evangelical schools, Glenny to Northwestern College in St. Paul, and Pettegrew to The Master's College and Seminary (John MacArthur's school) in Sun Valley, CA. So Glenny and Pettegrew turn out to not be fundamentalists. Perhaps this explains why they took so many neo-evangelical positions while they were at Central--they were closet neo-evangelicals. No wonder they had good things to say about neo-evangelical versions of the Bible, such as the NIV. No wonder they quoted favorably, and without any warnings or disclaimers, such liberal, neo-orthodox, and neo-evangelical writers as Daniel B. Wallace, Bart Ehrman, Harry Sturz, Eldon Epp, and Kurt Aland. Glenny leans very heavily upon Wallace, getting most of his material from him. Pettegrew, ironically, seemed to be worried in TBVD, p. 13, about KJV-only people being "less of a fundamentalist," but now it is demonstrated that neither Glenny nor Pettegrew are fundamentalists themselves. Teachers at neo-evangelical schools, such as Northwestern College and the Master's Seminary are not fundamentalists. Fundamentalists **separate** from neo-evangelicalism. A true fundamentalist is a separatist. A true fundamentalist takes a militant stand against the compromise of neo-evangelicalism; he does not join it.

It is of real concern to me that Central Baptist Theological Seminary, a school that has had until recently a reputation as a fundamentalist institution, would continue to include in her books writings by neo-evangelicals, Glenny and Pettegrew. It is difficult to imagine that Central could have had these men on the faculty for so long without knowing their neo-evangelical leanings; however, that might be possible. We are aware of teachers leaving other solid fundamentalist schools and going to teach at neo-evangelical institutions. It is not that unusual, and does not necessarily reflect badly on the fundamentalist school. However, by continuing to include writings by Glenny and Pettegrew in Central's books, the Seminary demonstrates a lack of wisdom and discernment, to say the least, and possibly a softening in the matter of ecclesiastical separation.

Writing in *The Testimony*, [Winter, 2003. Volume 43, No. 4] Bauder says that Central believes that Christian fellowship "must be limited among brethren who disagree seriously about the requirements of the Christian faith." We must conclude that either, (A.) Central does not believe that teaching in a neo-evangelical college is a serious breach of the requirements of the Christian faith; or, (B.) Central does not believe in limiting fellowship much in such cases. Either possibility indicates deadly compromise.

It may be true, as Kevin Bauder says, that the contributors "grew up in Baptist fundamentalism" and that they "have their theological roots in fundamentalism" [OBO, pp. 13-14], however, they are not all in fundamentalism today. This does not come as a surprise to me. Things are changing very quickly now in what is called "fundamentalism." We see formerly stalwart institutions of uncompromising and militant separatism beginning to compromise. It starts with a less than militant attitude and progresses on to endorsements and associations that would embarrass our fundamentalist founders and forefathers. The public use and toleration of liberal and neo-evangelical Bible versions such as the NIV, the NASB, and the NRSV is one step in the downgrade toward neo-evangelical compromise. I am no prophet, but if history is a guide to the future, then we can sadly but safely predict that the fundamentalist institutions that are beginning their tolerance of the new versions today will in twenty years be in the same compromised condition as today's Moody Bible Institute and the General Association of Regular Baptist Churches. They will be completely and totally neo-evangelical. Some of these so called, "fundamentalist" institutions have already begun to put neo-evangelical speakers on their radio stations. They have begun to have worldly "Christian" music on their radio stations and in their services. And some of them have already begun to "network" or "partner" with compromising neo-evangelical organizations.

Some Odds and Ends

Before confronting some of the more serious issues in OBO, we want to deal with some lesser aspects of this book.

OBO came out at about the same time as the first edition of our book, **Seventy-five Problems**, too late for us to review it at that time. In comparing OBO with TBVD, Douglas R. McLachlan claims that Central's work "has reached a new plateau in this present form." [OBO, p. 11] The editors say of OBO, "This current book constitutes a major revision and republication of" TBVD. [OBO, p. 185] There is no doubt that Central's 1995 effort needed improvement; however, the reader will search in vain for any improvement in Central's position in this new book. OBO may have reached a new plateau, but unfortunately it is a lower plateau, not a higher one.

In OBO, Central makes all the same errors that she made in TBVD, **plus some additional errors**. For example, Central repeats the error that none of the differences in manuscripts "affects the overall theology of Bible-believing Christians," and they "do no harm." [OBO, pp. 10, 121] This type of statement is often parroted by defenders of new versions, but the statement is false by any honest definition of words. How could eliminating or changing some of the passages which undergird doctrine not result in the weakening of the theological authority upon which Christians rest their faith? How could it not do harm?

Central repeats in OBO the error that God left the preservation of His Word to "natural processes." [p. 103] She repeats also the error of getting some doctrine from history rather than from the Bible. [pp. 103, 121-122] There is repetition of the error that it is acceptable to correct the Masoretic Text based on mere conjecture. [p. 114] And, there is the repetition of the error that the KJV is hard to read, quoting again the sales material put out by the New Living Translation. [p. 153]

We will not spend any more time on the above mentioned errors since we have already dealt with them in our previous pages.

One problem in Central's new book which deserves a little more space here is Glenny's repeated contention that many conjectures about the Masoretic Hebrew Text have been vindicated by the Dead Sea Scrolls. [p. 114] We have refuted this contention and have challenged Glenny and Central to show us even one example of any conjecture about the Masoretic Text that has been vindicated by the Dead Sea Scrolls. In OBO, Glenny attempts to offer some evidence of his theory when he writes, "For example, R. W. Klein says, 'Samuel's MT [Masoretic Text] is a poor text, marked by extensive haplography and corruption—only the MT of Hosea and Ezekiel is in worse condition.'" [p. 114]

This is an example of a conjecture vindicated by the Dead Sea Scrolls? This is no example. Please notice that Glenny says, "For example,..." He does not give us **an example**. Instead of an example, he gives us a quote. The quote is from a liberal textual critic about how he thinks there are words missing due to scribal errors in the text of Samuel in the Masoretic Text. We are still waiting for Central to give us an example of a conjecture which has been vindicated by the Dead Sea Scrolls. Keep in mind that OBO says, "**Many** of these conjectures have been vindicated by the discovery of the Dead Sea Scrolls." [p. 114] "Many," it says, but does not give us an example of even one. I do not believe that anyone's conjectures about the Masoretic Text have been vindicated by the DSS.

How did the Conflict Develop?

Professor Bauder claims to be giving a history of how the King James only controversy developed when he says, "Churches and fellowships that had been accustomed to hear the Scriptures read from one of the various newer versions began to pressure their preachers to use only the King James for public reading and teaching." [OBO, p. 15]

It did not happen the way Brother Bauder tells it! I say it kindly, but that is "spin." He portrays the KJV as the supplanter, and those who wanted to keep the KJV as those who cause all the trouble. If he had told it like it is, Bauder would have said, "Churches and fellowships that had once been accustomed to hearing the Scriptures read from their beloved King James Bible began to be pressured by the insistent pushers of the various new versions to accept those new translations for public reading and teaching."

That is the way it really happened. Brother Bauder seems to have forgotten momentarily that the KJV was here first, long before any of "the various new versions."

Why do we belabor this point? We do so because "King James only" people have gotten a bad rap! The people who hold to the KJV are not the bad guys. It is the insistent pushers of new versions who have caused the problem. These pushers of new versions have caused controversy and confusion in fellowships, camps, conferences, and churches. They demand that their new versions be used for public preaching and teaching. They denigrate the old King James in order to win their argument. They pretend to not be able to understand the KJV, and say they can not learn anything from it when it is preached. They quote seminary professors saying that the KJV has errors in it, but new versions are clearer and more accurate "because they are closer to the originals."

All informed people on both sides of the debate agree that the KJV is a good and accurate translation. All could accept the KJV as the center of Christian fellowship (something that can not be said for any of the new versions), but the pushers of new versions refuse to do that. They think that they must bring in the new versions even if it splits churches and divides fellowships.

We must be candid here to say that fundamental colleges and seminaries should accept their share of the blame for the conflict that has developed. We would not have anywhere near the amount of controversy that we have today if the fundamental schools had said, "The King James Bible is an excellent translation. We will not correct it in any of our classes or in our chapel. We will use only the KJV for all of our class work and for preaching. Whether the Critical Greek Text or the Traditional Greek Text is the best is a matter for scholarly debate, but we are going to use only the King James Bible for preaching and teaching."

Fundamentalist Christian colleges and seminaries are partly responsible for the fact that the controversy has reached today's level. The schools have **fed the fires** of controversy. Teachers in those schools have berated and belittled the King James Bible in their classrooms. Professors have been eager to point out "mistakes" in our Bible. Those same schools and professors have brought out books denigrating the King James Bible. Consequently, some graduates of some of those colleges and seminaries have now come to pastor churches where they are determined to get the churches to stop using the KJV and to start using a new version. All of these activities have contributed to the controversy. KJV defenders are not to blame for all of the heat which has been generated.

Not all controversy is bad. False teaching must be opposed. When the Bible is added to, subtracted from, or changed, there must needs be a fight. The pushers of new versions seem to regret that there is controversy, but they are unwilling to change their behavior—behavior that ignited and continues to feed the flames of controversy.

How Much Should We Care?

In the introduction to OBO, Kevin Bauder tries to define the "King James only movement." He says, "The main question is whether the debate is academic or doctrinal." He contends that the characteristic that marks the King James only advocate is that those King James people, both "moderates" and "extremists," make "the exclusive use of the King James Version and its underlying Greek and Hebrew texts...a doctrinal issue." He says the debate should be "academic," not "doctrinal." [pp. 18-19] Bauder seems to be saying that he and other new version pushers can tolerate those who believe that the KJV is the preserved Word of God in English **as long as they do not teach it**. It is okay to have the KJV as a **preference**; just do not hold it as a **conviction**. It is fine to believe that the underlying Hebrew and Greek of the KJV are the right texts, and that the Critical Text is the wrong one, as long as you do not believe it too strongly or say it too loudly.

I am reminded of a Baptist preacher who tried to tell me that choosing a version of the Bible is just like choosing chocolate ice cream instead of vanilla. He thinks it does not matter, and should not matter, one way or the other. And if it does matter much to you, then he thinks you must be a cultist. Now, it is time to get real! Nobody on either side of the issue looks upon the choice of a Bible as no more important than choosing the flavor of an ice cream cone, unless they are too incredibly ignorant to be taken seriously about anything. The differences in both Greek texts and English versions are so gargantuan that anybody who has read them **should** have a very deep bias, one way or the other. And yet, Bauder thinks that people with strong

271

convictions favoring the KJV are unreasonable and divisive, and should be opposed.

I do not believe that it is at all unreasonable for King James defenders to have strong convictions on the matter. They have, in my opinion, a much stronger case than the Critical Text/new version advocate. More and more, the new version pushers are breaking fellowship with "King James only" people, passing resolutions against them, and attempting to characterize them as those that "troubleth Israel" (I Kings 18:17). Why? Because the new version pushers fear "King James advocates" as those whose words might influence people to stop buying new versions, reject modern textual criticism, and go to "King James only" colleges and seminaries. (Having people no longer attending "King James only" schools is something Bauder would love to see.) [OBO, p. 157]

Scripture is the Basis of Faith

Throughout both TBVD and OBO, the Central faculty insists that real spiritual faith must be based on the Word of God. "Can the King James only theory be justified by an appeal to faith.... Did God say it?... They must first demonstrate that God has specifically promised the verbal (perfect) preservation of the text of Scripture." [OBO, pp. 22-23] The professors then go on to emphasize and repeat that unless there is a Bible promise that God will preserve the actual **words** of the original documents of Scripture, then there is an insufficient basis for the appeal to faith. They call "the appeal to faith" an "illusion," and say "genuine, biblical faith, however, must rest in the promise of God." They say that King James only advocates "have no legitimate right to appeal to faith," because it is asserted that the KJV-only position does not rest in any promise of God. [OBO, p. 158] Bauder insists that, "Faith is legitimate only when it rests in a sufficient object. When Christian truth is at stake, the legitimate ground of faith must be the promise and character of God." [OBO, p. 183]

I agree wholeheartedly and enthusiastically that biblical faith is based upon what God has said in His Word. The Bible is our only and sufficient standard for doctrine, faith, and life. "Faith cometh by hearing, and hearing by the word of God" (Romans 10:17). Furthermore, I have always insisted that what we believe about the text of Scripture must be based upon what the Bible says about itself and not upon modern textual criticism.

My question for Central Baptist Theological Seminary and for all believers in modern textual criticism is, "Why do you not base your faith upon the Bible?" Is this standard, which Central claims to believe, good only for KJV-only advocates? Does it not apply to you also? Why is it essential that KJV-only people base their faith on the Bible, but not that you should do so? Is this standard only for other people, but not for you? Did God exempt you, that you do not have to base your doctrine upon the Word of God?

The reason that we ask this question is that new version defenders do not base their position on the Bible. We have already pointed out that most of what Central teaches about Bible preservation, and about translations, is just a matter of opinion, and is not based on the Bible at all.

Central thinks she finds her doctrine of preservation in history (see problem #61, on page 179). Where does the Bible say that we should get our doctrine of Bible preservation from history? In OBO, Bauder again admits that his teaching on providential preservation "is not based on an explicit verse of Scripture. It is based on the evidence of history." [OBO, pp. 122-123]   Then, according to his own words, his faith in his doctrine of preservation is illegitimate, an "illusion," because "genuine biblical faith must rest in the promise of God."

The same can be said of Central's doctrine of "natural processes." There is no Scripture to support this doctrine. The Bible does not say that God would let nature take its course, so that some of God's words would be lost, so that man would have to guess at what God's words are, and so that we would not have a perfect Bible. As a matter of fact, the Bible declares the exact opposite of Central's view. The Bible says that God would be actively involved in the preservation of His Word (John 14:23, 26;   15:26;   16:13-15).   So, with no Bible statement that God would leave His Word to "natural processes," why does Central teach this?   Apparently, she thinks it is just fine for her to have faith in doctrines which are not taught in the Bible, but she has a higher standard for King James only advocates. Central's faith in her doctrine of "natural processes" is an "illusion," an illegitimate faith, because genuine faith and doctrine must rest upon the words of God.

We must further point out that the entire system of modern textual criticism is a doctrine and a belief not based on any words of Scripture. Where are the verses in God's Word that tell us that "the older manuscripts are better," or that "the longer readings are superior to the shorter ones," or that "the more difficult readings are better than the easier ones"? There are no Bible verses for any of these teachings with which men sit in judgment of the words of God. Liberal theologians invented the ideas of modern textual criticism, Westcott and Hort popularized them, and the Princeton scholars introduced them to conservatives and fundamentalists. These ideas did not come from God or from God's Word. If you search the Scripture from beginning to end, you will not find any reference, nor even an allusion, to the principles of modern textual criticism. And yet, the pushers of the new Bible versions have elevated these principles of modern textual criticism to the place where they have such faith in them that they are willing to throw out vast portions of the Word of God. They have such faith in modern textual criticism that they are willing to accept changes that greatly weaken all of the fundamental doctrines of the faith. Since modern textual criticism does not rest on any statements or promises of the Bible, belief in it is an "illusion," an illegitimate faith. Neither Central, nor anyone else, is entitled to base their faith in humanistic, naturalistic, modern textual criticism.

Most King James Bible defenders **do** base their faith on explicit promises and statements of Scripture. Of course, Central Seminary has already explained away and rejected these promises and statements as having nothing to do with preservation. Bauder says, "without exception," the passages we cite, "appear to be talking about something besides the written preservation of all of the words of Scripture." [OBO, p. 177]

Even though it has been so summarily and cavalierly dismissed, we assert here the promise of Psalm 12:6-7.

> *The words of the LORD are pure words: as silver tried in a furnace of earth, purified seven times. Thou shalt keep them, O LORD, thou shalt preserve them from this generation for ever.*

Since God promised to preserve His words "from this generation for ever," it is obvious that we have His promise that every generation has had all of the words of God. The text which every generation had was the Traditional Text, not the Critical Text. The Critical Text is a new text. The Traditional Text is the old text that every generation has possessed.

Some King James Bible defenders believe that the Received Text, in one edition or another, is, for all practical purposes, perfect and virtually identical to the autographs; and many of these defenders base their faith on Psalm 12:6-7 and other verses.

Other King James Bible defenders believe that the true words of God were all preserved in the multiplicity of manuscripts, though not necessarily in a single manuscript or in a particular reconstructed text; and many of these defenders base their faith on Psalm 12:6-7 and other verses.

Some King James Bible defenders believe, as I do, that the translators of the KJV were able to find all of the words of God. They found all the words of God, though perhaps not all in the TR; but they found all of the words among all of the witnesses. They translated accurately all of the words of God into English, so that we have in the KJV the inspired and inerrant Word of God, nothing added, nothing deleted, and nothing changed. I base this belief on Psalm 12:6-7 and other verses. If the King James Bible is not the preserved Word of God, then several generations of English-speaking people did not have all of the words of God. In my opinion this is inconceivable and inconsistent with God's promise. God preserved His words in Hebrew, Greek, Italian, Coptic, Syriac, German, Spanish, French, and many other languages. He preserved it in English, also. In English, God's Word has been the King James Bible for nearly 400 years. There has been no viable substitute, replacement, or peer. English, the most important language in the world, the language wherein the greatest work of God has been done, the language that has been the most universal, has not, during any generation, been without the words of God. God promised that every generation would have all of His words; and it is upon that promise that I base my faith. "His truth endureth to all generations" (Psalm 100:5).

The psalmist is speaking about the preservation of Holy Scripture when he writes, "For ever, O Lord, thy word is settled in heaven. **Thy faithfulness is unto all generations"** (Psalm 119:89-90). Yes, our faith in Bible preservation rests upon the promises of God. He promised that every generation of His people would have all of His words. Therefore, we know that the true words of God are the words that God's people have always had throughout all generations. The Elect Nation in the Old Testament and the Holy Spirit indwelt churches in this present dispensation have possessed, kept, guarded, and held dear all of the words of God. That is what God said would happen and that is what happened.

We are glad that Brother Bauder brought it up that genuine faith must be based on the Word of God. It gives us the opportunity to say that most King James Bible defenders base their faith in Bible preservation upon what the Bible says about itself, and the pushers of new versions do not. The Central teachers will, no doubt, say that my own position, basing my faith on God's promise to all generations, is tenuous and weak. However, it is stronger than Central's position since the faculty admits that they do not base their own position on any verses at all. (See our discussion of faith in problem #21, p. 74.)

Publicly Accessible?

Central downplays the idea that the true word of God has to be publicly accessible. Time and time again, the professors bring up the idea that the Bible does not demand the public accessibility of the true Word of God. [OBO, pp. 20, 105, 158] The reason the professors are downplaying public accessibility is that the manuscripts of the Critical Text were not "publicly accessible" before the 15th Century (Vatican manuscript) and the 19th Century (Siniatic manuscript). For all practical purposes, the Alexandrian Text did not exist for forty-five to fifty generations (forget about "publicly accessible"). Since it did not exist for the people to read, it can not be the text that God promised to all generations.

At least twice [OBO, pp. 14, 190], Central refers to the Law being found during the reign of Josiah (II Kings 22; II Chronicles 34). The Central professors would like to have us believe that every copy of the Word of God had been destroyed or lost for fifty years, until a copy was found in Josiah's day. If Central could prove that there were no copies of God's Word available for fifty years, that would mean that at least one generation did not have the Word of God. The Word of God, in that case, would not have been "publicly accessible." But, Central comes far short of proving such a theory—stating that something is true does not make it so. Most commentators do not believe that all copies of the Word of God had been destroyed or lost in II Kings 22. The Word of God was scarce, to be sure, but not completely inaccessible. Adam Clark comments:

It is scarcely reasonable to suppose that this was the *only copy* of the law that was found in Judea; for even if we grant that Ahaz, Manasseh, and Amon had endeavoured to destroy all the books of the law, yet they could not have succeeded so as to destroy the whole. Besides, Manasseh endeavoured after his conversion to *restore* every part of the Divine worship, and in this he could have done nothing without the Pentateuch; and the succeeding reign of Amon was too short to give him opportunity to undo every thing that his penitent father had reformed. Add to all these considerations, that in the time of Jehoshaphat teaching from the law was *universal* in the land, for he set on foot an *itinerant ministry*, in order to instruct the people fully: for "he sent to his princes to teach in the cities of Judah; and with them he sent Levites and priests; and they went about through all the cities of Judah, and taught the people, having the book of the Lord with them;" see 2 Chron. xvii. 7-9. And if there be anything wanting to show the improbability of the thing, it must be this, that the transactions mentioned here took place in the *eighteenth* year of the reign of Josiah, who had, from the time he came to the throne, employed himself in the restoration of the pure worship of God; and it is not likely that during these eighteen years he was without a copy of the Pentateuch. The simple fact seems to be this, that this was the original of the covenant renewed by Moses with the people in the plains of Moab, and which he ordered to be laid up beside the ark; (Deut. xxxi. 26;) and now being unexpectedly found, its *antiquity*, the *occasion* of its being made, the present *circumstances* of the people, the *imperfect state* in which the reformation was as yet, after all that had been done, would all concur to produce the effect here mentioned on the mind of the pious Josiah.

Some commentators believe that the book that was found in the temple was important because it was the autograph from the hand of Moses (Matthew Poole), or that it was a special copy of the Law kept in one of the holiest places of the temple (Barne's notes), or that it was a list of laws from Deuteronomy (Ellicott). Commentators are not even agreed about what "the book" was, much less that it was the only copy of the Bible in existence.

I would suggest that Central Seminary stop looking in II Kings 22 for proof that the Bible has not always been "publicly accessible." Clark was right when he said that it was not the last existing copy of the Word of God. (Read our discussion of why the discovery of the book in the temple is an example of miraculous preservation, problem #14, pp. 50-53.)

Will KJV Defenders Turn Out to be on the Same Side as Those They Oppose?

Those who study the issues of Bible preservation should use caution about generalizing too much about King James Bible defenders. It is not a monolithic group. All of them believe very strongly that the King James Bible should be used for public preaching and teaching, but beyond that, they hold various opinions. Personally, I have never met anyone who believes in the reinspiration of the KJV, or that the KJV translators were inspired. Yet, many proponents of new versions would have us believe that all, or most, KJV defenders are in that category. I have never met anyone, nor have I ever read the writings of anyone, who believes that the KJV is a new updated revelation which adds to or corrects the autographs, but according to some pushers of new versions, there is an abundant supply of such people. (They just can not name them!)

Kevin Bauder seems to think he would have the debate won if only he could get King James only people to admit that they do not know for sure that any particular Greek manuscript contains all of the words of God and only the words of God. This line of argument reveals a considerable amount of generalizing. It presupposes that all KJV defenders have believed that there is such a manuscript.

I have been able to find among King James only people at least eight distinct positions on the Greek, Hebrew, and English texts. Most KJV people never have believed that any extant Hebrew or Greek copy contains every word of God and only God's words. It does not help Bauder's argument at all that these KJV-only people exist.

Let us look briefly at several groups. **First**, there is a group of KJV people who know nothing at all about the Critical Text or the Traditional Text. However, they have read some of the new translations and they do not like them. They do not like it that the new translations leave out verses and large passages, including many doctrinally strategic verses. They do not like the fact that many verses have been changed in such a way as to weaken and water down many crucial doctrinal statements. Furthermore, this category of believers know that the new translations are inferior, having been produced by people from a wide spectrum of theological positions, everything from outright liberals to compromising neo-evangelicals. They know that this is the real reason that the blood of Christ is left out of certain passages, that the deity of Christ is missing from some verses, and that the virgin birth is slighted in some verses. These believers do not necessarily believe that the King James Bible is in every way perfect, but they believe that it is the clearest and best. They have an extreme distrust of all new versions. They are adamantly opposed to switching Bibles in their church and Sunday school. They want only the KJV in their personal devotions, in their camps, and in their youth programs. These people are KJV-only. They are tenaciously and vociferously opposed to all of the new translations and do not want to see them get a foothold among fundamentalist Christians. They accept the KJV as their final authority in matters of faith and life, and they do not want any conflicting authority.

There is a **second** group of KJV-only people who have studied the several Greek texts and believe that the Traditional Greek Text is the right text to translate, and believe that the KJV is the best translation of that text. They do not believe, however, that the TR or the Majority Text is perfect in any one printed copy. Consequently, they do not believe that the KJV is perfect either. However, they believe that the KJV is **almost** perfect, and that it is the clearest and most accurate translation that we have. Theoretically, they believe it is possible to (some time in the future) have a better translation than the KJV, but that none better exists today. They believe that the KJV is the best translation available, but not necessarily the best translation possible. Furthermore, they believe all other translations are very poor and dangerous. They are strongly opposed to substituting any of the new translations for the KJV in their church, in their camps, or in their Sunday school literature. Some of the best known and most influential defenders of the KJV have been (and are) of this position. They do not necessarily believe in the inspiration or inerrancy of any copy or any translation, but they believe that the Traditional Text and the KJV are, by far, the best, near to perfection, and so far above all others as to be beyond compare. This group is KJV-only because they oppose all the new translations, because they know those new translations misrepresent the Word of God, adding some, subtracting greatly, and changing much.

A **third** category of KJV-only people believe that the Textus Receptus, usually one of Beza's editions, is the perfect Word of God. They believe that all of the people who worked on the TR up to the point of the printing of that edition were able, collectively, to find all of God's words. They believe that all of God's words were preserved in the ancient manuscripts, versions, and translations and that God gave wisdom to such people, as Erasmus and Beza, so that all of the words of God were found and put into that edition of the TR. They believe, therefore that that edition of the TR is verbally identical to the autographs. This group further believes that the KJV is a very excellent translation of the TR. They are strongly opposed to substituting any other translation for the KJV, because none of the other translations is a trustworthy translation of the TR. They do not necessarily believe that the KJV is an absolutely perfect translation of the TR, but they believe it is the best translation, and they do not want any other.

A **fourth** category of King James Bible advocates believe in the Majority Text. They believe that if we exclude the few Alexandrian manuscripts (because they seem to be corruptions) and simply count the number of times a certain reading appears in the Byzantine manuscripts, that that will result in the correct reading. Many Majority Text defenders are strong KJV-only advocates because the KJV has in almost every case the majority reading. They believe the KJV is an excellent translation. They do not believe that it is an absolutely perfect translation, but that it is the best we have. They believe that all new translations, with the possible exception of the NKJV, are grossly inferior. Many in this category find many objectionable readings and notations in the NKJV, also. Most Majority Text/King James advocates adamantly favor the King James in pulpit and classroom.

A **fifth** group of King James only advocates are those who believe that the King James translators were able to find all of the words of God. We believe almost all of the words were found in Beza's fifth edition of the TR. A few words were found in some of the other witnesses. We do not know exactly what materials the translators had available, or exactly what their reasons were for using each word that they used since their notes and their printer's sheets seem to have been lost. However, we believe God gave the King James translators wisdom so that they translated all of the words correctly.

There are a few other minor positions among King James only people. Some are adherents to the new printed Majority Text, some believe in the inerrancy of the KJV and others do not, etc. However, we have taken enough space to show that King James only people are not monolithic. We do not all believe the same things, but it is safe to say that all King James advocates thank God for every person's choice of the right Bible. I am glad for every person who reads, loves, lives by, and defends the King James Bible, no matter how he arrived at that position.

Professor Bauder is mistaken when he thinks that all King James only people believe in a manuscript that has all of the words of God and only the words of God, and if they fail to come up with such a manuscript "then their whole position is falsified," and "they will turn out to be on the same side as those whom they oppose." [OBO, p. 22] The truth is that the vast majority of King James only people never made such a claim to begin with. The difficulty for Bauder and Central is not with getting KJV-only people to admit that they do not have a perfect Greek manuscript so that Central can win a debate. The real difficulty for Central Seminary and all pushers of new Bible versions is **the tremendous differences** between the new Bibles and the KJV. The amount of Bible material that has been eliminated or changed is vast.

Bauder says, "The proportion of words that are open to question is slight. The disputed passages are relatively insignificant. In any case, all of the various options support true doctrine." [OBO, p. 157] This statement by Bauder is absolutely false. He could not be more wrong! The disputed words and passages are **extensive, massive, very numerous, and earthshakingly important to doctrine**.

Some writers have accurately pointed out that the words eliminated from the New Testament alone are equal to the number of words in I and II Peter. The amount of material in the New Testament that is changed in meaning in most new versions is equal to the amount of material in the whole of the book of Hebrews. If a religious body or a publisher brought out a Bible with the books of I and II Peter missing, and if they said, "The reason we will no longer publish a Bible with I and II Peter is that we do not believe it is genuine; there is not enough evidence for it to be included," would we care? Would we not be ready to fight for that large portion of God's Word?

And suppose the words were all changed in the book of Hebrews so that none of it had the same meaning any more. Would we care? Would we not be ready to fight for that large portion of God's Word?

Then why do new version pushers find it unreasonable that we should fight for the many verses changed in the new versions? Why are we called cultists and Nazis when we are contending for the same Bible that God's people have always had?

The Bible is being attacked, sometimes by well-meaning people. It is being done piecemeal, one word at a time, or one passage or verse at a time. But it adds up to thousands of words. God's people know this is being done, and that is the real difficulty for Central Seminary and the other pushers of new versions. Their difficulty is not in winning a debate--it is that common, ordinary Christians know what they are up to.

The RSV, the NRSV, and Gender-Neutrality

Writing in Chapter 5 of OBO, Robert Milliman discusses translation theory and several new translations. He attempts to make the case for the need of modern textual criticism, saying that the Textus Receptus and the KJV came to us as the result of textual criticism. It was a type of textual criticism, loosely speaking, which contributed to these wonderful works. However, modern, naturalistic textual criticism it was not. The method which gave us the King James Bible was a biblical and spiritual method; whereas, the method which brought about the new versions is a naturalistic, humanistic method. The method which gave us the KJV says, "We have the words of God and God's people have always had them, because God has preserved His words." Modern textual criticism which has spawned the new versions, on the other hand, says, "We do not have the Bible yet; we are still looking for it. We have never had it, and neither has anyone in history with the possible exception of those who read the autographa." As a matter of fact, more and more modern textual critics are saying that there never were any autographs, at least not in the sense that fundamentalists have thought. [For a discussion of destructive modern textual criticism, review problem #22, pp. 79-88.]

Milliman tries to make the case for new versions by suggesting a test, of sorts. Try to read one of William Shakespeare's plays, says Milliman, without benefit of explanatory notes or marginal helps. He then concludes, "The unchurched person, the immigrant, the child, the television addict, and the secularized professional will read older versions such as the KJV with a similar degree of difficulty." [OBO, p. 148]

The answer to this problem is that the reader of the Bible **should** use explanatory notes and marginal helps. In fact, the reader should get a good Bible dictionary, or get a KJV with a good read-along-dictionary. No one, to our knowledge, has ever been opposed to Bible helps for the Bible reader. The reader will need these helps no matter which version he reads!

The answer for the person who can not understand Shakespeare's plays is not to have someone **rewrite** Shakespeare. Then what he would read would not be Shakespeare. The answer for the Bible reader is not to get a Bible that has been rewritten, because that will not be, in all cases, the words of God.

Central Baptist Theological Seminary, we are sorry to see, has now moved on to approval of gender-neutral language and of the New Revised Standard Version. In discussing gender inclusive language, Milliman says that gender-neutral equivalents should be sought for *brother*, *man*, and other New Testament words. He commends the NRSV for doing this. He says, "To the extent that it clarifies the biblical author's intended meaning, gender-inclusive language is a worthwhile goal." [OBO, pp. 146-147] Advocating for gender-neutrality is the natural consequence of a belief that the words of God are not as important as what the critic thinks God meant to say, or should have said!

Gender-neutrality is just one of the problems of the liberal NRSV. It is, of course, a rewrite of the old National Council of Churches Revised Standard Version. The fact that Central now has endorsed the RSV and the NRSV shows that she is moving away from her fundamentalist roots. Fundamentalists from 1950-1990 had nothing good to say about the RSV, for very good reasons. However, Milliman says, "In spite of these deficiencies [liberal attacks on the person and work of Christ], however, the RSV is, for the most part, a good, literal translation, often more readable than other versions such as the NASB." [OBO, p. 144]

The above statement in Central's book is very similar to saying, "Even though he cuts the tongues out of people who talk to the press, shoots all of his critics, and administers nerve gas to any who rebel, Saddam Hussein is really a nice guy. He is very predictable."

Milliman refers to the liberal Bruce Metzger, the chairman of the NRSV translation committee, as "the respected scholar." [OBO, p. 144] And concludes the matter by saying, "The NRSV...like the RSV before it [is] becoming the choice of many biblical scholars." Which tells us why we should be increasingly suspicious of, so called, "biblical scholars."

So, the plot thickens! Central has gone beyond endorsement of the NASB to endorsement of very liberal versions, and to gender-neutrality, which even some outright neo-evangelical denominations (Southern Baptist Convention) still reject. This progression (we are tempted to say "regression") shows that to begin to push **any** of the new versions is, indeed (no matter how vociferously it might be denied!), a slippery slope that leads down a grade to a denial of the words of God.

Inspiration and What God Said

I am surprised and saddened at some of the statements made by Kevin Bauder regarding inspiration. I consider these statements to be the most serious errors in OBO. There are two of these statements, both of them related to Central's view that only the "essence" or "meaning" of what God said is important, not the exact words that God used and preserved.

First, in arguing against the view that verbal inspiration requires verbal preservation in order to be useful and meaningful, Bauder gives us an example of what he considers inspiration without preservation. He says that God spoke before the flood "but no record of those divine words has been preserved." [OBO, p. 158]

We readily agree that God spoke to man at times when it was not recorded and not preserved, but that has nothing to do with any thing under discussion. We have never said that all of God's **spoken** words were preserved.

I do not believe that the example given by Bauder is a case of inspiration without preservation. In fact, I do not believe that there is any inspiration involved in God's spoken words which were not made a part of Holy Writ. I am not aware of any theologian who says that it is an example of inspiration when God spoke without the use of a human spokesman or human writer. None, that is, except Kevin Bauder.

A few theologians say that it was a case of inspiration when God spoke through the speaking prophets. Others deny that inspiration was involved when nothing was being written down by human penmen. There is no doubt that God's spoken words and the spoken words of the prophets were infallible revelation from God, even if those words were never intended to be inscripturated. It is possible to have revelation without inspiration. Most theologians have reserved the word *inspiration* to describe God's words penned by human authors.

As a freshman Bible student, I memorized, along with the rest of the class, Warfield's definition of inspiration. It says, "Inspiration is that extraordinary, supernatural influence exerted by the Holy Ghost on the writers of our sacred books, by which their words were rendered also the words of God, and therefore, perfectly infallible." Inspiration, then, would apply only to the writing of the Bible and would make certain that the words were the very words which God wanted.

But whether or not the word "inspiration" can properly be applied to the spoken words of God, where no human instrument is involved, those spoken words were never intended by God to be preserved in the Bible. Words spoken by God the Father, and by Jesus, but never recorded in the Bible, were never promised to be preserved as the Bible was.

Maybe Bauder is simply trying here to cloud the issue and distract people from the real force of the inspiration/preservation argument. It is a serious error, however, for a person in his position to promote a misunderstanding of the nature of inspiration.

When God motivated the penman of Scripture to write His words, **He did so because that was His way of preserving His words for future generations**. If God did not want the words preserved, and if He wanted only one generation to have them, He could have had all of His words delivered in only the spoken form. We conclude that inspiration and preservation are companion doctrines no matter how loudly this might be denied. [See problem #27, p. 126, for our discussion of this matter.]

Second, Bauder says that gospel writers recorded the **essence** of Jesus words, not His **exact** words, and therefore there are differences in what the several Gospel writers reported. Bauder says that Jesus' parable of the four kinds of soil as found in Matthew 13 and Mark 4, are examples of how Gospel writers report with conflicting words what Jesus said. He concludes that the differences in wording prove that only the **essence** and not the **exact words** are recorded. [OBO, p. 154] It proves nothing of the kind!

The only people who could see a problem between the words of Jesus in Matthew vs. the words of Jesus in Mark are people who either deny the Bible doctrine of inspiration or deny the Bible doctrine of preservation.

Our answer to Dr. Bauder is that Jesus said all the words that Matthew said that He said, **and** all of the words that Mark said that He said. He said it **both** the way Matthew reported it, **and** the way Mark reported it. As is always true in teaching and preaching, Jesus repeated things several times using slightly different words. This is even done in private conversation, and it is especially done in preaching. We come at the same truth, repetitiously, in slightly different ways, from slightly different directions, and with slightly different words, in order to emphasize it, and make sure that our hearers get it.

Jesus did the same thing. When considering Jesus' sermons, we should not assume that **all** that He said is reported by the Gospel writers, however, **all** of the words attributed to Him were actually spoken by Him.

It is troubling to read that Kevin Bauder, Associate Professor of Systematic and Historical Theology at Central Baptist Theological Seminary, believes and teaches that Jesus did not say the exact words that the Gospel writers say that He spoke. If Matthew or Mark, or any other author of any of the Scriptures, say that Jesus spoke certain words, **He spoke them!**

A Christian has no business saying that Jesus did not speak some of the words attributed to Him in the Bible. That is a very dangerous view. It is only a small step from the position that the Bible records only the essence, not the exact words of Jesus, to the position that fundamentalists should vote with different colored marbles to determine which words are genuine!

Dear reader, do you see where a denial of the Bible doctrine of preservation will lead? It will lead to a weakening of doctrine generally, and especially of the doctrine of inspiration.

Conclusion

It would be an understatement to say that OBO is not an improvement over TBVD. Central Baptist Theological Seminary retains all of her old problems and introduces several serious new problems.

Bibliology is the engine that drives the truck of theology. Central Seminary's engine needs an overhaul! Its rods are knocking, its valves are gasping, its pistons are cracked, and its blowing smoke!

APPENDIX 2

Misleading the Laymen

A Review of :
From the Mind of God to the Mind of Man

This 231 page book is published with the subtitle, *A Layman's Guide to How We Got Our Bible*. It was published in Greenville, South Carolina, by Ambassador-Emerald International. It has a 1999 copyright date.

The General Editor is James B. Williams and the Managing Editor is Randolph Shaylor. Apparently a special group was formed to write this book—something called The Committee on the Bible's Text and Translation.

THE WRITERS

There is an impressive group of writers: Ernest Pickering wrote the preface. Other writers were Mark Minnick, Paul W. Downey, John Ashbrook, John K.

Hutcheson, Sr., John Mincy, Mark R. Simmons, William H. Smallman, J. Drew Conley, and Keith Gephart.

Other names associated with the book (perhaps because they read the manuscript and made suggestions) are: David Beale, David Burggraff, Sam Horn, Rolland McCune, Douglas McLachlan, Larry Oates, and James Price.

It is obvious that the unstated purpose was to assemble a group of fundamentalist preachers whose very names and degrees would bedazzle and intimidate any who might disagree with them. The group is a sort of "last chance" or "Great White Hope" for putting a stop to King James only opinions. It looks like a "last ditch" desperate effort to try to get the laymen to embrace the Critical Text/Eclectic Text position.

I hold some of the men connected with this book in high esteem. Several of them have preached from my pulpit and would be welcome in my pulpit today. One who would not be welcome in my pulpit is Rolland McCune of Detroit Baptist Theological Seminary, who downplays the shedding of Jesus' blood. He takes the blood of the New Testament which was shed for many as a symbol of death. He follows R. B. Theime and neo-evangelical John MacArthur in de-emphasizing and minimizing the importance and efficacy of the blood of Christ.

McCune believes that "the **primary** significance" of the expression "the blood of Christ is death," thus assigning a **secondary** significance to the fact that Christ shed His literal blood. He believes that the blood of Christ is a symbol of His death and makes "no specific contribution to a full payment for our sins" because that was accomplished only by Christ's death.

McCune and Detroit Baptist Theological Seminary treat the King James Bible no better than they treat the precious blood of Christ. They believe there are many mistakes in the King James Bible.

However, we would appreciate some of the writers and some of the schools with which they are connected. I have belonged to the same fellowships and school association (AACS) as some of these men. I have been blessed by the writing and preaching of some of these men in the past. I do not count these men as enemies.

However, this impressive list of writers and "academicians" should be expected to have done a much better job and to have written more convincingly than they did in this book. There is nothing new in the book. It consists of all of the same tired warmed-over arguments which have been used against Traditional Text and King James Bible believers for the past several decades. One of the authors could easily have written the whole book without any help from the others. In fact, I consider the book to be a rather piddling performance to have been written by so many men with so many doctor's degrees!

THE COVER

The cover of ***From the Mind of God to the Mind of Man*** is a disgrace, having a picture of the Revised Standard Version. In the first edition of the book, Matthew 18 and 19 can clearly be read in the RSV pictured on the cover. In the so-called "third edition" (I have never seen the second edition), the picture has been blurred so that the RSV print cannot be read. This blurring was apparently done because the committee was embarrassed about using the RSV and are now trying to hide the fact that it is the RSV. The committee **SHOULD** be embarrassed. The RSV is a liberal, National Council of Churches version which has been rejected by Bible believers ever since it was first published in 1946.

To make matters worse, Drew Conley and company seem to agree with much that the translators did in the RSV (pp. 198-199). To be fair, it is mentioned that the RSV was rejected by conservative Christians because of its liberal translation of Isaiah 7:14, because "some of the translators" were liberals, and because it became the Bible of many liberal denominations. However, it seems that almost as many positive statements are made about the RSV as negative ones. For example, Conley says, "Many scholars consider the RSV to be an accurate translation." He also seems to appreciate the fact that the RSV translators were "convinced that the older manuscripts provided a far more reliable text basis (that is, readings closer to what the original documents contained) than did the few manuscripts available to the King James Translators." Conley also seems to like it that the RSV "updated English words that had either become obsolete or altered in their meaning since their use in 1611." Well, with all of these positive things being said about the RSV, perhaps the authors of ***From the Mind of God to the Mind of Man*** think that the fundamentalists made a mistake fifty years ago when they turned thumbs down on it, **AND HAD NOTHING GOOD TO SAY ABOUT IT!**

Of course, the RSV was made from the same manuscripts which gave us the NASB and the NIV, and there is **NOT** a dime's worth of difference between them. It's no wonder then that the RSV showed up on the cover of ***From the Mind of God to the Mind of Man***.

The graphics on the cover are highly suggestive and are intended to portray how various Scriptures brought down the very epitome of God's Word for us today. From top to bottom there are two lines of Hebrew, then two lines of Greek, followed by two lines of Latin, then two lines of Old English, then two lines from today's King James Bible, **followed by the picture of the RSV**. Again we say, this cover is a disgrace for a group of fundamentalists to publish.

CALLING NAMES, WHINING, AND REWRITING HISTORY

It was the intention of the committee to be less hostile than people often are when they discuss translations. Ernie Pickering says, in the Preface, that the book "contains a proper spirit" and does not make "attacks on the character of their opponents." Mark Minnick says, in the Disclosure, that the book was edited "to maintain a conciliatory tone" and he denounces the "ungracious and divisive tone, the character assassination and inflammatory speech of much of the current debate." We presume then that Minnick and the others will detest and denounce Central Baptist Seminary's language when McLachlan, Pettegrew, Beacham, and Glenny refer to King James only people as a cult, when they say that a King James only man is "less of a fundamentalist," and when they compare strong King James Bible supporters to the supporters of Hitler!

But the fact is that ***From the Mind of God to the Mind of Man*** fails in its stated desire to use a conciliatory tone, to abstain from character attacks, and to "heal the wounds." While talking about healing wounds, J.B. Williams in the introduction, refers to D.A.Waite, E. L. Bynum, Jack Chick, and Walter Beebe as "misinformers." [p. 7] "Strong advocates of the King James only position" are called "disseminators of untruth" and "disseminators of misinformation." [p. 4] Those who disagree with Williams about Westcott and Hort are said to be telling "lies." [p. 4] David Otis Fuller is said to be "another disseminator of misinformation." [p. 6] All of the above named individuals, and more, are then said to be those about whom we are warned in II Peter 2:1-3 and Acts 20:17-38— deceivers, exploiters, heretics, and grievous wolves. [p. 7]

So much for healing wounds! So much for a conciliatory tone!

Williams whines about the fact that visitors looking for a good church did not return after they found out that the church they visited did not use the King James Bible or did not believe the King James Bible was the inspired Word of God. Why whine about that? What else would anyone expect? The translation which is used and defended is reason enough for a person to decide which local church he will attend. **IT IS NOT A MINOR ISSUE.** There are many who will not attend a church that uses only the KJV. Does Williams think this is a problem? He does not say so.

Williams writes in both error and great bias about the above mentioned visitors, that "They were disappointed when they learned that the church and pastor held the same view held by Fundamentalist Christianity throughout the church age." [p. 5]

He means that the true people of God allowed for the use of more than one text all through the Church age. That is false. First of all, the new Critical Text manuscripts were not even found until A.D. 1480 and A.D. 1859. Furthermore, the true people of God continued to hold to the same Traditional Text after those Roman Catholic manuscripts were discovered. Not until 1881 was there a representation of the Critical Text translated into English, **AND IT WAS NEVER WIDELY ACCEPTED.** Nor was any other new English translation widely accepted by Fundamentalists until thirty years ago when the NASB and the NIV came out. Some fundamentalist **SCHOLARS** (maybe even most) believed the Westcott and Hort theory between A.D. 1900 and 1970. The issue was hotly debated. But to the rank and file fundamentalist Christians in our churches there was never any question about where they stood on new translations—they rejected them! Williams is rewriting history to try to fool the laymen!

WESTCOTT AND HORT

One of the sad things about ***From the Mind of God to the Mind of Man*** is the defense of Westcott and Hort. It is tragic to see these liberals defended over and over again by fundamentalists. Westcott and Hort are defended by Williams (p. 4), by Minnick (pp. 84-86), by Smallman (pp. 172-175), and by Gephart (pp. 211-213). Of course, ***From the Mind of God to the Mind of Man***, is basically a defense of modern textual criticism, so the authors felt that they must defend Westcott and Hort who were instrumental in popularizing this destructive approach to the text of the Bible. We are assured that Westcott and Hort never depart from "Fundamentalist doctrine," that they were scholarly and careful textual critics, and that they were not heretics nor apostates.

Some of the statements made by Westcott and Hort in their Bible commentaries are open to interpretation as to their exact meaning. These statements have been debated much in recent years, some stating that Westcott and Hort are heretics and others stating that Westcott and Hort are simply misunderstood. Personally, I believe that Westcott and Hort were intentionally obscure in a most Clintonesque way so as to be accepted by those of diverse opinions. I believe they intentionally wrote in such a way as to make their books acceptable to both conservatives and liberals.

What seems clear to me is that Westcott believed in universal incarnationism, that Hort rejected the substitutionary atonement, and that both Westcott and Hort were theistic evolutionists. Additionally, there is a strong likelihood that Westcott was a spiritualist.

Westcott believed that God was incarnate in all men. Man's real need was to come to the realization that God indwells him.   To develop within man the consciousness and the conception of the life of God, that was the goal.

Westcott's view of God being organically united to man, and of all men being united to each other in God, led to a practice of fellowshipping with dead saints. Both the living and the dead are a part of "the one life," and therefore, said Westcott, the dead may minister to us and we may minister to the dead. This Westcott did not do through mediums or clairvoyants, but through meditation, "fellowship of spirit with spirit."

Westcott's incarnation views are reported in a book by Dr. James Sightler, __A *Testimony Founded For Ever, the King James Bible Defended in Faith and History*__. [$21.00, postage paid, Sightler Publications, 25 Sweetbriar Road, Suite 1A, Greenville, SC, 29615] Dr. Sightler is a graduate of Furman University and Johns Hopkins University School of Medicine.   He teaches the History of Biblical Text Transmission at Tabernacle Baptist College. He is a good researcher, citing about 175 sources in his book. In the matter of Westcott's incarnation and spiritualist views (chapter 11), for example, Sightler cites Westcott's works, *__Lessons__ __From__ __Work__*; *__Historic__ __Faith__*; *__Gospel__ __of__ __Life__*; *__The__ __Gospel__ __of__ __the__ __Resurrection__*; and *__Christus__ __Consummator__*. He also cites works by the sons of Westcott and Hort, and many other sources. Those who get Sightler's book and read it will discover that Westcott had some very irregular and dangerous views, not in his youth only, as has been reported, but even in late life at the time of the publication of his Greek text, and following.

We repeat that it is tragic that fundamentalists are now defending Westcott and Hort. It proves once again that Modern Textual Criticism is a Trojan Horse which is bringing a destructive influence into Bible believing schools and churches. The stated purpose of the textual criticism of Westcott and Hort was to overturn the text of the King James Bible. The stream was polluted at its source.

FINAL AUTHORITY

Moving on to what the committee says about the Bible itself, we find some glaring weaknesses and unanswered questions. For example, Randolph Shaylor has a chapter on "Our Final Authority;" however, he falls far short of giving any assurance to the laymen that they have **ANY** final authority.

"Final authority" is an extremely important issue, so I was reading with great anticipation to see what the committee had to say.

After making the very excellent points that the Bible's authority comes from God Himself and that inspiration was the work of God whereby He gave us the authoritative originals, Shaylor never tells the laymen what **THEIR** final authority should be.

He makes the mistake of saying "nowhere does the Bible state or even imply" that copyists could give us copies that are inspired "in the same sense as the originals." [p. 22] But that is **EXACTLY** what the Bible says in II Timothy 3:15-16, where the Bible that Timothy had (either a copy or a translation) is included in the "All Scripture" which "is given by inspiration of God and is profitable..."

Shaylor is correct when he says that, "copies of these writings retain the quality of inspiration to the degree that they are accurate representations of what God gave in the autographs"; but we should go farther and say that it is possible (and even **CERTAIN**) that God could and did guide His people to know and keep His revelation so that we have a book which is as authoritative as the autographs would be **IF WE HAD THEM.**

Shaylor says, "This inerrancy extends to copies and translations to the extent that they accurately represent the autographs." [p. 23]   And we would add that the KJV represents the autographs to the **FULL EXTENT.**

Shaylor misses the truth slightly when he says, "That inspired **MESSAGE** is not limited to one translation or one language but is **PRESENT IN** any accurate translation." [p.27]

We would say, by contrast, "Those inspired **WORDS** are not limited to one translation or one language, but in so far as the English language is concerned, they are found in the King James Bible because it is an absolutely accurate translation."   If Shaylor had said that, he would have allowed the laymen to **HAVE** a final authority. He robs the laymen of their final authority when he writes that the laymen should rely on trustworthy translations [There is only **ONE** that is trustworthy in English.] and **seek the aid of those who are acquainted with biblical languages**." [p. 28, emphasis mine]

To have to consult Hebrew and Greek professors, of course, makes **THEM** the final authority. How is this better than what Catholics do when they make the church their final authority?

Only one thing could be more foolish than making Hebrew and Greek professors the final authority, **AND** that is to teach laymen **THAT THEY MUST MAKE THE ORIGINAL AUTOGRAPHS THEIR FINAL AUTHORITY!** No one has the original autographs, so how could they be consulted as a final authority? Even if we had the originals (which we don't) it would be utterly ludicrous for someone to say **ANY** Hebrew and Greek text must be the final authority for people who do not read Hebrew and Greek! I will go further and say that there are very **VERY** few college professors or seminary professors who can read Hebrew, Aramaic, and Greek well enough to say that the Hebrew and Greek text is their final authority. Anyone can look up the meanings of Hebrew and Greek words, but that is not the same as reading Greek or Hebrew. How can a Hebrew Old Testament and a Greek New Testament be the final authority **FOR A PERSON WHO CAN NOT READ IT?**

The people must have the Word of God in their own language, and they must make that Word of God their final authority. Failure to read, understand, believe, and obey the Word of God as delivered by God in one's own language is sin against a Holy God. Jesus commanded, "Search the scriptures" (John 5:39). By these words He did not mean search the originals nor search a copy of the originals. He was referring to the Bible that the people had, which was a translation. That was to be their final authority.

Two statements made by Shaylor are in glaring conflict. He says that the student of the Bible should "seek the aid of those who are acquainted with biblical languages." But then he makes this contradictory statement, that "the great truth of the Reformation [is] that the individual believer under the guidance of the Holy Spirit is competent to understand the Word of God." [p. 28]

Yes indeed, Shaylor speaks of the Reformation doctrine of the perspicuity of Scripture. That is the doctrine that the Bible is plain, clear, and understandable to the common, ordinary Christian with the help of the Holy Spirit. That doctrine asserts that we do not need church, priest or scholar to understand the Word of God, because God gave the Bible to ordinary Christians, not to scholars. God gave each believer the right and the responsibility to interpret the Bible for himself because he must rest his faith upon it and be judged by it. Since each person is going to be judged by the Word of God, he must listen to what God says, and not what someone else says that God says. Every man must look to the Bible as his final authority, and not to men.

Interestingly, the doctrine of soul liberty (a precious doctrine to Baptists) is related to the doctrine of perspicuity of Scripture. That is, each individual believer must believe and do that which he believes would please God, and he is under responsibility to find out for himself what it is that he should believe and do; and he **CAN FIND THIS OUT FOR HIMSELF BECAUSE** he can read and interpret the Bible for himself. So, when Ashbrook says that we must "turn to men with special training," [p. 108] that idea contradicts the Reformation/biblical doctrine of perspicuity of Scripture. People (especially laymen) are being tricked into thinking that they cannot learn what they should learn.

Both the doctrine of the perspicuity of Scripture and the doctrine of soul liberty **PRESUPPOSE AND DEMAND** that the believer have a translation of the Word of God in his own language and that he look to it as his **FINAL AUTHORITY**. Neither of these important doctrines can be a reality in a believer's life unless he has the inspired, inerrant Word of God in his own language.

DISCREDITISM

On another subject, the committee would have us believe that it disdains any denigration or "discreditism" of the King James Bible. [pp. 3, 8] We wonder if the committee is sincere about this since they do a considerable amount of denigrating of the KJV **THEMSELVES**.

For example, it is mentioned several times in the book that the Apocrypha was in the King James Bible in the beginning. The clear inference is that the King James translators thought that the Apocrypha was inspired Scripture and that the Apocrypha was put forth in the KJV **AS SCRIPTURE**. [pp. 45, 149, 155] The obvious intention of the committee is to lower the laymen's estimate of the KJV. **THIS IS DENIGRATION OF THE KJV.**

Of course, the inference that the Apocrypha was believed to be inspired Scripture by the translators of the KJV is totally and absolutely false. *First*, we should say that there is ample evidence in the writings and history of the translators to show that they knew the Apocrypha was not in the Canon of Scripture. There is not any evidence that a single KJV translator believed that the Apocrypha was inspired Scripture.

Second, in the original 1611 KJV, the Apocrypha was put between the Testaments, and not scattered throughout the Old Testament and attached to other books as it is in Roman Catholic Bibles.

Third, in the 1611 KJV, the Apocrypha was clearly set off in the index as separate from the Old and New Testaments.

Fourth, in the 1611 KJV, on the page where the Apocrypha began, the word "Apocrypha" appeared in large letters setting it off from both the Old Testament and the New Testament.

Fifth, in the 1611 KJV, on every page of the Apocrypha the word "Apocrypha" appeared twice, in both the upper left corner and again in the upper right corner of the page. This clearly sets the Apocrypha apart from inspired Scripture.

Sixth, the Apocrypha was never accepted as Scripture by even the Roman Catholic Church until the time of the Reformation. So it is just ridiculous to pretend that maybe the Protestant translators of the KJV accepted it as Scripture.

Seventh, the articles of the Church of England, as revised in A.D. 1562, stated that the Apocrypha was not inspired Scripture. It stated that Jerome's list of Canonical books was the correct list [***Kitto's Biblical Cyclopaedia***, Vol. I, p. 168]. The translators of the KJV were good Anglicans, as is pointed out several times by the authors of ***From the Mind of God to the Mind of Man***. Since they were noted Anglicans, does any one seriously entertain the idea that they held to the inspiration of the Apocrypha in defiance of their own church articles?

The KJV translators put the Apocrypha between the Testaments of their Bible because it was considered good to read and helpful, not because they thought that it was inspired. That was the same thing as had been done by many people for hundreds of years. Notes and study helps had been placed in many editions of the Bible all through the centuries, just as they are today. Hardly ever does any Christian say that these notes and study helps are inspired Scripture. The Apocrypha is probably as helpful as many of the notes that are put in our, so-called, "study Bibles" today.

In the Bible that I have here before me, on my desk, there is found some helpful material between the Testaments. Here are charts on Old Testament kings and prophets, charts on New Testament political leaders, articles on the Essenes and the Hasmonaeans, and an article on archeological discoveries. All of these items may be helpful, but I do not accept them as inspired Scripture, nor did the editor of my study Bible. The same may be said of the Apocrypha; none of the KJV translators entertained the idea for a moment that the Apocrypha was inspired Scripture.

Now, what I find disturbing is that I know the committee members, authors, and "academicians" of ***From the Mind of God to the Mind of Man*** know that what I have said about the matter is true. I have not said anything which is not common knowledge among preachers and teachers of the Word of God. John K. Hutcheson Sr. even admits, on page 120, that the KJV translators put the Apocrypha in a separate section. And yet, these men have put out a book for laymen in which they attempt to mislead those laymen into thinking that maybe the KJV translators believed the Apocrypha was inspired. At the very least, these men want the laymen to believe that it is a black mark against the KJV that the translators put the Apocrypha between the Testaments.

It is definitely a denigration of the KJV when the KJV translators are said to have "followed the Council of Trent." [p. 45] In reality, the Council of Trent had nothing to do with the Apocrypha being placed between the Testaments of the KJV.

It is definitely a denigration of the King James Bible when Mark Simmons says that "the inclusion of the Apocrypha by the translators leads one to believe that all eighty books are Holy Scripture." [p. 155]

It is a further denigration of the KJV when its underlying Greek text is called "The model "T" Ford of the New Testament text." [p. 106]

It is also somewhat denigrating of the KJV when the book teaches that our old Bible cannot be understood. Drew Conley says, for example, that the Bible reader "needs to find the words in which he thinks and talks, or he loses the meaning of what he reads." [p. 192] Another example is found in Mark Simmons words: "God's Word should be in the language of the people **so they can understand its commands**, savor its promises, relive the Bible stories, and carefully study its truth. This is extremely difficult when over four thousand words in the King James Bible are not found in even the best of our one volume English dictionaries today." [p. 153] Hutcheson says that we need to make sure "that each generation [has] a fresh English translation of the Bible **so that they could hear God speak to them.**" [p. 123]

Our objection to the quotes above is that the writers are pretending that the KJV can not be understood, and this is discrediting, belittling, and defaming. Most fundamental Baptists still use only the KJV, and do they not understand the revelation of God at least as well as those who use the NIV and other new versions?   How did the **VAST MAJORITY** of people learn any doctrine just twenty or thirty years ago before any of the new versions were at all popular? I do not believe that readers of the new versions understand the commands of God as well as readers of the KJV. I do not believe that readers of the new versions learn Bible doctrine better than readers of the KJV, especially in view of the fact that almost every Bible doctrine is weakened in the new versions.

The truth is that new versions are not made because people can not understand the KJV. And those who buy new versions do not do so because they can not understand the KJV. The motivation for making new versions is that publishers want to make money. And those who buy new versions do so because they have been "sold" by advertising. If anyone truly thought that he might have trouble understanding the "difficult" words in the KJV (there are only about two dozen of these), he could purchase one of the several King James Bibles that have the read-along dictionaries.

If the committee responsible for ***From the Mind of God to the Mind of Man*** was serious about not denigrating and discrediting the KJV, it would not say that maybe the translators believed that the Apocrypha was inspired Scripture. It would not say that the underlying text of the KJV is "the model "T" Ford of the New Testament text." And it would not say that the KJV is outdated, archaic, and cannot be understood.

So, again, I must question whether the committee's opposition to "discreditism" of the KJV is sincere. Perhaps they are only giving lip service to that opposition in order to appear "balanced," reasonable, and tolerant. If opposing "discreditism" of the KJV was a real goal, then why did they fail so miserably at it?

ERRORS

There are several other mistakes or overstatements in William's book.

IT IS STATED THAT THERE WERE THOUSANDS OF WORDS IN THE 1611 KJV WHICH ARE NOT IN TODAY'S KJV. [p. 147, 160] This is not true. Almost all of the words referred to differ only as to spelling and printing. Apparently the statement is made for its shock value.

IT IS SAID THAT THE KJV HAS BEEN REVISED AND THAT IT HAS GONE THROUGH AT LEAST FOUR MAJOR REVISIONS. [p. 27] This is not true. The KJV has never been revised. This is a myth that is repeated over and over by Critical Text/new version proponents. There have been many **EDITIONS** of the KJV, and in those many editions there have been spelling, grammar, and printing changes. Almost all of the changes have been of that sort. The few word changes that were made were almost all changes in the **FORM** of the same words. Nowhere in the history of publishing have such changes been called a revision.

Interestingly, ***From the Mind of God to the Mind of Man*** has been published in a "third edition," but it should honestly be called a "revision." The so-called "third edition" removes the writer's name from one chapter, partially rewrites the chapter, and makes other significant changes; and yet it is called a "third edition" not a "revision." Still the committee insists that the KJV has been "revised" over and over again, even though almost all of the changes have been in spelling, grammar, punctuation, or misprinted words.   What is going on here?   The committee is trying to destroy the faith that laymen have in the KJV in order to boost modern textual criticism and new Bible versions.

IT IS SAID THAT SINAITICUS IS A COMPLETE TEXT OF THE NEW TESTAMENT. [pp. 69, 172] This is not true.

Sinaiticus has most of all of the books of the New Testament, but omits large portions of some books. It does not contain Matthew 16:23; Mark 16:9-20; John 5:4; or John 8:1-11. It also does not have I John 5:7, Acts 8:37, and many other verses. In fact, Sinaiticus leaves out 3,455 words in the four Gospels alone.

It is also significant that Sinaiticus adds 839 words in the Gospels. It also changes, transposes, or modifies nearly 4,000 words. Additionally, Sinaiticus adds The Shepherd of Hermas and the Epistle of Barnabus.

So it cannot be honestly said that Sinaiticus contains a complete New Testament text.

IT IS SAID THAT KING JAMES ONLY ADVOCATES ARE RESPONSIBLE FOR CONFUSION AND DIVISION IN FUNDAMEN-TALISM. This is not true. When Williams points his finger and says, "This issue focuses on whether the King James Version of the Bible should be the only translation used by Fundamentalists," [p.2] he seems to forget that it is the new version advocates who have caused the confusion and division by bringing in something new. When Minnick accuses KJV only people of causing a "loud drum beating and tragic division," [p. 98] he seems to forget that it is the new version advocates who beat the drum. The strife and division has been caused by the pushers of the new translations. These insistent pushers of new translations have taken the attitude that all of us must listen to their Bibles in our churches, camps, classes, and conferences. "Listen, and keep your mouth shut about it," we are told. We are expected to listen and be quiet about it even though the new translations rob people of an understanding of God's Word.

When Williams indicates that the Bible version issue is the worst and most damaging issue in this century, he makes a huge overstatement. He specifically states that the Bible version issue is doing more harm to the cause of Christ among fundamentalists than liberalism, neo-evangelicalism, or the charismatic movement. [pp. 1-2] Brother Williams is being overly dramatic! The result is that the liberals, neo-evangelicals, and charismatics get a break—they are no more harmful than KJV-only advocates, according to J.B.

IT IS STATED SEVERAL TIMES IN THE BOOK THAT THE PURITANS WOULD HAVE NOTHING TO DO WITH THE KJV AND THAT IT WAS NOT ON THE MAYFLOWER. [p. 45, 121,139] This may be historically inaccurate, and it is an overstatement.

When I visited Pilgrim Hall Museum (the oldest museum in America) at Plymouth, Massachusetts, a few years ago, I noticed a very old King James Bible. It was displayed right beside William Bradford's Geneva Bible. I wrote to the museum to inquire about the KJV, "Did it come over on the Mayflower and to whom did it belong?"

Peggy Baker of the museum responded that the King James Bible was printed in 1620 and belonged to Mayflower passenger John Alden.

I wrote back to Mrs. Baker to say that "Since the Bible was printed in 1620, [and the Mayflower sailed the same year] I assume that the Bible was not brought **WITH** Alden on the Mayflower, but came later. Is this correct?"

Mrs. Baker responded very graciously, leaving no doubt that she believes that Alden brought the KJV with him on the Mayflower.

> The 1620 Bible was published early in 1620 and could very well have been brought on the Mayflower. We do not "know" with scientific standards of proof of ANY individual particular item that was on the Mayflower – there is no list of cargo or "this is what we brought." All we can do is make assumptions and educated guesses – that an item belonged to a Mayflower passenger is established by provenance and often confirmed by mention of a type of item in an inventory at time of death (although the inventory mention does not prove that, for instance, a Bible was this specific Bible and not another one), it was made before the voyage of the Mayflower, it is likely that it would have been brought then and not imported later, etc. So the answer is that we don't know absolutely and with proof in writing that there were any Bibles on the Mayflower but it is inconceivable given the nature of the passengers that there were not; certain items were owned by Mayflower passengers and predate the voyage, so assumptions and connections are made, etc.

I do not believe it can be proved that the KJV was on the Mayflower. And I do not believe that it can be proved that it was not on the Mayflower. Furthermore, it does not matter much to me whether it was on the Mayflower or not. But since the authors of ***From the Mind of God to the Mind of Man*** make such a big deal of saying that it was not there, as if this is another black mark against the KJV, we simply caution them–Hold on! **NOT SO FAST!** Don't be too sure!!

In any case the KJV **VERY QUICKLY** replaced all other Bibles, even the Geneva Bible. After the KJV had been out for about thirty years, the Geneva Bible would not be published any longer. By way of contrast, the NASV and the NIV have been out about thirty or forty years and neither of them is even close to replacing the KJV. We do not believe it will ever be replaced.

WILLIAMS ATTACKS J. J. RAY SAYING THAT IN HIS BOOK, _GOD_ _WROTE_ _ONLY_ _ONE_ _BIBLE_, RAY PLAGIARIZED BENJAMIN WILKINSON'S BOOK _OUR_ _AUTHORIZED_ _BIBLE_ _VINDICATED_. [p. 6] This is not true.

I was especially interested in this plagiarism charge because it was Ray's book which first raised my awareness of the textual issue back in 1967. The charge is not a new one. When I first heard the charge several years ago, I reread both of the books in question. When I first read William's charge I got out both books and examined them **AGAIN**. My honest conclusion is that there is no plagiarism of Wilkinson by Ray. In fact, I do not even see many similarities in the two books. Of course, both books deal with some of the same subject matter and many of the same facts, but I see no similarity of style or phrasing. Perhaps if Brother Williams had given some actual examples of what he is referring to, we might be able to understand what he is talking about and know why he has come to his conclusion.

In any case, both Wilkinson's book and Ray's book are very excellent. I recommend them. The fact that Wilkinson was a Seventh Day Adventist does not mean that we should reject the truths which he presents. Those who reject truth because they do not like the one who delivers it, do not love the truth.

MISUSING SPURGEON. . .

MARK MINNICK USED C. H. SPURGEON AS AN EXAMPLE OF A PREACHER WHO "FREELY MENTIONED" THAT THE KJV AND ITS UNDERLYING TEXT HAS ERRORS. [pp. 88-89] This is an overstatement. It is true, of course, that Spurgeon did from time to time correct the KJV, but he did not do this "freely" or often. Very often, in fact, he preached on those texts which are changed or left out of the Revised Version, the NASV, and the NIV. He did this without correcting the KJV or even mentioning that the Critical Text has a different reading.

An example is Spurgeon's sermon titled *Baptismal Regeneration*. [Memorial Library, Vol. 8, p.11] He took his text from Mark 16:15-16. Spurgeon was well aware that some critics had thrown the last twelve verses of Mark, chapter sixteen, out of the New Testament. So how did Spurgeon deal with the text? He did not say, "The passage is not in the best manuscripts." He did not say, "The critics are right to remove these twelve verses from our Bible." How **DID** Spurgeon deal with this text? **HE PREACHED IT.** For twenty-five pages he preached it and did not question its authenticity.

Another example of Spurgeon accepting as genuine a disputed passage is his treatment of Acts 9:5-6. The extreme textualists have ruled that portions of this passage are not in the "best manuscripts," and have expunged the words, "and he trembling and astonished said, Lord, what wilt thou have me to do?" On the other hand, defenders of the Traditional Text have defended the words because they are found in many manuscripts and ancient versions including The Old Latin (A.D. 200), the Vulgate (A.D. 380), The Syrian (A.D. 200), and "E" (6th Century). It is also recognized that the disputed words support the Lordship of Christ, therefore Dabney, Burgon, Hills, and others have defended them. The controversy was a long standing one even in Spurgeon's day.

Spurgeon's sermon on Acts 9:5-6 is titled *"Pressing Question of an Awakened Mind."* How does Spurgeon handle his text "Who art Thou, Lord?. . . .What wilt Thou have me to do?" Did he impeach the disputed words? Did he say, "These words are not genuine Scripture?" Did he say, "This is a poor translation, because the words are not in the original?" No, he said nothing of the kind.

How did Spurgeon treat Acts 9:5-6? **HE PREACHED IT!** He preached all of it without any alteration, correction, or omission. He preached it without mentioning the controversy over the passage. [The Treasury of the New Testament, Vol. 2 (Grand Rapids: Zondervan, 1950), pp. 780-784]

Still another example of Spurgeon rejecting the reading of the Revised Version and of the Critical Text is his treatment of I Timothy 3:16. The Critical Text, Westcott and Hort, the NIV, and the NASB all leave out that **"GOD** was manifest in the flesh."

Spurgeon preached on this text in his sermon titled, "The Hexapla of Mystery." Once again the "Prince of Preachers" preached on the disputed passage and did not change it or correct it. As a matter of fact, he defended the KJV reading saying:

We cannot spare a single word from it, and it would be a crime to add anything to it. . . . The first sentence is "God was manifest in the flesh." I believe that our version is the correct one, but the fiercest battlings have been held over this sentence. . . . We believe that, if criticism should grind the text in a mill, it would get out of it no more and no less than the sense expressed by our grand old version. God Himself was manifest in the flesh. [*The Treasury of the New Testament*, Vol. 3 (Grand Rapids: Zondervan, 1950), pp. 786-792]

Time after time, Spurgeon preached on passages that were not considered genuine by Westcott and Hort and by the translators of the new versions. In almost every case, the great Baptist preacher simply preached the words as they are found in the KJV. Usually he said nothing about the controversy, and sometimes he defended the King James reading. It is simply not true that Spurgeon can be included among those who "in many cases. . . freely mentioned" in a critical way the variants from the King James Bible.

Spurgeon did wrong in a few instances. He gave in to the pressures of liberal scholarship on an infrequent basis. But that was not his usual behavior. More often than not, he just preached the disputed words and verses without mentioning at all that they were in dispute.

Furthermore, Spurgeon seemed to frown on textual critics more and more as he grew older. In 1891, about eight months before his death, he spoke to his students at his college.

It is sadly common among ministers to add a word or subtract a word from the passage, or in some way debase the language of sacred writ. . . . Our reverence for the Great Author of Scripture should forbid all mauling of His Words.

No alteration of Scripture can by any possibility be an improvement. Today it is still the self-same mighty Word of God that it was in the hands of our Lord Jesus. . . .

If this Book be not infallible, where shall we find infallibility? We have given up the Pope, for he has blundered often and terrible, but we shall set up instead of him a horde of little popelings, fresh from college.

Are these correctors of Scripture infallible? Is it certain that our Bibles are not right, but that the critics must be so?..But where shall infallibility be found? "The depth saith, It is not in me" yet those who have **no depth at all** would have us imagine that it is in **them**; or else by perpetual change they hope to hit upon it!"

All possibility of certainty is transferred from the spiritual man to a class of persons whose scholarship is pretentious, but who do not even pretend to spirituality. We shall gradually be so bedoubted and becriticized that only a few of the most profound will know what **is** the Bible and what is **not**, and they will dictate to all the rest of us. I have no more faith in their mercy than their accuracy.

They will rob us of all that we hold most dear, and glory in the cruel deed. This same "reign of terror" **we will not endure**, for we still believe that God reveals Himself rather to babes than to the wise and prudent...We do not despise learning, but we will never say of culture or criticism, "These be thy gods, O Israel."

Do you see **WHY** men would lower the degree of inspiration in Holy Writ, and would fain reduce it to an infinitesimal quantity? It is because the truth of God is to be supplanted....whenever a man begins to lower your view of inspiration , it is because he has a trick to play, which is not easily performed in the light. . . . To these who belittle inspiration and inerrancy we will give place by subjection, no, not for an hour!

Spurgeon did not correct the King James Bible "freely," as Minnick says. An honest assessment would be that CHS was very restrained in making such corrections. He obviously believed that harm to his hearers could result by such criticism. It is also obvious that his general attitude was that the Bible, as he had it, should not be judged by men, even though he violated this standard himself sparingly and on an infrequent basis.

...AND DABNEY

Minnick also leaves the laymen with the wrong impression about Robert L. Dabney's view of the differences between the various manuscripts. Dabney did not believe that the differences were inconsequential. When Dabney wrote his illustration of the "ancient road" and how newly discovered data might change the wayfarer's opinion about where the old road had been (and concluded that the road was with "minute exceptions" right where it had always been), he was not saying that the differences between the Critical Text and the Received Text were inconsequential, or small. Dabney was saying that all of the newly found variant readings had legitimately moved the Received Text very, very little. In fact, the net result was that the correctness of the Received Text was substantiated **WHEN THE VARIANTS WERE PROPERLY EVALUTED**. The truth is that Dabney believed the differences between the manuscripts were **HUGE**. In fact, in the same article quoted by Minnick, *"The Doctrinal Various Readings of the New Testament Greek"* [**Discussions: Evangelical and Theological** (Harrisonburg, Virginia: Sprinkle Publications, 1982), pp. 364-365] he speaks of the great differences between the Sinaitic, Vatican, and Alexandrine MSS. saying that "the instances in which [these three] agree among themselves, are comparatively rare. The disagreements of the three, among themselves, are...not fewer than five thousand; and this, of course, excludes the minute variations of spelling and arrangement."

Dabney also knew that the Sinai, Vatican, and Alexandrian manuscripts differed more from the Traditional Text than they did from each other.

Dabney cannot be claimed as one who believed that the Received Text should be changed on the basis of the Westcott and Hort text, rather he believed that **THE TEXT UNDERLYING THE KJV PRESENTED EVERY FACT UNCORRUPTED.**

It is true that Dabney did not believe that the Textus Receptus had exactly the right word in every single instance. Almost all KJV-only people would agree with Dabney about that. The King James Bible is not based on the TR in every single instance. However, Dabney, who was an outstanding 19th Century Presbyterian scholar, cannot be placed in the column of those who thought that the differences between the Critical Text and the Textus Receptus were inconsequential. It mattered a great deal to him whether Matthew 8:1-11 was in the Bible or not. It mattered much to him whether Mark 16:9-20 was considered true Scripture or not. It was extremely important to him whether or not Acts 8:37; Acts 9:5-6; and I John 5:7 were to be considered as genuine. He also cared much that "God" be retained in Acts 20:28 and I Timothy 3:16. Furthermore, Dabney's opinion of modern textual criticism was that it was a waste of time at best and very harmful and destructive in its worst. His assessment of modern textual criticism is worth repeating here:

It may also be premised, that since critical investigations have reached the results admitted above, and since the most laborious research seems to give so small a promise of a definite end of debate on the remaining and unessential variations, one is not surprised to find that this branch of study has lost its interest with the more practical and vigorous judgments.   Such men feel that they have something better to do with their time and energies.   The minds for which criticism retains its fascination are usually of that peculiar and "crotchety" type found among antiquarians.   The intelligent reader is, therefore, not surprised to find, along with much labor and learning, a "plentiful lack" of sober and convincing common sense. [Ibid p. 352]

INSPIRED AND INERRANT?

Finally, we want to point out that the best statement in ***From the Mind of God to the Mind of Man*** is found in the last three sentences of Mark Simmons' chapter:

> *WE STAND IN THE PULPITS WITH OUR KJV AND WE HAVE GOD'S WORD.   IT IS THE INSPIRED, INFALLIBLE, INERRANT WORD OF GOD.   MAY WE BE CHALLENGED TO LOVE IT, LIVE IT, UNDERSTAND IT, AND DILIGENTLY STUDY IT AS WELL AS DEFEND IT!*

This statement, written by Simmons, is made the property of the entire Committee on the Bible's Text and Translation, in the "third edition" of the book.   It is a beautiful statement!   The trouble is that neither Mark Simmons nor the committee believe the statement. They do not believe that the KJV is the Word of God, inspired, infallible, and inerrant. How I wish they did believe it, but they don't!

Apparently the above statement is included in the book to make the laymen think that these men think more highly of the King James Bible than they do. All of the rest of the book shows that the committee, including Mark Simmons, does not believe this statement, except in a very qualified, limited way. They do not believe the KJV is the Word of God in the sense that the **WORDS** are God's words preserved and accurately translated, rather they think that the **MESSAGE** is there in some sense. They do not believe that the KJV is inspired, except in some euphemistic, lesser sense, because they think the inspiration leaked out when the manuscripts were copied and translated. They do not believe the KJV is infallible or inerrant; rather they think there are lots of errors in the KJV, and they are desperately looking for more errors in it, so that they can prove the need for modern textual criticism and the need for the new versions of the Bible.

In conclusion, ***From the Mind of God to the Mind of Man*** does not add anything new to the discussion. It says much that is untrue; tends to rob laymen of their final authority; defends men who were heretical; and promotes Bibles which are inferior. All of this is done to mislead the laymen.